BABYLON ★BY★BUS

BABYLON ★ BY ★ BUS

Or, the true story of two friends who gave up their valuable franchise selling YANKEES SUCK T-shirts at Fenway to find meaning and adventure in Iraq, where they became employed by the occupation in jobs for which they lacked qualification and witnessed much that amazed and disturbed them

RAY LEMOINE *and* JEFF NEUMANN

WITH DONOVAN WEBSTER

THE PENGUIN PRESS

New York

2006

THE PENGUIN PRESS
Published by the Penguin Group
Penguin Group (USA) Inc., 375 Hudson Street, New York, New York 10014, U.S.A. •
Penguin Group (Canada), 90 Eglinton Avenue East, Suite 700, Toronto, Ontario, Canada M4P 2Y3
(a division of Pearson Penguin Canada Inc.) • Penguin Books Ltd, 80 Strand,
London WC2R 0RL, England • Penguin Ireland, 25 St Stephen's Green, Dublin 2, Ireland
(a division of Penguin Books Ltd) • Penguin Books Australia Ltd, 250 Camberwell Road,
Camberwell, Victoria 3124, Australia (a division of Pearson Australia Group Pty Ltd) •
Penguin Books India Pvt Ltd, 11 Community Centre, Panchsheel Park, New Delhi-110 017,
India • Penguin Group (NZ), Cnr Airborne and Rosedale Roads, Albany, Auckland 1310,
New Zealand (a division of Pearson New Zealand Ltd) • Penguin Books (South Africa) (Pty) Ltd,
24 Sturdee Avenue, Rosebank, Johannesburg 2196, South Africa

Penguin Books Ltd, Registered Offices:
80 Strand, London WC2R 0RL, England

First published in 2006 by the Penguin Press,
a member of Penguin Group (USA) Inc.

Excerpt from "'Wild Boys' from U.S. Help Iraqi Relief Efforts" by Phillip O' Connor, *St. Louis Post-Dispatch*, March 28, 2004. Reprinted with permission of the *St. Louis Post-Dispatch*, copyright 2004. Excerpt from "U.S. Pitches In for Iraqi Kids" by Willis Witter, *The Washington Times*, March 29, 2004. Copyright 2004 News World Communications, Inc. Reprinted with permission of *The Washington Times*. This reprint does not constitute or imply any endorsement or sponsorship of any product, service, company, or organization.

Photograph credits
Page 14: Ray LeMoine; Page 90: Jeff Neumann; Page 188: © Spencer Platt/Getty Images;
Page 274: Maya Alleruzzo

Map illustrations by John Gilkes

Library of Congress Cataloging-in-Publication Data

Neumann, Jeff
Babylon by bus, or, The true story of two friends who gave up their valuable franchise selling "Yankees suck" t-shirts at Fenway to find meaning and adventure in Iraq, where they became employed by the occupation in jobs for which they lacked qualification and witnessed much that amazed and disturbed them / Jeff Neumann and Ray LeMoine, with Donovan Webster.
p. cm.
ISBN 1-59420-091-2
1. Iraq War, 2003—Personal narratives, American. 2. Postwar reconstruction—Iraq. 3. Neumann, Jeff. 4. LeMoine, Ray, 1979- 5. Coalition Provisional Authority—Officials and employees—Biography. I. LeMoine, Ray, 1979- II. Webster, Donovan. III. Title. IV. Title: Babylon by bus. V. Title: True story of two friends who gave up their valuable franchise selling "Yankees suck" t-shirts at Fenway to find meaning and adventure in Iraq, where they became employed by the occupation in jobs for which they lacked qualification and witnessed much that amazed and disturbed them.
DS79.76.N484 2006
956.7044'3092–dc22   2006046015
[B]
Printed in the United States of America

1 3 5 7 9 10 8 6 4 2

DESIGNED BY AMANDA DEWEY

For Hayder

Contents

•

Authors' Note

•

THIS BOOK IS TOLD from one person's point of view, Ray's, for the sake of readability, but we pooled our writing, insights, and recollections during its creation. It began as a magazine piece written in Ray's voice, and we decided to keep it that way. Nonetheless, everything we say here happened as we say it here.

—Ray LeMoine and Jeff Neumann

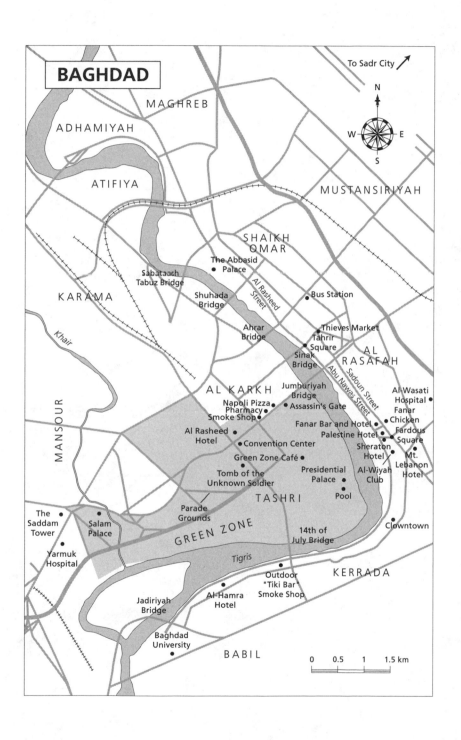

BAGHDAD

To Sadr City

N
W E
S

MAGHREB

ADHAMIYAH

ATIFIYA

MUSTANSIRIYAH

KARAMA

SHAIKH
OMAR

The Abbasid
Palace

Sabataach
Tabuz Bridge

Shuhada
Bridge

Al Rasheed Street

Bus Station

Ahrar
Bridge

Thieves Market
Tahrir
Square

AL
RASAFAH

Sinak
Bridge

Khair

AL KARKH

Jumhuriyah
Bridge

Abu Nawas Street

Sadoun Street

Al-Wasati
Hospital
Fanar
Chicken

Napoli Pizza
Pharmacy
Smoke Shop

Assassin's Gate

Fanar Bar and Hotel
Palestine Hotel

Fardous
Square

MANSOUR

Al Rasheed
Hotel

Convention Center

Sheraton
Hotel

Mt.
Lebanon
Hotel

Green Zone Café

Al-Wiyah
Club

Tomb of the
Unknown Soldier

Presidential
Palace

TASHRI

Pool

Parade
Grounds

The
Saddam
Tower

Salam
Palace

GREEN ZONE

14th of
July Bridge

Clowntown

Yarmuk
Hospital

Tigris

KERRADA

Outdoor
"Tiki Bar"
Smoke Shop

Jadiriyah
Bridge

Al-Hamra
Hotel

Baghdad
University

BABIL

0   0.5   1   1.5 km

BABYLON ★ BY ★ BUS

Prologue

•

"I've heard Judea is nice this time of year...."

T HE BUS BROKE DOWN again near Fallujah. This time it was only
for a few hours, but other engine and mechanical troubles had
already turned the advertised ten-hour ride from Amman to Baghdad
into a nearly twenty-four-hour epic. It was morning, just after sunrise,
and my companion, Jeff Neumann, and I jumped out to stretch our
legs and take a leak.

It was January 17, 2004. Nine days earlier, I had celebrated my
twenty-fifth birthday. Jeff was twenty-eight. During this time, Iraq
was experiencing a period of relative calm.

Jeff gestured up the road. "Look at that," he said, "a burned-out
tank."

A few miles ahead, the Sunni Arab city of three hundred thousand
hunkered low; a mud-brick skyline. Columns of thick black smoke
rose from somewhere inside the city, like spires punctuating the view

and adding a wispy counterpoint to the mosque minarets that spiked heavenward across the horizon. Fallujah is known as the "City of Mosques," and the Army's 82nd Airborne was now working the city's perimeter, with Fallujah's interior festering under insurgent reign. By the time we left Iraq, under threat of assassination, Fallujah would be at open war with the Americans, with heavily armed foreign jihadist and ex-Baathist guerrilla insurgents fighting the 1st Marines in bloody urban combat.

Baghdad was our ultimate goal. We'd entered Iraq on Highway 10 from Jordan, a super-slab across the desert—not unlike I-15 between Los Angeles and Las Vegas—that cuts east-west across the featureless heart of Iraq's western al Anbar province, an area about the size of Connecticut. Due to the number of roadside ambushes and bombings taking place there, Highway 10 had recently become one of the most dangerous stretches of pavement on earth.

But if Anbar and Fallujah were in a state of anarchy, it was being benignly overseen by the encircling 82nd Airborne troops, who were keeping their distance and avoiding civilian interactions at nearly all costs. Both sides understood that Fallujah was set to explode, and even a small interaction gone wrong could escalate into violence with deadly speed.

Anbar was a no-man's-land, and anyone traveling there was assumed to be aware of its dangers: It was definitely a "travel at your own risk" situation. Back in Amman, as we'd boarded the bullet-pocked bus, everyone had been watching everyone else from the corners of their eyes.

At the Jordanian-Iraqi border, there hadn't even been security: No tanks, concertina wire, or armed guards were visible to imply Iraq was at low-intensity conflict. Nobody even came out to inspect our bus. Inside a grim blockhouse, a pair of tired and bored-looking Passport Control clerks, Arab men in full-length, dark-gray dishdashas, moved through their fluorescent-lit room as if underwater.

They stamped our passports without looking up.

AT THE TIME, in January 2004, American government statements out of Iraq contained news of "terrorists on the run," overlaid by images of happy Iraqis, gentle breezes, and warm sunshine. In this version of occupied Iraq, democracy and freedom were flowering in the land of the Tigris and Euphrates. This Golden Age was being underwritten by a nation-building effort run by the American-led Coalition Provisional Authority (CPA), whose noble work was being slowed only slightly by a few foreign jihadists and Baath Party "dead-ender" guerrillas, lonely fighters who were losing resolve as their support in Iraq continued to evaporate.

Across the past months, though, this picture hadn't seemed in sync with the daily news out of Iraq. With a steady frequency, bombs were going off, killing Americans in Baghdad and beyond. And any time the Iraqis announced they would expand training for the Iraqi police or military, those registration drives were being met with gunfire or suicide and car bombers. So, in late 2003, we decided to go to Baghdad and see for ourselves. Had we known Iraq was set to collapse into all-out war, we might not have gone at all. But that's irrelevant now.

FOR THE TWO OF US—Red Sox fans to the point of painful cliché—the road to Baghdad started in the South Bronx; more specifically in Section 336 of Yankee Stadium on the night of October 17, 2003: Game 7 of the American League Championship Series, or ALCS. "The Stadium," as Yankee fans call it, is known as "The Toilet" by Red Sox fans, since, seen from above, it resembles a giant commode. On this night, the usual antipathy between these two sets of fans was amplified by a tied-up series: Both the Red Sox and the Yankees had won three games. After the Red Sox won Game 6 to tie and force a decisive Game 7, the team had their best hope for a World Series in seventeen years.

Compounding the anticipation, Game 7 was to showcase the greatest postseason pitching duel in decades: current Red Sox ace Pedro Martinez versus former Red Sox ace Roger Clemens. From New Jersey to Maine, every media outlet hyped Game 7 as more than a mere athletic event. In New York, the headlines read things like "Showdown in the Bronx" and "Do or Die." On that day, across the Northeast Corridor, regular life simply stopped for millions of people, including us. All everyone cared about was the 8:17 P.M. game time. After a few hours of trying, we scored tickets at the last minute. Nothing beats October baseball in the Northeast. The traditional red-white-and-blue bunting was unfurled around the mezzanine and box seats. Then the sun slipped from the Bronx sky, and the night grew cold. We could see our breath as Yankee Stadium began to fill, and everybody in the place remained standing as Pedro and Roger walked out of their bullpens to do long-toss warm-ups in the outfield. By the time of the National Anthem, with its F-16 flyover, we had butterflies in our stomachs, which we were trying to quell with several seven-dollar beers. As we mingled among the New York faithful, it didn't take long for us to start getting harassed by Yankee SuperFans, with their wind-suited, satin-jacketed bada-bing humor—"Hey Bos-tuuun? What's Bos-tunnn eva won . . . *eh-oooohhhhh.*" Life was great.

The Red Sox took an early lead, knocking Clemens out of the game and holding their edge behind a steady Pedro on the mound. Soon, we became magnets for showers of tristate saliva and thrown beers, and we were celebrating and high-fiving with any Red Sox fans we could find. Talk was already circulating between us about who would be driving the first leg of the trip to Miami for Game 1 of the 2003 World Series against the Marlins. "Sticky Van," our trusted old friend—a classic white Ford F-150 cargo van that we often slept in, only to awaken stuck to the floor—was our ride of choice, as it had been on so many cross-country adventures before. In anticipation of victory, we gathered with our friends and other Red Sox fans on the left field lower deck, where we were provided our own (somewhat abusive) police detail.

Then things went wobbly. Not long after our route to Miami was planned (a hard charge down I-95, as the World Series would start in two days), the Yankees rallied to tie the game. And the rest, well . . . sucks. In the bottom of the eleventh, Aaron Boone blasted a game-winning home run into the left-field stands only a few yards from us. We didn't even stick around long enough to see Cap'n Jeetz emerge from the Yankee dugout to do his patented "victory chop."

On our ride home down the FDR, tears were flowing. We were broken. Drowning our sorrows with bourbon at a bar in the East Village, we contemplated our future—or fresh lack thereof. We had no regular jobs, nor were we looking for any; we weren't done with school, and we weren't getting any younger. At about 3:00 A.M. I turned to Jeff and said, "Bad as this feels, it isn't bad at all. It's an opportunity to make some decisions. Make some new plans."

"I had no plans beyond the World Series. You know I hate thinking ahead."

THE NEXT AFTERNOON we woke up in our Brooklyn loft and retreated to our rooftop refuge. Our building's old, unused water tower had been converted by an artist into a sitting area with two comfy wooden benches, and it offered the best view of Manhattan for miles. Below us was a major sanitation depot, and the sweet smell of garbage in transit filled the air. A scrawny, crackhead hooker trolled the street below. Despite the benches and the views, at the moment our loft seemed to rank among the most unlivable places in America. The nearby stores were often out of everything that hadn't been canned or bottled by Goya. A twenty-minute walk would get you to the nearest health food store. We sat on the roof, nursing our hangovers with a few beers.

"Must we endure another painful winter?" Jeff said. "I can't. I have to leave."

"New York?"

"The whole East Coast. America even. I'm over it. I don't know. Maybe go to the Middle East."

"It's pretty boring there right now."

Jeff liked to live in a place, be it Boston, New York, or California, for a few months only to fail at whatever he was trying to do, and then pack his bags for an international destination. The prior winter, a humbled Jeff had retreated from the city after dropping out of the School of Visual Arts in midsemester. Now I planned on joining him as a New York failure.

"Another retreat, huh? I think I'll be joining you on this one," I said.

"Fuck you, the Middle East was my idea." It was common for us to argue about who thought of what first.

"Asshole, I've been saying I wanted to go to the Middle East all summer and you know it."

Neither of us spoke. We stared at the endlessly interesting Manhattan skyline. Airplanes were cruising above the city.

"I can't believe the Sox lost."

"Imagine how many shirts we'd have sold and cars we'd have flipped if the World Series was in Boston."

"No shit."

SINCE 1999, the Red Sox had provided me with a decent income, not to mention a lot of Jeff's.

Back in the summer of '99, I'd been a vendor inside Fenway Park, selling Cokes in the stands during games. That October, the Red Sox had faced the Yankees in their first-ever ALCS matchup when, just hours after the series was set, a friend and I silk-screened the words "Yankees Suck" on a white T-shirt in a blue athletic-bold font. The night before Game 1, we sold three hundred shirts between the hours of 1:00 A.M. and 3:00 A.M. to fans camped out at Fenway awaiting the sale of tickets. From that night on, "Yankees Suck" T-shirts have been sold outside Fenway after every home game, along with later iterations that read things like: "WWJDD?" ("What Would Johnny Damon Do?"), "Yankees Suck, Jeter Swallows," "Jeter Sucks A Rod," or other similarly pithy phrases we could generate. Beyond all the other T-shirts, though, the "Yankees Suck" shirts have become, in their way, famous: gaining mention in *Sports Illustrated, The New York Times, The New Yorker,* and dozens of other national publications.

Most games, we had roughly twenty people selling shirts on the sidewalks and street corners around Fenway. Generally, they were old friends or younger brothers of old friends. "Work" consisted of standing and hocking shirts for an hour after games. The T-shirt operation wasn't a normal business, with profit as the bottom line. For us, the bottom line was fun, with a nightly "suck" of our gross profit going toward collective good times. The money gave us the freedom to do things like traveling on a whim or attending big playoff games.

I'd actually met Jeff in 1996, outside Wetlands, a now-shuttered bar and club downtown in New York City, back when I was still in high school. Then I would see him around at music shows up and down the East Coast. Growing up, Jeff mostly lived in the greater Washington, D.C., area, including Arlington and farther south in Richmond, Virginia. When we met, he was living in northwest Washington, D.C., working as a bicycle messenger and playing guitar in a few bands. He picked up his global travel habit with these bands; touring gave him a chance to see Europe, South America, and the Pacific Rim, plus a good chunk of North America. In 1998, he moved to Boston to make a new start and remove himself from what had become a negative environment: a situation that culminated with a long jail sentence for his best friend and his longtime girlfriend leaving him for a guy who loved penny loafers and had greaser hair. In Boston, he promptly enrolled in—then dropped out of—Northeastern University, where I was also enrolled as a student.

College kids in Boston have two major enclaves, the Mission Hill area of Roxbury, near Northeastern, and Lower Allston near Boston University. Neither of these neighborhoods can be described as nice, though the Hill is the slightly more dangerous of the two. I'd moved to Boston as a student from my family's home north of the city in 1997, the year before Jeff arrived permanently. We lived in similar Mission Hill triple-decker apartments. Our circle of friends was drawn from the various colleges in town, as well as from the music scene we'd both grown up in.

Over the next five years, we lived in a succession of houses on the Hill, the most notable of which we called the "38 Calumet Street Gentlemen's Club." The GC was part imperial England, part Tijuana backstreet strip club, part Explorer's Club, and part bookie desk. It also functioned as a sometime casino and—for one pleasant, fuzzily memorable February—an opium den. A black stripper named Cookie lived with us for a time. It was at 38 Calumet Street that many of our worst ideas—parties and debacles too humiliating to mention—came to fruition. But it was also at the GC, even more than in college, that our true education began, generally over our card games. GC poker nights would attract a collection of the city's young entrepreneurs, drug dealers, writers, musicians, college dropouts, yuppies, couch surfers, real surfers, skaters, Sullys, designers, artists, middle-aged street hustlers, day traders, and the occasional MIT or Harvard students.

With all the T-shirt cash funneling through the house, these games were huge for the college crowd. This was before anyone with ESPN and the Internet had made poker their own, and our game was one of the few in town. It was during these events that we learned to calculate risk, appreciate the power of the individual, and develop the nerve to face failure and financial defeat. The 38 Home Game also gave many of us the opportunity to take money from a pair of Oxy-Contin dealers/sniffers—the pills sold for eighty dollars apiece—who joined the game from time to time.

BACK ON THE ROOF in Brooklyn, Jeff said, "Hey, at least we don't have to go back to Boston."

I nodded and recalled my hatred for Boston's postcollege scene. Once you turn twenty-two in Boston, everybody leaves, and those left behind are either younger than you or establishing their careers in fields that neither Jeff nor I had any interest in. We'd done everything we could in Boston, and now we'd outgrown it. We were in a phase in which we were too young to be taken completely seriously in New York, but too old to be hanging out with the students in

Boston. The Red Sox loss aside, our life situation in October 2003 was as bleak as it had ever been. Our friends and families knew it, and they wanted little to do with our problems. And we didn't ask them for help. Our girlfriends—frustrated by our drifting and traveling—had moved on to what they believed were greener pastures. "Let's get out of here. We haven't paid rent in three months," I said. Our Brooklyn loft was a scam. The elevator didn't work and the place wasn't legally habitable. Our landlord knew he'd broken the law, and he'd stopped trying to collect rent weeks before the playoffs. "It's time to plan another trip."

For the past few years, Jeff and I had been using the baseball offseason to travel. We'd been to some sixty-odd countries each: everything from a weekend in London to multimonth trips to Latin America, Europe, and Asia. We'd grown tired of the Lonely Planet scene, though, and never wanted to meet another Dutchman who liked "Goa Trance" and Ecstasy. There's this stupid romance with Thailand's fake exoticism, or Guatemala's "culture," or Prague's cheap prices that really aren't cheap. At the moment, nothing sounded less appealing than sitting on a beach in some backpacker hotspot.

We also didn't want to go somewhere "untapped" like Rangoon or Patagonia, which didn't figure into prominent current events. We had grown up in D.C. and Massachusetts respectively, politics were in our blood, and since 9/11 foreign affairs had come to the forefront of American politics. We wanted to go somewhere that mattered, someplace where we could see firsthand that concept called the Global War on Terror.

The T-shirt thing showed us that anything is possible and we figured: Why not try and work in humanitarian aid? Help people dig wells, build infrastructure, or distribute food and medicine—anything, really—and, lately, we'd been looking for these jobs in the hottest of spots: Gaza, Baghdad, Kandahar, Peshawar . . . any place that would have us. We combed humanitarian and Non-Governmental Organization (NGO) websites, searching for jobs, but they only wanted Ph.D.s. Instead of applying online for a job half a world away, we decided to apply in person.

It's not accurate to pretend Jeff and I were simply two do-gooders trying to help babies in the third world. We also enjoyed the world's sleazy side. Ever since high school, when I'd first gone to Tijuana (always Jeff's favorite city after New York), I've had an attraction to the darkest corners of the world. During Iraq's looting, the thought of loading up a stolen Lamborghini with Persian rugs and Baathist booty had crossed our minds. Stupid, I know.

When I say we were stupid I don't mean that we didn't know anything. With all our free time we had the chance to read and read and read. Our stupidity lay not in a lack of knowledge, but rather in our application of that knowledge toward dumb ideas, like buying stolen sports cars in Iraq to transport rugs, or selling offensive T-shirts on the sidewalk, or going to Gaza to get a job.

So it was a combination of political curiosity, a willingness to work for free, and a love for bad schemes that made us set off for the Middle East, with Iraq looming largest in our sights. I said to Jeff, "We can stay home and do nothing. Blow money at bars and sleep till noon. Or we can go see what interests us most. Seems like an easy choice to me."

"You're right. Hemingway didn't stay home. Orwell didn't . . ."

"Hey, it's what we have to gain—though in Iraq we've probably already missed the looting. And I've heard Judea is nice this time of year."

A date was set: We'd spend New Year's 2004 in Tel Aviv; then we'd press on for Baghdad.

As a Jew, the idea of going to Israel also seemed a rite of passage. I felt that I had to see the Holy Land at least once if I was going to call myself Jewish. The Second Intifada was raging and now seemed as good a time as ever to confront the land of Zion and its discontents.

For us, in order to understand America and her growing entanglement in the Middle East, we had to see the conflict firsthand. Watching Middle Eastern events on the news and reading about them in newspapers and books suddenly seemed too remote and antiseptic. The money was there. So we went.

FALLUJAH BREAKDOWN

(Photo by Ray LeMoine)

BOOK★ONE

"And there's a chance things'll get weird . . ."

1

.

W HEN I SHOWED UP to meet Jeff in Tel Aviv on New Year's Eve,
I hadn't seen him since just after Game 7 back in October.
Jeff had been in the Middle East for three weeks. For the last few days
he'd been traveling in Israel with his grandmother and her church
group, assisting them and providing a little youthful energy, and at
the same time experiencing a version of the Holy Land that's been
well scripted by American religio-tourism companies, commercial
entities that guide the faithful to all the Old and New Testament
photo ops while avoiding the intractable present-day troubles wher-
ever possible.

There Jeff was, up the sidewalk. As I got closer, I could also see he
was wearing the same shoes as me. Two friends, who haven't seen
each other in months, now on a sidewalk half a world away from

where they last saw each other, and both wearing the same brand-new sneakers.

TEL AVIV is one of those places that feels familiar, even if you've never been there before. It's a Bauhaus version of Art Deco Miami or classicist-modern Sydney. The beaches are great, the sun is hot, and the architecture is excellent. The girls are beautiful, too. In fact, Tel Aviv may have some of the best-looking women on earth, but many of them have been in the Israeli Defense Forces (IDF), and they're a bit guarded.

Both Jeff and I really wanted to like Tel Aviv. It wasn't easy. There is a ferocity in even the garden-variety Israeli: a streak of individualistic self-importance that often leaves them seeming not only unhelpful but flat-out mean. Even their dogs are vicious. And then there's the expensive food. A pizza costs twenty dollars. A cup of coffee is three dollars. Even the simplest foods are ridiculously expensive, especially considering that all over Israel are kibbutzes where people farm for no wage at all, so shouldn't food cost *less* there?

The same bars you find from New York to Barcelona to Hong Kong also exist in Tel Aviv. It's a bar that now circles the globe like the Tropic of Cancer—a minimalist, sleek lounge. Even the music is the same: minimalist techno and ironic dance punk.

We saw and found some funny things while urban lurking in Tel Aviv. There was a place called Chinky Beach where you could eat bagels and smoke weed. Our hotel sat on Dizengoff Square, home to Tel Aviv's crust punk community. Aside from doing heroin and drinking canned beer, Dizengoff Square's crusties could be counted on to pick a fight with virtually anyone who walked by. One day, we watched two punks in black leather jackets as they pummeled each other for an hour.

What made Tel Aviv unique was all the weaponry. The Apache attack helicopters that flew south down the beachfront toward Gaza. Or the assault rifles everyone seems to carry. Israel is always at war. That's one of the things we realized as we walked the streets of Tel Aviv. Israel/Palestine is a conflict, where the two sides are fighting for two different things: Security versus Land. The Israelis want their national and personal security, while the Palestinians want their land back. Both sides have their sets of solid arguments.

Both sides have extremists, too, people who—when peace shimmers for a rare moment—step in to ruin it. Both sides also have leaders who are married to the conflict.

In the Holy Land, the one thing you cannot sugarcoat, polarize, or politicize is the bloody, guts-strewing reality of the violence there. Underneath the propaganda on both sides sits certain wrenching truths, and these realities are reinforced every day by another new tide of death. But we didn't go to Israel to pick sides.

In the case of Israel, occupation is never an easy business. The IDF are definitely brutal in their military dominance over 3.5 million Palestinians whom they have effectively trapped inside the Palestinian Territories. The IDF are among the world's greatest human rights violators. And yet they're faced by Islamic militants who have no problem using children as suicide bombers, often against other children. Both sides engage in acts that all human beings—no matter their nationality or religion—should condemn.

In Tel Aviv, New Year's Eve was dead because they operate on the Jewish calendar. There was nobody in the bars and nightclubs; there was no celebration. Everywhere we searched for fun was deserted.

One of the only people we saw on the street, in fact, was a heroin addict lying against a wall in a downtown underpass, with a needle jammed into his left forearm. We took our pictures with him, just to immortalize the moment as a low point for the three of us. But we were pretty let down. Our grand plan for New Year's in Tel Aviv was a bust.

Things got a little better when we stumbled upon a group of teenage Arab rappers down by the beach. We told them we were Americans and they broke out a bottle of absinthe. "Now listen to our rhymes," one said before breaking into a verse. "Israelis keep us down/they actin' like clown/we gonna take them down . . . I love 2Pac!"

We told them that 2Pac sucked and Biggie was God, before continuing down the esplanade.

AFTER NEW YEAR'S EVE, we headed to Jerusalem to see the sights and figure out how to see the West Bank. Staying at the run-down Faisal Hostel, where Jeff had stayed the week before, just opposite the Old City's Damascus Gate, we began talking with some members of the International Solidarity Movement (ISM) about the current situation in the West Bank. After the recent suicide bombing of a bus stop near Tel Aviv, the IDF had encircled and cut off the city of Nablus, the home of the suicide bomber. We found a couple of ISM girls, Sara and Samantha, who knew of a way to sneak in and were leaving the next morning, and they invited us along.

Around noon the next day, we went from the Old City to the West Bank border in a couple of minibuses, the vehicles most commonly used for travel between West Bank cities, then switched to a service taxi, which dropped us off at the Huwwara checkpoint just south of Nablus. Since the city had been closed off by the IDF, after wasting about an hour in line at the checkpoint we headed back about a quarter mile to the taxi waiting area. Luckily Sara spoke fluent Arabic and found a man willing to drive us on back roads over the mountains and into the West Bank in his van. So we set off with these two ISM activists and three Palestinians we'd met at the taxi area who were trying to get home.

A partially blocked tunnel ran under an Israeli-only highway between West Bank settlements, and as soon as we'd shut the van's doors the driver took off, tearing through the tunnel at high speed. We headed up a steep hill, only to be confronted head-on by an IDF jeep carrying three paratroopers. At gunpoint, we were told to get out of the van and were given a mild interrogation. "What are you doing here? . . . Can we see your passports, please?" Jeff and I were getting laughs from the soldiers more than anything else. We told them we were on our way to Iraq, which they found equally maddening and confusing. One soldier asked, "What do you want to see there? Or here?"

"We have no idea what we're going to see in either place," Jeff said.

Then the paratroopers turned to the Palestinians—and they really gave it to them. They stuck guns in the Palestinians' faces and gave them what seemed like very serious warnings, accompanied by a few extra threatening gestures. In English, the paratroopers told us how dangerous it was to be inside Nablus. He told us to get out of there. Backtracking in the van, we were relieved we hadn't been detained.

This experience was about as far away as a person could get from the Israel Jeff had recently experienced with his grandmother and her church tour group. His three days with them in Jerusalem and over to Qum'Ran and Ein Gedi hid many truths about this place and its always roiling conflict. In the American Church Tour Version of Israel, a strange fusion of evangelical Christianity and Zionism, all Arabs are reduced to being street peddlers, friendly waiters, and the smiling face of "Holy Land" souvenir shops.

After hanging around for a half hour back at the taxi area, we headed up the same road again, because, according to the driver, the IDF had a "shift change" at 4:00 P.M. We kept saying this was the dumbest thing either of us had done, and we were right. But this time we passed safely through the tunnel, then hung a hard left onto a dirt and stone trail, with another van carrying a Palestinian family hoping to get home following close behind us. The road was so rutted, the terrain so rough, we couldn't believe this shitty van was actually making it. Then we were in plain view of the highway below. Above us, not two hundred yards up a steep hill, we also saw we were in plain view of an otherwise hidden IDF outpost.

It was getting dark now. But what a sunset. The sun was dipping behind the mountains across the road: red and orange, with visible individual beams of light shooting everywhere. "Biblical," we kept saying and laughing. It was like something you might see signaling a monumental event in the Bible.

A green jeep with blue lights spinning on top suddenly began to tear down the hill toward us. Luckily there was a barbed-wire fence separating them from us, and, fortunately, it looked like their road veered off into another direction through some rough terrain just ahead. Still, fear tingled my spine. Our van sped up through an olive grove and climbed, back tires bouncing and spinning, up another mountain. Everyone inside kept looking frantically in all directions for any sign of the Israeli troops.

Shortly after crossing the mountain, we arrived at a small West Bank village called Tell, where we all let out a huge sigh of relief, even though "safety" for us was a sealed-off combat zone that had been averaging a few Palestinian deaths a day for the last two weeks. Just down the road from Tell, Nablus remained encircled and under siege by the IDF. As we drove into the city, we let Samantha, the activist from Sweden who'd hitched a ride with us, off at an ISM safe house, then we kept on toward the city center.

Nablus, a city of two hundred thousand, the largest in the West Bank, had an eerie feeling. There wasn't a soul on the streets. Clouds of black smoke billowed from the burning tires of street blockades. An M1 Abrams tank spotted us and followed us with its turret cannon until we were out of sight.

Just past the tank and to the right was the hotel where Sara suggested we stay, which also happened to be the only one still open in the whole city. Actually, it was a nice hotel, but empty and really quiet.

We talked the guy at the front desk into letting us split a single room three ways, for thirty dollars. The only sign of the fighting was a single bullet hole in a hallway window. We threw down our small packs in the room and headed outside. It was now dusk and a little drizzly. There were three or four Palestinians hanging around in the narrow alleyways that led into the city's central market square, which was only a couple of blocks from our place. Also in the central square were the tank and some burning/smoldering tires.

Tank treads had shredded the pavement, and the fountain at the square's center had been repeatedly crushed and smashed beneath the tanks, which had left their tread marks across it. We started walking directly for the tank and its gun slowly turned in our direction with that mechanical "grrrrrrr" sound you imagine it making. There was also a Humvee-type vehicle parked nearby. We stopped for a minute to talk to a guy named Lloyd, who turned out to be from San Francisco and who was there as some sort of witness for a Christian aid group.

In the alleys of Nablus's Old City we got tea from some really friendly guys, talked with them a little, high-fived them all, then walked farther in. Minutes later, two Humvees started shooting large-caliber bullets down the street, red tracers slashing the dusk over our heads. We ran and hid behind a dumpster. A few more bursts of gunfire erupted, and then it was dead silent again. The Palestinians we'd been talking to had coolly split up the side streets and away from the Israelis.

Twenty minutes passed before one of us decided it was a good idea to head back for the central square, where the tank had been and the gunfire had come from, because that was the way back to the hotel. As we got back to the city's center, we spotted two Red Crescent ambulances parked where we had been talking to Lloyd an hour or so earlier. One of the drivers from the ambulance crew said a seventeen-year-old boy, Naji Sayeef, had been shot dead, bullet wounds to the neck and head. We lied and told the drivers we were journalists (Sara once interned at the *Cairo Times*) and the guys let us ride along to the site, the Balata refugee camp.

The clinic we pulled up to was riddled with huge bullet holes— from an IDF drive-by. We spent about twenty minutes inside and got all of the details on the killing: Supposedly Naji Sayeef was in the wrong place at the wrong time and the IDF soldiers had shot his head off. The bullets exploded his head and neck. Earlier that day, another Palestinian kid had also been shot, but he'd survived. According to the clinic workers, neither kid was doing anything wrong. With the story told, the two guys in the clinic offered to take us into the camp.

Balata, founded in 1948, was one of the first Palestinian refugee camps. Its entrance had a huge Hamas banner strung across the road. A huge metal loudspeaker bolted to the exterior of the camp's mosque was blaring a pissed-off-sounding voice in Arabic. A group of guys with megaphones walked around the corner, yelling Naji's name and saying all kinds of stuff in Arabic.

We lurked around in the narrow streets, passing Hamas and PFLP graffiti, and ended up at the home of the ambulance driver's friend. The building was run-down. It looked more like a shrunken public-housing project than a refugee camp. Our host was a young man with a beard. Inside, just past the apartment door, was a huge, floor-to-ceiling painting of our host's dead brother, fronted by a pair of crossed AK-47s. The man told us his brother had been killed several years earlier during the Intifada's worst fighting, at thirty-one years old. He'd been killed defending the camp's gates from invading IDF troops. On the opposing wall was a cap-and-gown graduation photo-graph of his other brother, a lawyer, who was in jail and hadn't been heard from for a long time. We listened to stories of Israeli injustice for over an hour. The whole thing had a staged feel, as if the same litany had been told in the same way to many foreign observers be-fore us. Finally, we said our good-byes. Back in the hotel we watched bad Egyptian pop videos on satellite TV in the lobby, trying to regis-ter all that we'd seen in the past seven or eight hours.

The next morning we awoke to the sounds of bustling street life: horns honking, people yelling and moving. The Israelis had gone, the hotel concierge told us as we checked out. Jeff and I decided to walk the roughly three miles from downtown to the nearest Israeli secu-rity checkpoint. From there, we could get a taxi back to Jerusalem.

In less than twelve hours, Nablus had gone from a desolate shell of abandoned buildings to a vibrant, crowded city. Where tires had smoldered the night before, vendors now sold fruit, batteries, and just about anything else you could imagine. Jeff looked around, amazed. "It went from a postapocalyptic horror movie to São Paulo overnight," he said. "Where do all these people go during a siege?"

As we walked from town we passed the former Palestinian Au-thority (PA) office compound. The wreckage was stunning. An acre-wide, four-story building had collapsed on itself following Israeli bombing in April 2002. Tank shells and large-caliber machine-gun bullets had Swiss-cheesed what remained of the building's walls. Though it had been destroyed less than two years earlier, the compound felt like a Roman ruin. Weeds and wildflowers blossomed in the rubble.

In the courtyard of the compound an unexploded bomb sat among the rubble. "Is that a five-hundred-pound bomb?" I asked Jeff.

"Don't know. Probably. Could be even bigger."

"Never heard you not know a military fact."

"My dad was a Marine, not Air Force. I was never really around bombs, man."

After pulling some artifacts from the rubble as souvenirs, including a tear-gas can, a red beret, and a poster of Arafat, we kept on trucking. The road to the checkpoint was lonely, dotted by auto shops, housing blocks, and the occasional underfed school. A juice shop was open and we got fruit smoothies. The shopkeeper spoke some English. We asked him where everyone goes during the IDF sieges.

"They stay inside . . . no lights," he said. "They hide from windows and sleep on floors."

A group of Palestinian teenage schoolgirls came into the shop. They giggled and gawked at the two Americans. "Ameri-kee," the shopkeeper told the little girls and they all laughed.

Upon reaching the checkpoint, we jumped in the line to pass out of Nablus. No matter where you go in Israel/Palestine, IDF checkpoints are messy affairs. As usual, a makeshift holding cell on the side of the road detained a dozen or so young Palestinian males inside a rectangle of concrete barriers fifty yards square topped with triple-strand coils of concertina wire. As we waited in line, we watched IDF soldiers call one of the detained guys forward. The soldier kept his M-16 pointed at the head of the Palestinian as he walked toward them. The soldiers told the man to stop walking when he got within a few feet of them: The one soldier never wavered with his rifle.

An hour later we crossed back into Israel, but not without getting told by an IDF guard that we were stupid and naïve and had "a death wish." Just beyond the checkpoint was an IDF military base. The Israeli flag flew above the dusty fort, and a dusty taxi area stood just beyond that. We negotiated with a Palestinian taxi driver to take us back toward Ramallah, where the next permanent IDF checkpoint is, after which we'd have to negotiate with another taxi to take us to Jerusalem.

The ride back through the rolling hills of the Holy Land couldn't have been on a nicer day. God's Country looked splendid with its endless groves of olive trees, though all the razor wire and the checkpoints did mar the effect. Every ten minutes or so, we'd pull up to a mobile IDF checkpoint with camo netting, Israeli flags, guns, and concrete reinforcements, and either we'd have to leave the cab, walk through the checkpoint, and then secure our next ride, or a soldier would come up and check our papers and passports.

In Palestine, it seemed that a lot of the best views, the highest bluffs, and the most fertile-looking soil had an Israeli flag stuck into it. These were the illegal Israeli settlements in the West Bank, and there were lots of them. "These settlers have great taste," Jeff said. "Every mountaintop has the Star of David and a subdivision. Imagine being a Palestinian and waking up every day in your dusty, run-down house with twenty siblings and looking up at the nicest, prettiest land, only to see the Israeli flag and a line of tract houses?"

The Israeli settlements aren't arbitrary. For the Israelis, much of their security from West Bank violence comes in the form of these topographically advantageous locations. And their surrounding buffer zones—enforced by IDF soldiers and weapons—certainly serve purposes beyond securing housing. For instance, the line of large settlements between Jerusalem and the Jordanian border has not only snatched some of the Jordan River valley's best farming soil for the Israelis, these linked outposts also offer Israelis a safe way of passage between Israel and Jordan.

Many people, including Jeff and me, see Israel's Gaza pullout of 2005 as both an easy appeasement to the Palestinians and a sacrifice Ariel Sharon made to secure his legacy in greater Israel, as it helps secure the much larger class of illegal Israeli settlers on the West Bank. By negotiating to toss the Gazans back their small area of land in the south, Sharon has seen to it that the major West Bank settlements, most of which are far larger and more strategically located, continue to exist and may yet become permanent.

IN EVERY WAR, bystanders like to pick sides. And with Israel/Palestine, both sides have their merits and their embarrassments. Eventually, pretty much anyone can be dragged into the dispute and forced to choose his side.

Nine months earlier, for example, the ISM reached a peak of international notoriety when a twenty-three-year-old American named Rachel Corrie chained herself in front of an IDF bulldozer and was crushed to death by the Israeli soldier driving it. Corrie was a passionate crusader for Palestinian rights. Her death was tragic. In the end, though, it was the preventability of Rachel Corrie's death that made it so awful.

Intoxicated on that white-lightning mix of Israel/Palestine real-estate politics and religion, Rachel Corrie wouldn't get out of the way of the dozer. The equally intoxicated Israeli bulldozer operator wouldn't stop . . . and together they created an eternally pointless loss. In the end, Rachel Corrie's death did nothing to slow the cause of Israeli security or promote Palestinian freedoms. All it did was kill Rachel Corrie. In the Israel/Palestine conflict, you don't need to be religious to become enmeshed.

After our brief glimpse into the Israeli/Palestinian conflict, all we knew was that we were more confused than ever. It was time to go to Iraq.

2

•

War Disneyland

"It's almost like being at Walt Disney's version of Arabian
Nights. *I lived in a villa that was originally owned by a
Republican Guard colonel . . . it had six bedrooms, two and
a half baths, two balconies. We had a hot tub on the
top-floor balcony. We had a huge galley kitchen. . . . We lived
very large in downtown Baghdad."*
—*an American Civil Affairs soldier on Green Zone living*

AFTER A WEEK traveling around Jordan—we went to the port city
of Aqaba and to Wadi Rum, where *Lawrence of Arabia* was
filmed—we made our way north to the national capital of Amman
and began searching for a bus to carry us to Baghdad. We found one
just before sundown on January 16, 2004, and climbed aboard.

The bus was packed. Suitcases and plastic bags full of food and
clothes were jammed into the overhead bins, with the arms of coats and
strings and straps dangling down above the seats. Old, leathery men
with kaffiyehs wrapped around their heads or necks stared at us, and
the young children stared at us. The vehicle itself had been promoted as
a "five-star bus . . . of course, my friends," which meant zero considering

everything in Jordan is sold in this manner. Actually it was a lemon with a sick engine, crappy seats, and no ventilation or suspension.

Just after we crossed the Iraq border, around 1:00 A.M., the bus broke down (again) in a dusty little settlement. Curious, we followed the other passengers and hopped off our wounded bus. The town was like a big, dark junkyard; crumbling buildings sat ringed by scrap metal and rusting auto parts; sporadic light shot across the scrubby brown landscape from flood lamps powered by gas-fueled generators. A tumbledown falafel stand was open, and we stumbled toward it, half drunk from a bottle of whiskey we'd been sipping on the bus. Jeff bumped into a young Iraqi, who stopped, wheeled around, and started shouting at him. We ignored him and kept walking. We bought sandwiches. On the way back to the bus, the Iraqi youth and a few friends stared at Jeff and flashed a knife in the air. We got right back on the bus.

The night was punctuated by intermittent engine failures. By sunrise our highway speed had been reduced to twenty miles an hour. Along this very same Highway 10 big-time journalists and contractors often traveled in armored convoys between Baghdad and Amman at speeds exceeding one hundred miles per hour and at a cost of five hundred dollars per head. That was out of our price range, hence the fifty-dollar bus. Plus, we weren't that worried about security. Word from the peaceniks we'd met in Jordan and Israel, a few of whom had just come from Iraq, was that Baghdad was pretty safe at this time. It was true, early 2004 would prove to be a relatively quiet time of the war.

As the sun began to rise, we saw our first burned tank and jeep carcasses, blackened and rounded steel hulks that became more numerous as we approached Baghdad. As the sun rose higher, the highway widened to four lanes and traffic increased. We made it to

Fallujah by about 10:00 A.M., then our sick bus began to crawl even slower. It would take us six hours to cover the last forty-five or so miles to Baghdad. By two that afternoon, we were stuck in our first Baghdad traffic jam. Iraq has seen an increase in the number of cars on the road since the end of Saddam Hussein's reign with its 100 percent car tax; now smuggled-in vehicles with Turkish, UAE, and EU license plates were nearly as common as Iraqi ones.

Our voyage finally ended around 4:00 P.M. at the city's central bus station, where chaos ruled. Hundreds of minibuses were coming and going across a broad swath of pavement the size of several football fields. While we were picking up our luggage from the bus's undercarriage, a female fellow passenger who spoke English offered to split a cab. We told her we wanted to go to the Al Rasheed Hotel inside the Green Zone, one of the few hotels there we knew by name.

"That's Saddam's house," she said. "Now Mister Bush house!" Her head was wrapped in a flowery scarf, face showing, and she looked flinty, but she was laughing at her own joke. We'd soon learn that Iraqis love jokes, especially ones about Saddam, gays, Bush, sex, and donkeys . . . roughly the same things Americans tell jokes about.

We knew about the Green Zone: that walled-off seat from which Ambassador Bremer and the Coalition Provisional Authority (CPA) administered Iraq's occupation. It was also the center of America's nation-building effort in Iraq. During Baath rule, it had been the core of Saddam's government, complete with palaces and parade grounds. There was even a zoo, where a U.S. soldier had gotten his hand bitten off by an underfed tiger.

The Green Zone . . . War Disneyland, the beating heart of the occupation and a megafortress that insulated the CPA's policymakers from the Iraqi policy-livers. Its outer walls were quite possibly the ugliest vista in Iraq. What the white picket fence is to suburbia, the fifteen-foot concrete blast wall is to occupations in the Middle East. These walls—the same kind as that which separates the West Bank from Israel—completely encircle the Green Zone. The walls are imposing, uninviting, and send an unambiguous message to the Iraqis: Keep Out.

OUR TAXI LEFT us out at one of the Zone's major checkpoints, called the Al Rasheed Gate for its proximity to the hotel of the same name. Never had we seen a more threatening militarized position. It made the Nablus checkpoint in Palestine look tame. What had once been the road leading to the Rasheed had become a few hundred yards of no-man's-land, layered by razor wire and flanked by a roadblock of mega-sandbags called Hesco Barriers. A guard tower, with a heavy machine gun poking from it, oversaw the scene. Just outside the gate's entrance, Iraqi hustlers tried to sell falafel, cigarettes, candy, school supplies, watches, and other looted goods to anyone in a buying mood.

A maze of razor wire spilled out onto the street and Jeff promptly ripped his jeans on it. From an opening in it walked a youngish blonde, the prettiest woman we'd seen in weeks.

"Backpackers in Baghdad? Wow, now I've really seen it all," she said and giggled. "Where are you guys going with those big packs? You know you'll have to empty every single thing."

"Can we stay at the Al Rasheed Hotel?" Jeff asked her.

"No." The girl smiled at our sublime ignorance. "It's been closed since Wolfowitz was rocket-attacked there this past summer. C'mon, I'll take you guys to a hotel."

The blond girl had a driver, a casually dressed Iraqi man, and we all packed into his car. This was the second woman to help us in an hour and we were beyond thankful. "Thank you so, so much for saving us at that checkpoint," I said.

"No problem," she turned from the front seat and extended her hand. "I'm Marla. Nice to meet ya."

It only took a few minutes to get stuck in traffic again, this time on a bridge that spanned the brown Tigris River. We peppered Marla with questions, which she answered as fast as we asked. She had been in Baghdad since the initial invasion, and had been in Afghanistan before that. She was twenty-seven and from California.

"What do you do here?" Jeff asked.

"I run an NGO," she said. Marla fumbled through her stuff and handed us two business cards. "We keep track of civilian casualties in war zones." According to her card, she was Marla Ruzicka from the NGO called CIVIC.

"You must drink a lot of coffee," I said.

"Why do you say that? Because I move so fast?"

"You're a spaz like me."

"I have a lot of energy." She laughed. "How much money do you want to spend on a hotel?"

"Cheap. What about the Palestine?" Jeff dropped the name of a hotel we'd read about in *The New Yorker.*

"Ohh . . . it's expensive there, but there are cheap-o ones right by it. I'll take you. So, what are you guys doing here?"

"We don't really know yet," Jeff said. "We want to work."

"E-mail me and we'll get together. I might be able to help you boys."

Marla led us to a hotel compound and our first night in Baghdad turned into a celebration. After checking into the Al Rabei Hotel, across from the Sheraton and Palestine hotels, we cracked open a bottle of whiskey. The room had a boom box and we blasted the only

CD we still possessed (Jeff had left all his CDs on the bus) and took up seats on the balcony of our room to enjoy some nineties indie rock—Built to Spill and Archers of Loaf. Visuals were provided by the shockingly vast darkness that was Baghdad at night. From our perch in a narrow strip of hotels between the militarized and secure Green Zone and the encircling destroyed city—known to all Western occupiers as the Red Zone—we had a view of Iraq's two worlds: those of the Coalition and the Iraqi people. Despite being a sprawling city of six million people, now being overseen by an occupying government made up of the planet's most powerful nations, the city had virtually no electricity, with only the rare privately owned generator providing light. In the night, Baghdad looked like a sparsely populated desert. Circling in the dark sky, two Black Hawk helicopters patrolled up and down the Tigris, reminding us that this was a war zone.

"Mission accomplished, amigo," I said to Jeff. "From a Brooklyn roof to a Baghdad balcony . . . we did it."

"Cheers," Jeff said; then he lifted the bottle. Tired from the twenty-four-hour bus ride, we passed out soon after.

THE NEXT MORNING we were awakened by an extremely loud explosion. A suicide car bomber had hit the Assassin's Gate checkpoint. Curious, we walked the few miles to the scene. When we got there, the landscape was full of the things we'd, in retrospect, like not to have seen. There were smoldering frames of cars and a deep crater, a blood-splattered passenger bus and body bags filled with corpses, and bits and pieces of clothes. We couldn't believe the scope of destruction. Twenty-six people had been killed, over one hundred injured.

The Assassin's Gate bombing was definitely shocking, but the scene surrounding it felt incomprehensible. What was this place, where twenty-six people could be sliced to oblivion by shrapnel from a bomb set off by their countrymen?

We went out for a walk and soon found a street full of Internet cafés and black-market moneychangers. Jeff and I fired off e-mails back home and drank gallons of complimentary Iraqi tea, all to a background of deafening Arab pop. We bought bootleg DVDs, a fresh phenomenon in Iraq, where a new, digitally based, free-market economy was quickly expanding. We picked up an American kung fu/ Western movie starring Hong Kong actor Jackie Chan with subtitles in Chinese and Arabic. In a way, that's what the Iraq War under the CPA had become: a pointless, violent movie in multiple languages.

We gave ourselves two weeks to find jobs in Iraq. After lunch at the Sheraton, we set off for the Green Zone's Convention Center to look for work. Reaching the cavernous Convention Center took a fifteen-minute cab ride to the still-opened Al Rasheed Gate, and then a forty-five-minute wait in a line of Iraqis to get through the checkpoint. Despite what we'd already seen that morning, we failed to realize that one of the most dangerous activities in the world is waiting in line in front of a U.S. military checkpoint in Iraq. Thousands of people have been killed by suicide bombers, car bombs, and drive-by shooters while waiting in various lines during the war.

Finally, after being searched by three different Iraqis while leaving through a sandbag maze, we were introduced to the 82nd Airborne, who ran the Al Rasheed Gate. The soldiers were happy to see two fellow young Americans and made small talk with us about hometowns, sports, and women.

We crossed through the Al Rasheed checkpoint and into the Green Zone to find an oasis of calm. We stared down a wide, empty road. On our right side stood the Al Rasheed Hotel. On our left was our destination, the Baghdad Convention Center, a huge concrete bunker guarded by the elite 82nd Airborne and encircled by sandbags, iron fences, and razor wire. It was the only Green Zone building in which Iraqi citizens could enter and interact with their Western rulers, after navigating a hundred-yard gauntlet of checkpoints, metal detectors, X-ray machines, and security pat-downs.

Once inside the Convention Center, we marveled at the lobby's tile mosaics, especially one that featured Saddam Hussein in Nordic dress, throwing little atomic symbols into the air while on horseback. We laughed and headed off on our job hunt.

The Convention Center was home to such noble operations as UN Oil for Food, the U.S. Agency for International Development (USAID), and DFID (the U.K. version of USAID), as well as Bechtel, MCI, Freedom Radio (Baghdad's pop music and propaganda broadcast station), and Royal Jordanian Airlines. It was also home to the CPA offices of Human Rights, NGO Assistance, Detainee Issues, and Civil Society, and a U.S.-funded/Iraqi-anchored propagandist television station, Al-Hurrah. As the site of CPA and Iraqi Governing Council press conferences, journalists always milled about like vultures looking for scraps, dressed in cargo pants and Ex-Officio safari shirts with notebooks in hand and pens at the ready.

At the Iraqi Assistance Center, or IAC—a "help desk" that looked like a hotel registration counter—an Iraqi guy listening to Bon Jovi (the Iraqis love Bon Jovi) gave us worker applications and a flyer for a Procter & Gamble job fair later in the week. Iraq's unemployment was over 60 percent and jobs with the Coalition were the highest-paying and therefore the most coveted.

Jeff and I split up. The unfriendly Bon Jovi fan directed me to the CPA's NGO Assistance Office. When I walked in, a pretty female soldier, a sergeant, was sitting on the edge of a desk and wearing her full desert camo battle dress uniform (BDU), with one leg and desert-combat-booted foot dangling above the floor as she held court in an office full of Iraqi women. Slim, athletic, and in her early twenties, with olive skin and long brown hair, she reminded me of the cute IDF soldiers we were constantly being rebuffed by back in the clubs of Tel Aviv.

She looked over at me, somewhat surprised to see a young, scrubby Westerner in her office. I said hello and asked, "Do you need any help? Like, with work here."

She stood up and walked over to me. We introduced ourselves. She was Sergeant Jody Lautenschlager. "We actually do need some help. Do you have any experience in development and aid?" she asked.

"Sure. I was just in Palestine with the Red Crescent," I said, semi-lying. I flashed back to our night under siege in Nablus, with the ambulance crew, when that seventeen-year-old kid had been killed by the IDF patrol.

It turned out that the two people who'd been heading up the NGO capacity-building initiative for CPA were quitting and leaving Iraq in just a few days, and Jody needed to fill the positions. She told me a little about the jobs, something about capacity building and civil society, to which I nodded as if I knew what she was talking about.

"There is no doubt in my mind that I can handle the job." There was a lot of doubt. "My friend Jeff is here with me. He can fill the other position."

"Great. When can you guys start?" she said. She was grinning. "Oh, and we can't pay you."

"When can we start? . . . Now. And about the money, that's fine."

So that was it, we had jobs: NGO coordinators and capacity

builders for the CPA's NGO Assistance Office, whatever that meant. We exchanged e-mail addresses, and I let Jody get back to work. Jody started referring to us as the "dirty Berkeley hippies that stumbled in."

I sprinted out of Jody's office. I found Jeff in the basement, at Bechtel's office, filling out an application. The room's fluorescent lights and plastic furniture were pretty low-budget for the world's premier construction company. Cheap bastards. As if that billion-dollar, no-bid contract hadn't provided them enough cash to buy a few lamps.

Jeff looked up as I entered the office.

"Hey, I think we got jobs," I said.

"Wait, I'm almost done."

"It looks like we got hired by the NGO office."

"Without resumes?"

"Yeah, as volunteers. Well, we need to send resumes. This female soldier just kinda hired us. C'mon, she's still in her office, you can meet her."

Jeff met Jody and was impressed. She was a fast talker with endless information. We talked for a few minutes. Before joining the Army, Jody had been a trainer at Starbucks in Seattle. She sure wasn't lacking ambition, and rattled off a few things she was working on: getting the UN back to Iraq, coordinating with the U.S. Embassy in Jordan, building an NGO database, and establishing NGO centers across Iraq. It seemed a little odd that the CPA didn't have qualified people to fill such a position.

THE CPA WAS AN overwhelmingly Department of Defense–run affair, with a sprinkling of foreign officers and grunts running around and being used by the Pentagon whenever the Americans needed to show a "more international" (which meant less American) face or motive or excuse. Despite being called a Coalition, the CPA was 90 percent American. The CPA had trouble filling its ranks and had to draw from conservative think tanks like the Heritage Foundation. Most of those hired were young, forcing one Army officer to say, "Shit, this place is run by a bunch of goddamned interns!"

Before the CPA's occupation of Iraq, the Pentagon had never run a nation-building project. In fact, one of George W. Bush's first-term campaign promises had been that he would avoid "engaging in nation building." Now, building a nation in Iraq, he'd made a fateful decision: The Department of Defense would run the occupation. Historically, all previous American occupations and rebuilding efforts—from the Philippines and Cuba to Germany and Japan after World War II—had been overseen by the State Department, usually with an American general serving as a figurehead.

When the CPA took control of Iraq, the State Department's post-war plans were publicly tossed out the window, and the DoD shoved itself into power, seemingly without a plan, unleashing one of the great ironies of postwar Iraq. To create democracy in Iraq, the Bush administration had chosen to use the one American societal tool that wasn't democratic: the military and its chain of command. This would become one of the major contributors to the ultimate failure of the CPA.

But in those first days and weeks, Jeff and I were just pleased to have jobs, and we were sincerely ready to help build civil society in Iraq. After saying good-bye to Jody, we left the Convention Center. We walked out toward Saddam's old Parade Grounds, with those two huge scimitar swords thrusting out of the earth and into the sky. "Man, I wish we had some weed," I said. "What a perfect spot to smoke a victory blunt."

. . .

A WHITE HYUNDAI BUS with a purplish roof drove past, filled with soldiers and civilians. It stopped just ahead of us and a soldier got off. We asked him about it.

"It's the Green Zone shuttle," he said. "Comes every half hour all day. Runs less at night, though."

So the GZ has its own transit system, like the monorail at Disney World. Since the bus had already moved on, we trekked on foot, planning to catch the next one we saw. The Green Zone has two major landmarks, the Convention Center and the Republican Palace. In between are scores of bombed-out palaces and former Baath Party ministries, as well as some parkland, housing complexes, and an abandoned zoo.

We approached a gold-domed mosque that straddled a Green Zone road. It was home to Titan Corporation. As we walked closer, two American employees were standing outside, smoking cigarettes. We chatted with them for a few minutes; they said, if we wanted, Titan would let us up on the roof to get a good look at the Green Zone layout, as well as see the remnants of "Shock and Awe." One of Titan's jobs was hiring Iraqi translators for the CPA. And since every Iraqi that worked for the CPA had been hired as a translator, Titan was responsible for nearly all Iraqis working inside the Green Zone.

From the roof of the Titan offices we could see more bombed-out buildings, some columns of smoke, a sky full of helicopters, and the partially completed Mother of All Battles Mosque, which Saddam had been building when he was overthrown. We also saw that the next Green Zone bus was coming. We hustled back downstairs and jumped on at the Titan stop for a little tour. Next stop was the Green Zone Café, a former gas station whose parking lot was full of Hummers and armored SUVs. From there we passed the CASH (Combat Support Hospital), the finest in Iraq, now only admitting military and CPA officials. There were also more destroyed palaces lining the route, many with blast zones that implied puncture by Tomahawk cruise missiles.

ROUGHLY THE SIZE of Central Park, at around four square miles, the Green Zone occupied Baghdad's core and was its most prized real estate. Since the fall of Saddam, it had been transformed from the Baathist seat of power into Washington, D.C., on the Tigris. Pentagon-run, militarily secure, and Iraqi-serviced, the GZ was the opposite of the chaos and anarchy that was Baghdad. There were four entry points to the Green Zone: one, across the 14th of July Bridge, led to the posh Kerrada and Jadiriyah neighborhoods; another western checkpoint led to Baghdad's most dangerous stretch of road, Route Irish, which cuts across the rich Mansour neighborhood en route to the airport; and the last two checkpoints were on the same road, about half a mile apart, the Rasheed Gate and Assassins's Gate. All of these entry points have since been the targets of innumerable bombs.

Our bus reached the Republican Palace in midafternoon. We got out to gape. A huge, imposingly domed structure meant to impress all who gazed upon it, the palace was the former seat of the Baath Party, became the CPA's headquarters, and would later be turned into the U.S. Embassy. Inside were the architects of a liberated Iraq. After Baghdad fell in April 2003, the country was put under control of the Pentagon's Office of Reconstruction and Humanitarian Assistance (ORHA), with Lieutenant General Jay Garner in charge. Three weeks later, though, the White House changed course and created the Coalition

Provisional Authority, which was to provide stability and security to the people of Iraq, put together and support the provisional Iraqi Governing Council, create a network of Iraqi ministries to fairly oversee Iraq's resources and needs, and then—when all was stable and prepared—set into motion responsible Iraqi self-governance through democratic processes.

For this job, President Bush selected the bureaucrat and former ambassador L. Paul "Jerry" Bremer III to run the CPA. Brylcreem handsome, and apparently teleported into Baghdad from the early years of the Nixon administration, Bremer was cut from the same sociocultural fabric as both George Bushes: a Yale grad with ties to Wall Street and Republican Washington. Before taking over the CPA, Bremer was head of Kissinger Associates, a consulting firm run by former secretary of state Henry Kissinger. Bremer's area of expertise is terrorism risk assessment. After 9/11, Bremer also announced the founding of Crisis Consulting Practice, his own terrorism risk-consulting firm, on October 11, 2001.

For those actually interested in diplomacy, the idea of placing a terrorism specialist in charge of rebuilding a democratic Iraq seems a bit strange, especially considering there was no history of terrorism in Iraq at the time of his appointment. Under Bremer, terrorism came to Iraq with a vengeance.

Maybe Bremer's selection was meant to reinforce the premise that Iraq remained part of the Global War on Terror (GWOT). And Bremer, with his experience assessing terrorism, had the jargon of threat and fear down perfectly. Who better to put on CNN or Fox or Dave Letterman than a guy whose job it was to scare corporations into paying him to assess their terror risks? From his first press conference on, Bremer mixed fear and diplomacy, overlaid with a mirage of nation building. He also did his best to uphold the myth that the growing number of insurgents in Iraq were associated with the people who'd attacked the United States on 9/11.

Wearing desert tan combat boots, matching khaki pants, a blue blazer, shirt and striped red tie, Bremer set the CPA dress code. By the time we arrived in Iraq the Bremer Look had fully penetrated the CPA. Like a news anchor wearing a suit jacket and tie but naked below the desk, the Bremer Look suggested both serious work and slightly reckless adventure. Considering that most Iraqis wore plastic sandals, and didn't live in palaces or travel by helicopter, they associated the Bremer Look with American arrogance. Standing outside the palace and watching the parade of mini-Bremers going about their business, Jeff and I imagined them phoning or e-mailing home and telling their loved ones, "It's a dirty job, but somebody's gotta do it."

Fact is, most CPA combat boots never left the Green Zone. The Look, like the CPA itself, was all image. As long as people at home turned on the TV and saw Bremer or Dan Senor, his spokesman, booting and blazering through Baghdad, the propaganda fit the press release. With the Pentagon controlling Iraq's reality in America, all the CPA had to do was present a credible situation, complete with swashbuckling diplomats, dead terrorists, and smiling Iraqis, and the American people would go back to their real-estate deals, celebrity worship, and fad diets. The CPA and Bremer were keeping the lid on the fire in an election year.

Gaining access to the palace where Bremer lived and worked was virtually impossible, even for U.S. citizens. The 1st Marine Expeditionary Force, with a secondary ring of Nepalese Ghurkas, guarded it. Every approved visitor to the palace had to have his identity reconfirmed upon arrival and then was signed in and out. We didn't know

anyone who could do that, so on that first late afternoon in War Disneyland we simply stood awestruck by Bremer's fortress within a
fortress.

With its palm-tree-lined backdrop against the sun's late-day glow,
the Green Zone took on a palpably relaxed, postcard feel. The streets
inside the Zone were calm and traffic-free, the opposite of the chaos
outside the gates.

3

·

You Will Not

W E CAUGHT THE NEXT SHUTTLE back to the Convention Center. Jody had told us to register with the U.S. Consulate. Housed just down the hall from Jody's office, the consulate was a small room staffed by three women from the State Department. A middle-aged lady ran the place. Her name was on her badge: Beth Payne.

"What the *hell* are you boys doing here?" She didn't seem to be joking.

"Wanted to try and find some work."

"Do you have any idea where you are? This is Baghdad: a war zone, not a work zone." She seemed angry at us; it made a sharp contrast to Jody's friendliness. "This is *not* a safe place for you. Do you know how dangerous it is here?"

Feeling cocky, I answered: "We've just come from the West Bank, so we have an idea."

"This is not the West Bank. Iraq is not Israel. You have no business being here." Now, visibly annoyed at our arrogance and ignorance, she launched a tactical strike. "You will not get badges! You will not get housing! You will not find employment!"

Shocked by her fury, we cowered for a moment in silence.

"Where are you staying? I can't force you to leave, but I advise against staying for long."

We provided Beth all our info, and she huffed and puffed around her office like an angry mother. Jeff gave me a pissed-off and confused look. What was this lady's deal? Later, we'd realize that Beth wasn't in the military and didn't have to adhere to any bullshit policies. She was offering us the truth as she saw it. Few people at the CPA ever did the same, and instead hid the truth from us out of either ignorance or mindless fealty to policy. As we made our way out of her office, Beth firmly stated: "Iraq is the most dangerous place on earth. It is no place for two college dropouts!"

We left joking about Beth's bitchiness. "Now I really wish we had weed. Let's go back to our hotel and relax." That was code. By relax, I meant enjoy the sweet science of antianxiety pills: a stashed-away mix of Valium and Xanax that we had left over from a collection gathered during our stay in no-prescription-necessary Jordan.

"Yeah, Beth Payne made me anxious."

"I'm antianxiety."

BACK OUTSIDE the Green Zone walls, the contrast was stunning. After spending a day in the GZ bubble, you could almost forget that

Baghdad is a city in anarchy. Traffic choked every intersection. From every angle, Iraqis tried to get our attention—"Hello, Mister! *Mister!*"

A newspaper article from a few months earlier mentioned one-dollar boat rides across the Tigris. It sounded like a good way to enjoy the sunset. We decided to give it a try.

4

•

RIGHT OUTSIDE THE GREEN ZONE, a young, oddly dressed Westerner was climbing out of a taxi at the same spot where we'd found Marla. Scraggly bearded and about our age, the guy was in rough shape and a little disoriented.

"Um, are you guys Americans?" he asked.

We introduced ourselves, and he did the same. "I'm Charlie Crain, a freelance journalist. I wanted to register with the consulate. Do you know where that is?"

"Too late. We were just there and they close at five P.M., plus the lady there is a bitch. Don't let her ruin your day."

"Oh . . . What do you guys do here?"

"Nothing yet, we just got here yesterday. We know a little about the town, after a drinking session last night with some folks. You wanna go for a sunset cruise on the Tigris with us?"

"Sure."

And then we were three.

WE WALKED DOWN Haifa Street, a major Tigris frontage road, and found a bunch of boatmen. Sunset on the river seemed like a good time and we had yet to "tame" the Tigris, which was generally our first order of business whenever we arrived in an area with a sizable river. Despite its putrid stink and diarrhea-colored water, the river was the most peaceful place in Baghdad.

Down by the river, we haggled with an Iraqi in an athletic jump-suit who was around our age and had a pistol sticking from his belt. He wanted five dollars, we offered him two dollars, and struck a deal. As we began boarding the leaking boat, I playfully grabbed the gun from the boatman's belt. Charlie looked like he was about to cry. It was a fake gun; a lighter, actually. I thought it was real. The boatman offered me a cigarette and laughed. Charlie laughed, too. Jeff took a photo of me holding the day's issue of *Stars and Stripes*. The head-line read: "U.S Now Considering Possible Iraq Elections."

On the boat, Charlie told us this trip was his first real expedition beyond the U.S. border. The previous spring he'd finished his MA at Northwestern University's journalism school and decided to try his hand as a full-fledged freelance war correspondent instead of riding a night desk in a small-town newspaper office, awaiting news of DUIs and domestic violence. It was a bold move. He didn't know who he'd be writing for yet; he didn't have any relationships with editors will-ing to publish his work, other than a tentative hookup at the *Raleigh News-Observer.* He was like us: He'd come to Baghdad for the adven-ture and opportunity. We liked him immediately.

As the boat shoved off, Charlie said that after flying into Istanbul, he'd traveled overland by taxi into Iraq. Somewhere along the way, a Turkish cab driver had stolen his luggage. He'd bought his new wardrobe in Dohuk, Iraq, and his getup was standard Iraqi: a kind of sleazy, generic, disco-Arab look of 100 percent polyester and nylon. Sanctions prevented the latest sartorial trends from coming to Iraq, and as a result the national garb possesses the distinctive essence of late-1970s pimp. Still, it beat the premium adventure clothes from REI that so many of the other Americans wore around the Green Zone. So not only was Charlie not supported by a news-outlet foreign desk, he didn't have the clothes for the job, either. We liked him more because of it.

People we met in the Green Zone kept calling the rest of Iraq the "Red Zone," as if once out there in The Red, nothing could be trusted or believed—and everything you might touch was deadly. For some reason, during our first month in Baghdad, we found this exceptionally funny, and we kept sarcastically saying in a Texas accent, "Dang, ya'll live in the *Red* Zone."

Charlie was soon annoyed by how much we said it, as well as our other new catchphrase, "You will not!" Which was understandable. Jeff and I have been hanging out so long—and across so many different backdrops and experiences—that we sometimes run out of new things to say, so to keep conversation going we lean heavily on new catchphrases or lines from movies or notable quotations from daily life . . . just to break the silence. What made it funnier was that no one in Baghdad other than the Americans called Iraq the Red Zone, and Americans spoke the words with fear, as if to enter it was to risk being set upon by the locals and eaten over a bed of shredded lettuce, like so much kebab. Of course, most Iraqis thought the same thing about people inside the Green Zone.

The fabled Tigris River splits Baghdad more or less down the middle north to south. For all its fame, the Tigris is actually a pretty sad-looking, thick, muddy waterway reminiscent of nothing so much as chocolate milk with the smell of sewage. The river's banks, especially along the eastern side where they're traced by Abu Nawas Street, used to be prime real estate before the invasion, but many of these houses were destroyed during the "Shock and Awe" campaign or the subsequent UN Headquarters bombing the previous fall. Now the street was closed off and riddled with checkpoints, blast walls, and razor wire, staffed by zealous and heavily armed Iraqi men, private security workers hired to protect the Baghdad hotels nearby.

Saddam had many palaces alongside the Tigris, most with over-emphasized, phallic-looking domes, some with fishing ponds, and all with the same Islamic-Miami color scheme and feel. When looking downstream from central Baghdad along the river, you could see the fires from oil refineries in and around the Dora district, which at night put an eerie orange glow over the southern part of the city. Seafood fare from the river was offered on the sidewalks fronting the river, still living fish on wooden carts in small tanks holding an inch or two of water to keep them alive—the fish were surprisingly tasty.

The urban sprawl of Baghdad is home to nearly six million residents of all tribal and religious backgrounds and affiliations. Nearly half of that population lives in the Shi'ite slum of Sadr City, formerly Saddam City, now renamed after the famous Shia martyr Grand Aya-tollah Mohammed Sadiq Al Sadr, who was executed by Saddam in the 1990s. Sadr City takes up the northeastern corner of Baghdad, sepa-rated from the city center by a series of military canals. The western bank of the Tigris is home to many former members of Saddam's Baath Party who live in the stronghold Mansour district. Mansour is also the city's wealthiest area, with the modest Shia/Christian neighborhoods of Kerrada and Arasat on the river's east side coming in close behind.

The sunset cruise wasn't bad. We motored up and down the river for a time in the setting sun, getting our bearings and figuring out what was where, especially in relation to the Green Zone. After the boat trip, dinner plans were made. Charlie came back to our hotel and over a bottle of Scotch joined us in some early evening poker. Jeff quickly passed out from Xanax and alcohol. I pressed Charlie on his story. Chicago bred, he did his undergrad at the University of Chicago. His views on the war were very different from mine. He was a hawk and proinvasion. But despite these differences of opinion, we both hoped the occupation would succeed; we wanted a democratic, free, and secure Iraq. Charlie was much more optimistic about this than I was.

Even though the twenty-four-hour cable stations and a bunch of the big newspapers called this era Postwar Iraq, people in the Red Zone had already started to grumble that the real war was just beginning. In January 2004, the insurgency was still a toddler. Hope was still in the air. In Iraq's teahouses, restaurants, and bars—both inside and outside the Green Zone—many journalists, contractors, profiteers, and Iraqis thought the CPA had a shot at avoiding a long-term guerrilla war and establishing democracy.

Jeff woke up and we decided to go across to the Palestine Hotel's bar for a drink. The Palestine was the same drab brownish-sand color that the majority of buildings were in Iraq. It still bore scars from a tank shelling in the spring of 2003 that killed two cameramen, one from Reuters, the other from the Spanish news outlet Telecino. Jeff pointed out the holes from our balcony, less than one hundred yards away. We knew about the tank assault from the news, but it resonated with us because of a series of dispatches by Jon Lee Anderson, who wrote his stories in *The New Yorker* and often made references to it. Jeff kept staring and pointing at the holes, which were round and were spattered with shrapnel scars. "No fucking way that wasn't intentional!" he said.

IN THE LOBBY of the Palestine, some war trash lurked about, including a guy named Dave, whom we would soon nickname Sketchy Dave. He was wearing a ratty leather jacket and looked to be in his late twenties or early thirties, with a goatee, receding hairline, and semilong hair. Over a beer he gave us a rundown of the whole Red Zone scene.

"There are two major hotel compounds, here and the Hamra, across town," he said. "The CIA stays at the Baghdad Hotel, and they're always getting attacked. There are no girls here, so get ready to jerk off a lot. I've been here for a while and know everyone. There is great chicken across the street. You guys hungry?"

We were.

Moving to the restaurant across the street—a place he called "Fanar Chicken"—Sketchy Dave's stories kept coming. He told us about a troop of European clowns who drank too much, but who helped a lot of Iraqi children. Then he went on about his plan to start a bike messenger company in the Green Zone, like in San Francisco, where he was from, and tried to recruit Jeff. He said he'd been to Burma, Nepal, Liberia, and more, and he was currently about to get a job with Agence France-Presse (AFP) in Basra as a photographer. His stories sounded a little too crazy to be true, but he was certainly right about the food. For three dollars you got a fresh and well-seasoned roasted half chicken, cooked over an open flame, rotisserie style, with an amazing array of spices. Iraqi chicken proved to be about the best deal for the money I'd ever had. Not only that, but for that same three dollars a huge hummus, fresh salad, and pita tray, called a mezze plate, arrived on the table before the chicken and rice.

"The food in Baghdad is pretty good," Dave said. "I'll take you guys to get the best fruit juice and dessert after this."

After paying the bill for all of us, Dave popped out of the restaurant and hailed a cab like he was on Madison Avenue instead of Sadoun Street. In our naïveté, we assumed this was both normal and safe, so we came along.

Baghdad at night is under unofficial curfew. After dark, the city's bustling markets, sidewalks, and roadways become ghost town–deserted. Our cab hurtled at about sixty miles per hour around Ali Baba Circle and toward the Christian neighborhood of Kerrada before screeching to a halt at a corner juice shop. It was closed.

"Fuck," Dave suggested.

We decided to go back to Fanar Bar, which was on the second floor of the Fanar Hotel, and just a few doors down from our hotel.

Sketchy Dave knew everyone everywhere, but as we entered the Fanar, people seemed apprehensive upon seeing him. That didn't stop us, being gullible morons, from making plans to rent an apartment with him in Kerrada.

We ordered beers and a narghile water pipe, commonly called a hookah in college dorm rooms worldwide and known as *sheesha* in the Middle East. A sweaty, middle-aged American sat down with us.

After saying hi to Dave he greeted us: "Andrew Robert Duke, nice to meet you." He wore wire-rimmed glasses, had a mustache, and was dressed for cubicle chic: pressed trousers and a striped, short-sleeved dress shirt. He even wore a sleazy necktie. Sketchy Dave called him Dilbert of Arabia.

"What are guys doing here?"

"Not too sure. Think we're doing aid work with Iraqi NGOs."

"Great," he said. He smiled as his eyes twinkled. "Maybe I can help you. I know this guy, great guy, a French-Lebanese fellow named Hassan, who is trying to airlift in ten thousand soccer balls and a few tons of rice. Right now they're in a hangar in Kuwait just waiting for a ride. The bastards at BIAP [Baghdad International Airport, formerly Saddam International] won't call me back."

The Duke, as we immediately started calling him, was one of Baghdad's most memorable characters. Originally from Colorado, he was in Iraq mainly to wheel and deal. Out came Charlie's notebook: Charlie's first real source. This made the Duke even more animated. He had even more stories than Dave, and the whoppers just kept coming. I don't remember any of them, though, because I was drinking myself into oblivion.

During our time in Iraq, we spent (at least) a few nights a week at the Fanar Bar. Dark and sleazy, with booth seating and narghile pipes at every table, the place was about as timeless a wartime watering hole as one could find in Baghdad. British mercenaries sat with Washington lawyers from firms like Patton Boggs, while a senator from Romania ate shish kebabs with Lebanese profiteers and German reporters. John F. Burns of *The New York Times* would be at a table with Jon Lee Anderson from *The New Yorker,* two great war correspondents, far from home, enjoying a drink while swapping sources and info in a seedy bar. Serbian mercenaries would be talking Vlade Divac and Slobo's trial at The Hague with State Department contractors. The same Serbians had been killing so many Muslims a decade ago that NATO bombed their country. Now, they were getting paid by NATO countries to manage Muslims. It's funny how things work out.

The Duke held court in the Fanar Bar like no one else. He was born for this war. We loved his style. In America, he was just another businessman, always playing some angle. In Iraq, he was the Duke. During our time in Iraq, the Duke popped up everywhere, from the pool at the Republican Palace to a snooker room in a private gentlemen's club. Mostly, though, we saw him at the Fanar.

"Welcome, Jeff and Ray," he'd say. Then, like a master host, he'd introduce his companions for the evening, "This is Dieter from *Die Welt*. And his friend, Uter. I know you know Charlie." Then he'd recount the day's best anecdote about Iraq gone mad. "They are trying to rip me off at the Palestine. They locked all my stuff in my room and won't budge."

Other times, he'd offer up a scheme: "I've got ten palettes of fruit juice. Do you guys want them? Iraqis are thirsty. I'll just give them to you."

THAT NIGHT, in what now seems like many moments of questionable judgment, Charlie, Jeff, and I agreed to rent an apartment with Sketchy Dave. He said he knew a place in Kerrada that was housing a bunch of foreigners. He gave us the address, and we agreed to move in a few days later—we'd already paid for several nights at the Al Rabei. Dave claimed that for two hundred dollars a month we'd have a two-bedroom place with security.

ON TUESDAY of our first week in Baghdad, Jody e-mailed us saying we should come to the weekly midday NGO meeting, which would be followed by a good-bye dinner at the Green Zone Café for the two people whose jobs we were taking.

The NGO meeting was held at the Convention Center, inside a big conference room. We arrived a few minutes before it started, and Jody waved to us from across the room. There were three hundred to four hundred Iraqis there as well. Sheikhs in traditional dress sat next to gray-suited old Iraqi men. Some women wore full abayas and had greenish-looking face tattoos; others dressed in Western-style blouses and jeans, and wore no head scarves at all.

The room was a cross section of Iraqi society. It quickly became clear that our new beat was far from the top of the CPA's Iraq-building agenda. Everyone who spoke had a list of complaints about the CPA and its U.S. overseers. While the Oil Ministry looks like a Vegas strip hotel, the CPA's entire civil society support effort in Iraq consisted of just this one open public meeting per week. Under Saddam, Iraq had no NGOs, no unions, no environmental controls, no minority-rights groups . . . nothing. The Americans and their CPA staff were starting a free country from scratch, and we were now the interface.

From the looks of the meeting, the only thing the CPA was providing was Jody, a few Army personnel, a loose group of translators, and worried-looking international aid workers. The people whose jobs we were taking, Dustin and Esther, both gave farewell speeches. They looked run-down and defeated. Esther was Danish, Dustin an American. A female soldier, Lieutenant Heather Coyne, gave a speech in Arabic and English that was direct and impressive. But those Iraqis in attendance kept shouting over the speakers, arguing with one another. The room vibrated with combative energy.

Meeting Lieutenant Heather Coyne was the highlight of the day. She was Jody's mentor and ran the CPA's civil society building initiative in Baghdad. The projects she was working on included opening women's resource centers across Iraq and a new Iraqi NGO center in Baghdad. In about twenty seconds she gave us a rundown of what our job would entail. No one ever said so much in so few words. In short, we were to help build and support the coming wave of new Iraqi NGOs. Jody said she'd try to get us housing, as well as official ID badges, and, ideally—eventually—some pay for our efforts. In the meantime, we could set up our offices in the NGO Assistance center down the hall. "You should go meet the Iraqi women who currently work there," she said.

A ring of Iraqis, four deep, surrounded Heather to ask questions. We let her work the room.

"Damn, she's a genius," Jeff said. "Now that's a fucking soldier."

"Wow. Maybe we will win the war on terror. Look at her, she's having four different conversations, in two languages, at once." Heather was talking in Arabic to an old guy with droopy red eyes in a sleazy, shiny gray suit.

"Red Eyes is getting animated," Jeff said. "Let's get out of here."

THAT EVENING WE WENT to Dustin and Esther's farewell party, at the Green Zone Café, a converted gas station located in the dead center of the Green Zone. Jeff and I arrived at the party too early: The caterers were still setting up amid the café's neon lights, plastic chairs, and dirty tile floor. Soon, the café began filling with people ready to celebrate Dustin and Esther's contribution to a new, democratic Iraq. It was open bar, free beer and wine, which was a relief given that beers were usually $4.00 at the café, which is about $3.20 more than anywhere outside in the Red Zone. We took advantage immediately.

"Hey guys . . ." It was Jody, perky and smiling. "What'd you think of the meeting?"

"It was crazy, totally out of control."

"The Iraqis aren't used to being able to speak their minds," Jody said. "And they have no idea of how to act in an open forum. They've never had that before. So, are you guys ready to work?"

"Definitely."

The pop song "Hey Ya" by Outkast came on the café's stereo, which was tuned to the American military station out of the Green Zone: Freedom Radio.

"Here, come meet Dustin and Esther," Jody called us over. She introduced us to the departing NGO coordinators. They wanted nothing to do with us. They acted like we had the plague.

"What's the job like?" I asked.

"Frustrating," Dustin said.

"Where are you going from here?"

"I'm going to South Africa and Dustin's going back to the States," Esther said.

They gave us a few more one-word answers, then walked away. That was our introduction to the international aid community of Iraq.

Dinner was a raucous affair, at least for us, who were enjoying the free drinks. Everybody was well informed, and the policy talk was great.

Then a mortar shell crashed our party, hitting somewhere nearby. For such a small piece of artillery, it sure packed quite a punch. The explosion sent everyone diving for cover. It's impossible to say where it landed, but it was close. Everyone stayed down.

Another mortar shell crashed in, and for a few long minutes we all sat silently, waiting for the next incoming blast. Finally, we began to feel confident enough to get out from beneath tables and behind chairs. In just a few more minutes, the bash kicked back into gear. It was going to take more than a few mortars to shut down the party that was the Green Zone at night.

5

·

Clowntown

JEFF AND I showed up at the apartment Dave had arranged for us in Kerrada, the middle-class Christian/Shi'ite neighborhood along the river south of the Green Zone, at two o'clock the next afternoon. Dave was nowhere. We talked to Sam, the heavyset and imposing Iraqi who owned the place—and who carried two Kalashnikovs with him at all times, as well as a .45 pistol—and Sam said we could leave our bags in his office while we waited for Dave and Charlie. He told us there was a tea shop and Internet café up the street, which sounded like a good place to burn an hour or two.

We thanked Sam and told him to send Charlie or Dave down to us when they arrived, and we'd all get moved in.

Ninety minutes later we returned to the guest house, but there still was no sign of Charlie or Dave. As we looked around, it became obvious that our new home was more a youth hostel—with mini-apartments rented to transient Westerners and Human Shield leftovers—than an official apartment house. Kids were everywhere, all internationals, hanging out, smoking, and acting as if we all weren't in Baghdad together. The air was thick with unpleasant arrogance.

We walked back to Sam's office to look in on our bags. When I checked my pack's zipper and lock, I saw that my towel had been stolen. Earlier that day, I'd strapped the towel to the outside of my bag, as it was still a little wet, and now somebody had gone and snagged it.

When I asked Sam about my missing towel, he said that Dave had come and gone, and that he had taken my towel as well. Sam also said that Dave had backed out on the apartment, claiming he'd gotten a photo gig with AFP and was heading to Basra. Sam noted that Dave never carried a camera. And in fact, we'd never seen him with a camera, either. What kind of an asshole steals a towel? And who hires a war photographer who never carries a camera?

"Did that asshole Dave really steal my fucking towel?" I asked.

In the next hour Charlie backed out on the apartment, too. Still, Jeff and I had nowhere to go, and we felt we had to move in, especially since Sam kept telling us, in a sort of strong voice, "You promised, my friends, you promised." Considering he had four guns on his person and Jeff and I had a LeatherMan tool between the two of us, we felt we had little room to argue. We agreed to a two-hundred-dollar-a-week deal.

"Two weeks up front," Sam said. He caressed the metal on one of his AKs.

We paid. Sam smiled. He hugged us and gave us each an Arab male kiss: pressing his cheek on each of our cheeks. Given we were now family, we asked him if we could take some photos holding his guns.

"OK, Habibi," he said. Habibi literally means "my baby," but across Arab cultures it is a term of close friendship used among men. He offered us cigarettes. I obliged. Jeff and I both got our requisite insurgent photo snapped, complete with red-and-white-checkered kaffiyehs wrapped around our face.

Our new digs were basically a run-down suite: two rooms, a small cooking area, and a semiworking toilet. But its location was prime. We were only a five-minute, one-dollar taxi ride to the 14th of July Bridge checkpoint entrance to the Green Zone.

Now we had a home. So we set about becoming good denizens of fallen Baghdad by joining other CPA staff in their nocturnal rounds. That night, Fox News was hosting a big party at the Sheraton Hotel in the Green Zone, which was advertised to have an open bar.

On the way, we invited a few soldiers from the 1st Armored Division who were guarding the hotel along for the party. We'd become friendly with them during our stay across the street at the Al Rabei Hotel, as they were bored guys standing for hours on end. One of the guards, a cut Puerto Rican from Miami named Sanchez, said he'd try to get up to the party later, but at the moment he was still on his shift.

"This job ain't that bad," he said, after we'd tried to convince him to play hooky. "Most days, like today, I just frisk journalists going in and out of the Sheraton. Sometimes I get to go on a patrol inside a Bradley Fighting Vehicle. But I miss pussy, and I miss my family." Jeff told Sanchez that he missed that stuff, too.

The Fox News party was on the second-floor mezzanine of the hotel. There were sofas and chairs as in any hotel lounge. Floor-to-ceiling windows looked out on the square where the Saddam statue was pulled down during the war's early "Mission Accomplished" days. Funny how all the major TV networks and news outlets were based in the hotel, and the statue that became iconic in the fall of Baghdad stood just outside its windows. From their rooms at the Sheraton, CNN could have spat on the site. There were hundreds of Saddam statues in Baghdad. But it was the one on the news outlets' doorstep that got filmed and became the icon.

By the time we got to the party's bar, people were already getting wasted. In the middle of the din, one woman from Fox broke out her acoustic guitar, and she was playing and singing along kind of woozily. Marla was there. She introduced us to a guy from *Newsweek*, Joe Cochrane, who she knew was a big Red Sox fan.

"These guys are from Boston," Marla told Joe as she pointed at us, ever the socialite. "And Joe bartended at a party I threw in Kabul"— now she pointed at Joe. "You'll like these guys, Joe." Then she giggled, waved at somebody else, and disappeared into the crowd.

We talked for a few minutes, telling Joe about Game 7 of the ALCS and the chain of events that had brought us to Baghdad.

"You guys were at Game 7? No shit," he said. "I was stuck covering SARS."

Joe was based in Bangkok. His boss was Fareed Zakaria, the prodigy who edited *Foreign Affairs* magazine in his twenties. Now Zakaria was the editor of *Newsweek International* and the international affairs columnist for *Newsweek*. Zakaria was also one of our heroes. "The guy gets everything short of a twenty-one-gun salute when he comes to town," Joe said, trying to explain his boss's pseudo-dignitary status. "Great guy, though. How do you guys know Bubbles?"

"Who?"

"Marla . . . Bubbles. Her nickname is Bubbles. Because of her Californian flaky social skills," Joe said. "In Kabul she was dubbed Bubbles and it stuck."

"We met her trying to check into the Al Rasheed."

Joe laughed. "How'd *that* go? Not too well, I presume."

"Marla saved us the trouble."

We were jealous that Joe had such a great job and boss. Then he began telling us about his life in Bangkok, and we grew even more envious. He lived the life, complete with drivers and all expenses paid. Whenever we'd been in Bangkok, our accommodations had been bug-infested, two-dollar-a-night joints on Khao San Road, global capital of Backpacker Trash (BPT) society. The Khao San scene draws from a depthless pool of humans from around the world who believe showering is optional and daily access to warm sun, dirt weed, cheap beer, and inexpensive curries and stir-fries are critical for life support. It's a place where white guys from Ohio or Germany can dress in sarongs and dreadlocks without either irony or self-consciousness.

Joe said he'd never even been to Khao San Road. We toasted him for it.

"Right now, we're about as far from Khao San as it gets," I said.

And that was true. Baghdad was the Anti-Bangkok. If the BPTs use Thailand as an escape from reality, Baghdad is reality in IV-drip form, twenty-four hours a day. Real, lethal, and constant, Baghdad was our escape from the escapism we'd been living during our T-shirt baron years on the BPT circuit. It's urgency and relevancy were intoxicating. It felt a long way from Fenway.

Fox News threw lots of parties, Joe told us. So did the other networks. This being our first major journalist shindig, we were impressed by the level of drinking. All the people there looked like nerds on safari: Eyeglasses and something tan with pockets were required, as were too heavy boots with knobby soles. But that was fine. It was far better than the steroid-pumped, bouncer-on-safari vibe of the American and British "Security Contractor" mercenaries, or the NASCAR-on-safari style of the finest from Halliburton's KBR unit.

People had little to do at night in Baghdad, what with the city's unofficial curfew and all. So they drank. You could get cans of beer with 10 percent alcohol content for eighty cents a pop. The local liquor, arrack, is Iraq's version of ouzo or Turkey's raki, and tastes like black licorice. It could be had for one dollar per bottle. Drugs were harder to come by. Iraqi culture is intolerant of the weakness associated with drug addiction. But if weed, hash, Ecstasy, and cocaine were hard to get, Iraq had a Valium problem, mainly because it was manufactured and sold there in hundred-milligram liquid form, a bottle of which costs less than one dollar. Also, every pharmacy carried it and no prescriptions were required, à la Tijuana. On the cap it read: "Made in Samarra, Iraq." Valium was the perfect drug for Iraq: Reality was so intense that some nights it was impossible to relax without it. Within days, my signature cocktail became a shot of arrack and a shot of Valium with a dab of water. Jeff called it an Arab Tom Collins.

OVER THE NEXT FEW WEEKS, we started cutting our teeth at the new job. Our office was in a back room of the Convention Center, right across the street from the Al Rasheed Hotel and in the Green Zone across from Saddam's former palace.

Lieutenant Heather Coyne and Jody had arranged for us to get our own cubicles. With fluorescent lights and bare white walls, it could have been in any office park in America, were it not for the blown-out windows covered in construction plastic that had been stapled to the old window frames. The harsh Iraqi sun and the windblown orange dust that gusts all across Iraq had already turned the window plastic a sickly orange.

The Green Zone was a constant reminder of 9/11, right down to the offices and desks of soldiers and civilians. Among them, "Wanted Dead or Alive: Bin Laden" posters were the most popular. Jeff hung up a picture of Sox slugger Manny Ramirez to lighten the mood.

In our office, the other NGO Assistance cubicles were occupied by two Iraqi women—Sawsan and Ibteesam. Sawsan was in her mid-forties. Her job was to create a database for the more than three hundred Iraqi NGOs that had registered so far with the CPA. Sawsan wore bright, flowery clothing. Rarely peeking from behind her file-strewn desk, seemingly always hunkered down typing, she would prove to be a calming force. Ibteesam, or Ibty as we called her, was in her late twenties or early thirties. She lived in the Green Zone and had been an Iraqi translator for Titan until Jody hired her as a sort of protégé. Her job appeared to consist of chatting on Microsoft Instant Messenger.

Our Internet connection was not a secure DoD line, which meant it was much faster than most of the other Convention Center and palace computers. MCI actually provided the server. MCI also had an office across the way in the Convention Center and sold cell phones with 908 numbers, making a call to Jersey local and a long-distance call anywhere else in the States inexpensive.

Ibty was supposed to be running the office, and she always told Jody she was. But whatever she was doing on Instant Messenger wasn't very effective. The office was in shambles. Still, we liked her. She wore flowery headdresses and had a round face with beautiful olive skin. Like so many Iraqis, she had this dark, dry sense of humor.

Technically, our office was an arm of the Iraqi Assistance Center

(IAC). Overseen by Army Civil Affairs, the IAC had fifty-seven Iraqi translators on staff. One of the Iraqis on the translation staff was a Kurdish cross-dresser named Adams. He always wore women's scarves to cover his Adam's apple, as well as women's blouses and thick makeup to hide his five-o'clock shadow. He also used the women's bathroom. But he was a great translator, and over time he became our full-time unofficial translator.

Taken aback by Adams's flamboyance, we wondered how he was still alive. Iraq under Saddam wasn't exactly the West Village, and Iraqi culture in general is pretty homophobic—at least publicly, though behind closed doors this may be another issue. It's fairly widely said that Arab men often have their first sexual experience with other Arab men. This might be out of necessity, since many Arab women are basically locked up from age fourteen and then provided with an arranged marriage. We still hadn't seen an Iraqi girl our age walking the streets of Baghdad.

For the first few weeks on the job, we got the office organized: holding focus groups and starting regular open-house meetings for Iraqi and international NGOs and military operations; coming to understand the database for Iraqi reconstruction; and familiarizing ourselves with the welter of acronyms and paperwork designations used by the military joint task force and the CPA.

UNFORTUNATELY, the room where our cubicle sat was actually divided into two different bureaus. Our office, NGO Assistance (NGOAO), was the front half. A handwritten sign on a piece of copier paper taped up in the hallway in front of our door was the only evidence that we were there at all. The other half of the room belonged to

CPA's Office of Detainee Issues. They operated behind us, and were separated from us by a chin-high cubicle wall, which was fortified on their side by an office blockade: shelves, desks, tables, extra partitions, paper and supplies, and file cabinets. What kind of office needs a blockade?

It didn't take long to find out. When you share office space with the visitor-relations arm of Abu Ghraib prison, some disgruntled former guests or the families of current guests are going to come and see you. Every ten minutes of every day, our office was assaulted by another crying, screaming Iraqi, demanding to know where another Iraqi was. Needless to say, this created an awkward tension between the two offices: One side of the cubicle wall was there to help Iraqis; the other represented the torturing, degrading, and occasional excruciating killing of them.

Jeff said the blockade was like the fence on the TV show *Home Improvement*. When we peered over at our neighbors, we'd only see their eyes and forehead. The coupling reinforced to us that the CPA hadn't put much thought into things. In this one room, Iraqis were made to equate humanitarian-aid NGOs with Abu Ghraib. As time went on, we began to wonder if this was a deliberate slap in the face to the international NGO community after it had voiced opposition to the war. Whatever the reasoning, the fact remained that the Oil Ministry was like an enormous resort hotel, and the NGO Assistance Office shared an impossible-to-locate room with representatives for American torturers.

The Abu Ghraib scandal had yet to break, but rumors were ever present. And journalists like Letta Taylor from *Newsday* were persistent, always asking us to recount anything we heard about misdeeds that crossed the office DMZ. But despite all the wailing of visiting Iraqis in our office, we really didn't yet know how the other half lived.

. . .

MOST DAYS AROUND DUSK, we'd get a cab back to our apartment. Everyone else there had a strong ultraleft militant peacenik ideology. We tried to avoid them at first, having learned our lesson with the ISM in Israel. But people being people, we eventually found a few of them to be pretty friendly beneath the zealotry of their politics. After a few days at Sam's, we saw that the most prominent group was Circus 2 Iraq, which took up most of the floor above us. Led by a young British law student named Jo Wilding, Circus 2 Iraq was composed of a bunch of Euro peaceniks who had come to Baghdad to make Iraqi kids laugh, a goal they never stopped mentioning.

"Wait, you guys are a circus?" we asked Jo when we met her.

"Yeah, a circus. You guys work for the occupation?"

"Yeah, we do NGO coordination for the CPA."

"Why would you work for the CPA?"

"Because it's our country," I said.

"You support the war?"

"No."

"Then how can you work for them?"

"Life is full of contradiction and compromise," I said. "It's not like we're hiding behind ideals, we're just trying to help. The CPA offered us work doing something we could do, so we're doing it."

"Nah," Jo said. She wasn't buying.

THERE WAS ANOTHER CLOWN sitting in the room with us that first evening: Luis, a hash-loving Frenchman. Luis was the friendliest and most accepting of Jeff and me. Sensing a political debate brewing between us and Jo—who obviously had a taste for such interaction—he stepped in: "Politics are nothing," he said. "Americans treat politics as an argument, like sport. Always yelling on TV. All politics is really negotiation."

"So . . . I want to negotiate," Jo snapped back.

"At least we're doing something besides smoking hash and drinking moonshine," Jeff said to Luis. The clowns had a makeshift bong made out of one-liter soda bottles. They were adept at using it.

After an hour or so of chatting and deflecting their political barbs, I think we found a common ground through the great social equalizer—alcohol. When it came to drinking, these clowns were hard-core.

"You ever see that movie *Shakes the Clown*?" Jeff asked. "That's you guys."

"Who?" asked one of the clowns, a guy named Pete, though he spelled it Peat. He was an accomplished war-zone juggler.

"There's a movie about this hard-living clown, starring Bobcat Goldthwait. Never mind . . ."

"Tell me."

"Shakes is a scumbag clown like Krusty."

"Oh."

Peat, it turned out, had been a war junkie for a few decades, ever since he fought for the Brits in Northern Ireland. Due to the poor diet endemic to most war zones, not to mention the British public dental program, he'd lost all his teeth and now wore dentures. Probably in his late thirties, Peat had leathery skin, a receding hairline, and a scraggly goatee, and he dressed like a shipwrecked clown. Jo and Peat had found each other on the Internet.

In a northern English accent Pete kept saying, "I luuvvv chilldruun!" Then he'd take a long swig from a bottle of Iraqi booze that featured a naked girl on every label. "I'm collecting all the ladies. This is Cassandra . . . would you like to meet her, boys?"

Of course we did. So we got a tour of empty bottles, each with a different naked woman on the label, strewn about the room.

Luis had also joined the circus through the Internet. Tall and tan, with a goatee, Luis was a consummate stoner, always moving and talking slowly. His lifestyle was familiar and comforting. It was the opposite of the nicotine- and caffeine-fueled, overachieving and over-working CPA lifestyle. Being around Luis was like a vacation.

Luis said there was a fourth clown sleeping in the other room. The door was open and eventually the man started snoring. A video camera shared the mattress with him. "That's Sam," Luis told us.

Jo didn't drink or smoke any hash during the party. She hacked away busily on a laptop PC. Her serious, determined attitude slightly cramped the mood. But if not for her entrepreneurial spirit, well, the party—not to mention Circus 2 Iraq—would never have happened.

6

·

Order 45

J EFF GREW UP in a football house divided. His mother was a Dallas
Cowboys fan, his father a Washington Redskins fan. Since his
childhood and adolescence were spent in Virginia, he eventually
chose the Skins.

I grew up in a near-complete football vacuum. Where I came
from, north of Boston, everyone worshipped at the church of baseball, and after the basketball Celtics and hockey Bruins, the eternally
mediocre football Patriots were a distant fourth, our state's pathetic
sporting afterthought. Compounding the embarrassment, the Pats
played in Foxboro, in the southern hinterlands of Massachusetts.
During my first twenty years, they commanded no loyalty from me.
In fact, my college girlfriend's father had Redskins season tickets.
He had also clerked for Chief Justice Rehnquist and wore pink Polo
shirts. That was enough for me. I defected from New England to

become a Skins fan. Their home field, RFK Stadium, was the Fenway of football, filled with knowledgeable, loyal, diehard fans. It was an easy transition to make.

This all changed in 2001, when a quarterback named Tom Brady came to New England. After piloting the Patriots through a fairy-tale run in the playoffs, Brady led his team into Super Bowl XXXVI, where they were underdogs against the St. Louis Rams. In the Super Bowl, as per usual that year, a last-minute field goal by golden-footed Adam Vinatieri secured their first title, setting off the best sports riot of my lifetime.

The night of the Patriots' 2002 Super Bowl victory I joined the festivities. Down at Northeastern University, on Hemmenway Street, thousands of drunken college kids were going nuts. It was at this glorious moment—as a group of us threw dozens of "Rams Suck" T-shirts into the frenzied crowd—that I became a true Patriots fan. Women flashed breasts, men smoked cigars, and people passed joints and bottles of booze. People tried to flip cars, light fires, and celebrate in an orgy of destruction. It was one of the few times I ever enjoyed being at Northeastern.

Slowly, Jeff had come around to liking the Patriots, too. When the Pats made it back to the Super Bowl in 2004, though we were in Iraq, we had to watch it, even if for us this meant making the ultimate sacrifice: hanging out with private-security contractors.

On February 1, 2004, the best Super Bowl party inside the Green Zone was advertised to be at a messhall called Wolfpack Staging Area. Hidden in the shadow of a bombed-out palace, Wolfpack was a series of trailers that housed the best KBR buffet in the GZ. The game didn't start until 2:00 A.M. Iraqi time—it was technically February 2— and to gear up for it we passed the hours in our Convention Center office eating MREs (Meals Ready to Eat) and listening to our one CD.

The Green Zone wasn't filled with people from New England. Many of the contractors were from the South. So it was really no surprise that when we arrived at Wolfpack we were the only Pats fans there. Everyone else was rooting for the Carolina Panthers.

Which was fine, because we didn't want any association with the SKOAL-dip set who filled the hall anyway. It felt more like a truck stop than the Middle East. Only a few Army soldiers were there. Instead, there were a dozen or so fat contractors from KBR and the like. The least-cool guy had an extreme goatee, an "Iraq World Tour" T-shirt on underneath an open flannel, acid-wash jeans, desert combat boots, and a rainbow-colored NASCAR hat.

Despite a glorious Pats win—the final score was 32–29—the contractors and the armored SUVs they rode in on ruined the affair for us. And the fifty pounds of fried chicken they consumed during the game wasn't easy on the eyes.

IT MAY SEEM that our whole time in Baghdad was spent drinking with journalists, laughing at war profiteers, and smoking hash with clowns. But actually we did work. In the end, it was our work that would come to define our time in Iraq. There is no point in romanticizing what we did. We thought we were helping Iraqis. We were wrong. Because of our failure, we'd leave the Middle East in a state of regret. But our story does offer a window into the misguided ideals and rank ignorance that drove us.

At the end of January, we dove headfirst into NGO coordination and so-called capacity building. We were to be the CPA's interface between Iraqi and Western Non-Governmental Organizations wanting to help out in post-Saddam Iraq. Every day was a new meeting under a different umbrella. Some meetings were set up by Jeff and me, like our weekly ones for medical and environmental NGOs. Others were set up by Heather Coyne, such as the Sunday "Civil Society Working Group." Still others were set up by the military, CPA, or USAID: "Women for Women" was a memorable one. Another, convened by USAID, focused on "Transparency."

Almost all of the meetings were at the Convention Center, which served as the primary zone for Iraqi-American interaction, since it was the only place in the Green Zone where ordinary Iraqis could go. Before long, hundreds of Iraqis knew our names. A walk through the Convention Center turned into an endless meet and greet. As "Mistah Jeff" and "Mistah Ray," we couldn't walk five feet without a hug, a kiss, and a long handshake, followed by a barrage of questions we couldn't answer. Iraqis we didn't know would seek us out, bringing us photographs, papers and documents, prayer beads, and even flowers. It made us feel important, even though on the CPA food chain we were at the absolute bottom. Fact is, no Americans in-country had less authority than we did. Even the lowly peaceniks had blogs. But if we had no real clout, there were also no Americans who had more Iraqi contacts and friends than we did. We quickly learned not to make any firm promises to any Iraqis, only to try to help.

Our office soon became a refuge from the Convention Center's chaotic town square vibe. Ibty served as our minder, kicking out anyone who didn't have a scheduled meeting. The NGOAO was still a mess. Sawsan wasn't keeping pace with the NGO database. Ibty did nothing except play bouncer and use Instant Messenger.

We decided that our first goal was to create a model for humanitarian-aid distribution. As it turned out, a large stockpile of humanitarian aid was being stored in the Green Zone, nearly all of it donated by Americans and sent from a single post office in Warwick, Rhode Island. This came to be so because an American Army Civil Affairs officer named Sergeant Grimley in Baghdad—whose father was Warwick's postmaster—put out a call to arms. Working through his father, Grimley used the post office—and the goodwill of the people of Rhode Island—to open the taps so American goods could pour into the Green Zone. The stockpile was housed just down the road from the Convention Center at the Humanitarian Affairs Control Center, known by all as the HACC.

The aid was collecting dust, and our role was to find reliable Iraqi NGOs to distribute it. If an Iraqi NGO filled out an aid request application and had it approved by our office—meaning Jeff or me—one or both of us would go out with the NGO, gather up the goods for distribution at the HACC or BIAP, deliver the aid where it was supposed to go, and, when we returned to the office that evening, file a roughly five-hundred-word field report on the day's activities. The ultimate goal of this was to establish a blueprint for reliable, managed, large-scale aid distribution. Then, if any international organization, like the UN or a large international NGO, wanted to come in and work with Iraqi NGOs, they'd have a tested pathway for the flow of assistance, complete with reports and histories of earlier runs.

But there was a problem with this: Bremer's Order 45. During CPA rule, Bremer signed into effect one hundred Legal Orders. These Orders affected all aspects of Iraqi society. Order 45 required all Iraqi and international NGOs to register with the CPA. If an NGO did not register, then a series of tariffs would be levied on all goods associated with them moving in and out of Iraq. What this meant was that aid groups had to register or be taxed into oblivion.

For Bremer and the CPA, the point of Order 45 was to control the flow of aid and humanitarian information in Iraq. While NGOs can be useful in a postconflict country—providing the basic goods and services provisional governments can't—they can also have inconvenient side effects. If, as the CPA intended, military force was being used to establish a democratic government, NGOs might step in and—without approval—publicize tribal inequities and plights, horrible events, or unpleasant human-rights accidents that the CPA might prefer weren't aired to the world. Therefore, under the guise of controlling security threats, the best way to keep leverage on all NGOs—both international and Iraqi—was to register them and monitor their activities.

International NGOs understood that were they to register with the CPA under Order 45 their mandates would be compromised. One Italian NGO coalition pointed out that Order 45 violated Article 63 of the Geneva Conventions—as well as UN Security Council Resolution 1483—a declaration that an occupying force should not be an "obstacle . . . [to] the Red Cross and those organizations operating to guarantee essential services to the civilian population." However, the rule of Paul Bremer in Iraq apparently superseded any other rules. Consequently, international NGOs stayed away from registering with the CPA in droves, and instead decided to keep a low profile so as not to be aligned with the CPA.

It made sense that Iraqi and international NGOs didn't want to register with the CPA, since any NGO registered was entered into the public record. And since each group had to be listed under an individual's name and with a local address, all of which was posted online at www.cpa-iraq.org, this relationship with an increasingly disliked occupier was seen as public official affiliation with the CPA, which amounted to a death sentence for that individual.

. . .

To state the obvious, Jeff and I groped our way toward a grim understanding of humanitarian aid from a starting point of complete ignorance. We had no training and little understanding of the competitive world of NGOs. Aside from reading a book by Médecins Sans Frontières, plus journal and magazine articles and some books on Africa, we had little grasp of the politics and financial infighting between international aid groups.

Postconflict transitional societies always need high levels of civil society support and rebuilding. This was especially true in Iraq, a country without a national identity and emerging from thirty years of totalitarian rule. During Saddam's Baathist rule, Iraq had no civil society as defined by the London School of Economics: *"Civil societies are often populated by organizations such as registered charities, development non-governmental organizations, community groups, women's organizations, faith-based organizations, professional associations, trades unions, self-help groups, social movements, business associations, coalitions and advocacy groups."* None of these organizations existed under Saddam.

For the CPA, creating an intact Iraqi civil society should have been of paramount importance. The point of the occupation, it was always the CPA's contention, was to nurture Iraq's population toward self-determination. Order 45 helped force many of the NGOs best organized and trained to handle postconflict underground, where they could help Iraqis only on a far smaller scale.

No group felt Order 45 to be a symbol of U.S. hypocrisy more strongly than NCCI (NGO Coordination Committee in Iraq), which represented the international aid organizations OXFAM and CARE, among others. NCCI's website said it served as "the vehicle for the UN" in Iraq, representing fifty-plus large international NGOs. As its website also stated, NCCI's core spheres of concern were aid with

1. Health
2. Education
3. Water and sanitation
4. Food and nonfood item distribution
5. Rehabilitation and engineering

Immediately, NCCI met trouble. NCCI played the middleman in negotiations between the CPA and the UN Assistance Mission for Iraq (UNAMI). Yet because they didn't want their work restricted by the CPA, NCCI refused to register with the NGO Assistance Office, as they were supposed to do under Order 45. Consequently, meetings between NCCI and the CPA in Baghdad were frustrating affairs, where NCCI was forever pointing out that, thanks to Bremer Order 45, Iraq was the most difficult place on earth for NGOs to work.

Watching all of these negotiations from front-row seats, Jeff and I never saw a clear reason why the CPA wanted to make NGOs work as hard as possible. Several factors, however, are worth mentioning. In the run-up to the invasion of Iraq, many of the world's most prominent NGOs—like OXFAM and Médecins Sans Frontières—came out with strong stances against it. It is a bedrock tenet of humanitarian-aid providers, and one of the key understandings that has allowed them to work all over the world for the past quarter century, that no NGO is to take a political stance, and that NGOs are only to minister to those who can benefit from their help.

On top of violating the "No Politics" thing, NCCI's arrogance was legion. It didn't help that NCCI's Iraq mission was headed by a crabby Frenchman named Philippe Schneider. Idealistic French crusaders didn't mesh well with the buttoned-down realist crowds at the State Department or in the military chain of command.

In early February, Jeff and I sat in on a Working Group meeting with Philippe of NCCI, his cohort/girlfriend Claudia, and an undercover Canadian Mennonite crusader, as well as Jody and Heather, among others. All Philippe did was bitch about Order 45. We well understood his frustration, but his attitude was annoying. While fiddling with a walkie-talkie, Philippe squirmed in his seat as Heather told him that Order 45 still wasn't being changed.

Trying to change Order 45 was a guy named Max Primorac, a personable, palace-based D.C. lawyer, who had been working on it for months under contract from ACC (Arab Cultural Committee). "Max is still working on it," Jody kept saying as Philippe sighed, grunted, or looked to the sky in frustration.

Jeff and I probably didn't help matters, though. During the meeting we were showing each other some just-developed photos of a party thrown by a couple of Army Civil Affairs officers a few days earlier. The party had taken place in an old Baathist official's villa in the Green Zone, which this sergeant friend of ours had taken over as his house. It was like an arsenal inside: Every kind of Iraqi weapon you could imagine was there, hung on the walls alongside some old Iraqi Republican Guard uniforms and Saddam portraits. There was also a big-screen TV, a great stereo, and a lot of booze. So after a few drinks, Jeff and I had started putting on Republican Guard uniforms and pulling different weapons off the walls and snapping portraits of each other.

During the meeting, Claudia, Philippe's second in command, saw us passing photos back and forth beneath a table and laughing. When she saw Jeff in one photo in Iraqi uniform and brandishing an

AK-47 across his chest, she sniffed and, in a dourly thick accent, said: "This is not the work of a humanitarian."

After the meeting broke up—or more like evaporated—I sent Philippe a harsh e-mail, noting that by maintaining his high humanitarian morals he was only harming those people he claimed to want to help: the Iraqis. Eventually, my e-mail was forwarded to Heather and Jody, and I was made to apologize. I didn't have the authority to say the things I had said to Philippe. Sorry, Philippe.

CONTROL OF THE CPA'S humanitarian relief effort fell on the U.S. Department of State's Agency for International Development (or USAID). Sticking to a very broad mandate, USAID was tasked with handling much of Iraq's civil society building. Its mission was to implement programs in four strategic areas:

1. Restoring essential infrastructure
2. Supporting essential health and education
3. Expanding economic opportunity
4. Improving efficiency and accountability of government

NCCI's and USAID's mission statements seem to share a lot of common goals and interests. For an outsider, it would be easy to confuse the role of the humanitarian NGO with that of the government occupier. An NCCI–USAID partnership would have been relevant to creating a better, healthier, stable Iraq. But USAID was an arm of U.S. policy in Iraq and was guided by American national interests rather than humanitarian goals.

Every Sunday morning, for example, at the Sunday Civil Society

Working Group meeting, you could see how little the U.S. government was actually offering the Iraqi people. Cochairing the meeting was USAID's Office of Transition Initiatives (OTI), which existed, according to its mandate, to coordinate efforts between international organizations—the United Nations, and so forth—and the Iraqi people under the management of the CPA.

With a budget of $190 million, OTI had more cash than any other civil society building group, and far more than any international organization or NGO. In the early days of the occupation, it was OTI's cash handouts that did the most to bolster Iraqi civil society. By the time we got there OTI was less generous. Some of OTI's programs were merely exercises in propaganda. At one point, OTI even set up a so-called arts council that doubled as a CPA propaganda machine. This "arts council" hosted an art show at the Convention Center, with many of the works taking the form of posters promoting the CPA: doves flying with Iraqi and American flags, Iraqi police kissing babies . . . and so on.

Sarah Brewer, a D.C. lawyer, usually attended Sunday Civil Society Working Group meetings as OTI's representative. Once, after another frustrating discussion about why more NGOs weren't being encouraged to help with civil society building and in fact were actually being driven off by policies like Order 45, Sarah Brewer finally couldn't help herself. She answered a question about why the international aid community was shut out of Iraq by saying, "Every postconflict situation is different," as if that would explain everything.

"Yeah," Jeff said. "This one's different because the entire international aid community has been shut out."

After that, Sarah Brewer never acknowledged Jeff or me as human beings. If we were the only three people in a Convention Center hallway, she would act as if she was there alone.

. . .

BY EARLY FEBRUARY, Jeff and I could already see the seeds of Iraqi dissatisfaction germinating. The U.S. government and its CPA in Iraq didn't seem to care that using an army to achieve humanitarian aims sends the wrong message to the local population. Tanks and machine guns are never associated with hospitals and schools. If the Pentagon-powered CPA insisted on using Army Civil Affairs units instead of NGOs to lead Iraq's rebuilding effort, confusion was going to be the result. Bremer's Order 45 became our introduction to the wholesale misdirection of power that was the CPA.

On February 3, at our weekly Tuesday general NGO meeting, Jeff and I announced our initial aid program and handed out our first NGO Assistance applications for humanitarian-aid distribution.

A town-hall-style affair, the NGO meeting was stressful, crowded, and chaotic. On this Tuesday, as on most, more than four hundred Iraqis were in attendance, and they all wanted to be heard. By the end of that day we had more than one hundred applications filled out and returned.

With the new NGOs now registered and our NGO Assistance Office approved and ready to go, it was time to figure out exactly what we had to distribute. For that, we had to find Sergeant Grimley's secret stash at the HACC.

The HACC, Army Civil Affairs' big compound in the Green Zone, was located between the palace and the Convention Center. The HACC served as the coordination center for Civil Affairs projects in Baghdad and beyond, and also housed the stockpile of donated goods from Sergeant Grimley's father at the PO in Warwick, Rhode Island. The HACC was an all-military affair, as opposed to the Convention Center, which was equal parts CPA and military. Because of this, the HACC compound had a distinct and disciplined feel and none of the Convention Center's chaos. Still, set among palm trees and hidden behind high blast walls, the HACC minipalace—which previously housed some component of the Baath Party—was more office park than military base.

It fell on Civil Affairs to do a lot of reconstruction work. Civil Affairs repaired roads, cleaned up parks, and refurbished schools. If there was good news in Iraq, it was Civil Affairs' reconstruction efforts. The Army's reconstruction and humanitarian programs were different from the CPA's. Unlike the CPA, the Army had a functioning budget and had the chain-of-command orders that could get things done. Not as corrupt and hollow as private-sector efforts, Civil Affairs was the bright spot of the occupation. Because they were working hands-on with Iraqis outside the Green Zone, many Civil Affairs soldiers built deep bonds with Iraqis.

Some of the programs Civil Affairs was implementing had more success than others. Some of its non-successes had to do with the condition of Iraq's infrastructure before the American invasion. And, of course, part of the problem was that it's hard for a conquering army to change helmets and be seen as a humanitarian force. That negative association would end up crippling many Civil Affairs efforts. The majority of Civil Affairs soldiers we met, however, worked hard and created good projects to help Iraq. Mostly drawn from the Army's reserve, Civil Affairs citizen-soldiers were often older and had more life experience than their infantry counterparts.

Understanding the difference between reservists and active-duty troops was key in understanding postwar Iraq. Reservists tended to fit into the bureaucratic structure of the CPA better than active-duty soldiers. They usually had more real-world work experience and could easily take a desk job at places like the HACC or work in the field on Civil Affairs projects.

Of course, active-duty troops were a far superior fighting force to the reservists. You could really tell the difference. For instance, an 82nd Airborne company guarded the Convention Center. These guys were in top-notch shape, and were as sharp and gung-ho as soldiers get. To keep their edge, they spent their time off lifting weights and playing basketball or soccer. The company's commander was a young West Point grad we called Lieutenant Mikey. Every few days Mikey would stop by our office to chat, and any subject could come up, from sports to politics to family life. Having an intelligent, honest guy like Mikey in charge of the Convention Center made it feel safe. With the 82nd you knew what you were getting: a hard, fighting-fit combat unit.

The reservists staffed many of the Convention Center's offices. The current Iraqi Assistance Center staff was nearing the end of their tour of duty. While Jody, Sergeant Jay Bachar, and their coworkers were excellent, the incoming troops would soon illustrate the negative aspects of using reserve forces. They were most epitomized by Lieutenant Colonel Weaver, a grandpa stress counselor from Florida. In his midsixties and seemingly afraid of "Eye-Rakkis," Lieutenant Colonel Weaver stood no chance of getting anything done in the IAC in our opinions. He brought a frightened, uncomfortable vibe to the whole office. He even had the IAC entrance sealed off with a velvet rope like a nightclub, making it as unwelcoming as possible. At the Convention Center, Iraqis noticed the new closed-door policy, and Civil Affairs and the IAC soon became associated with the arrogance of the CPA.

But on that first Tuesday of our new NGO Assistance aid program, when we showed up at the HACC to do an inspection of Sergeant

Grimley's stash from Little Rhody, the reservists were working hard to help Iraqis. They showed us the stockpile, and told us we had the run of the warehouse.

We tore into the boxes. "Let's see what we have," Jeff said.

Inside the boxes was a mish-mash of used garments, many of which celebrated New England–centric sports and sporting teams, as well as toys and school supplies. From a clothes box, Jeff pulled out a New England Patriots jersey and put it on. We laughed; the shirt was way too tight. He pulled it off and tossed it back into the box.

"Looks like we'll be separating and organizing all this shit ourselves," he said.

"Just like after a night at Fenway when we'd have to dump thirty boxes out and fold all the shirts again. I hate boxes. Let's do it tomorrow. I can't stomach it after that meeting, it was too hectic."

"Fine, let's go look at those applications and choose an NGO to go out with."

"Yeah," I said. "We'll turn some Iraqi kids on to the Pats."

SADR CITY KID RUNNING WITH FLIP FLOPS ON ARMS

(Photo by Jeff Neumann)

BOOK★TWO

House of Cards

7

·

Going Broke

J EFF HAD NO MONEY LEFT. In fact, he'd been borrowing off me since Jordan, and now, in early February, I was out of money to lend. I only had about two hundred dollars in cash left, and Iraq had no banking system: There were no ATMs, no check cashing at bank branches, and no Visa advances at hotels.

For Bremer and his crew, the dollars flew in by the duffel bag and reinforced box on chartered private jets or Army C-130 aircraft, direct from the United States Treasury. For Jeff and me, without an unlimited budget or an air force at our disposal, it was time to get frugal or get out.

Jeff was particularly stressed, since on top of having zero dollars, he was also in debt. Bad luck had done him in before we'd left on the trip. During the fall, he'd been living in California and playing poker full-time. On the side, he smoked weed and went to Tijuana, usually with one of his harem of girls who drove Audis and BMWs. He'd get down there and leave me these great voice mails: "Yo, I'm in TJ. Won a G in L.A., then drove all night to get here. You know I love border towns. TJ is the greatest. Fuck New York! Wish you were here . . ."

In November, he'd sold all his possessions—including his four-thousand-dollar road bike—as insurance that he could afford our trip. But instead of saving the money, which totaled about ten grand, he tried to turn it into more. So he went to a place he liked to call his office, officially called the Commerce Casino, which is in Los Angeles, and settled in to the life of a poker "professional."

Commerce Casino is the world's largest poker room, and is located in South Central Los Angeles, probably America's largest ghetto. One time, I was pumping gas across the street from the Commerce, having just played a few hands and downed some bad casino buffet and a couple of mai tais, and this black hooker jumped into my rental car and started fooling with the radio.

"I'll suck your dick for twenty dollars."

I declined and told her to get out of the car.

"I be givin', you know, massages and stuff, too," she said. She was now rifling the change dish in my car's center console.

"Thanks, but no thanks," I said. She got out.

That's the kind of place Commerce is.

Once on Commerce Casino property, things get no more wholesome. Over the years, the parking lot of Commerce has been the scene of numerous murders and countless robberies. Inside, it's equally nasty: You enter to see hundreds of low-limit poker tables, where neon lights paint ugly hues onto the balding or scraggly heads of the gaming world's degenerates.

The Commerce is nothing like the glamour and glitz of ESPN's

poker programs. Its tables are filled by poor Asian and Hispanic immigrants who're playing poor blacks and poor whites. No one wins
in those low-money games. The house cut is so high that even the
best players lose over time. Like the dog track, a methadone clinic, or
Central Booking (New York City's prearraignment jail), Commerce is
filled with debased and desperate humans: crack addicts, male street
hustlers, homeless winos, petty thieves, deranged sociopaths, hookers, us . . . you name it. The honest gambler is a myth.

Commerce's high-limit tables attract a different but equally un-
seemly crowd. Make no mistake: Poker is gambling, not sport. Jeff
would play in the high-limit section, in games like $40-$80 and pot-
limit Omaha. Fall 2003 saw poker's ascent to the mainstream. There
had been one season of the World Poker Tour, and ESPN was about
to throw its chips into the pot. Owing to all the notoriety, there were
a lot of unschooled new players floating around, and most of them
were still finding their game. On TV a few had gotten lucky, which
only seemed to draw in more of the uninitiated. Jeff noticed the number of new young faces on the TV before I did. "I hate the Internet
jocks," he said. "They don't know how the game flows, they don't
watch what's played . . . they suck."

At the Commerce, Jeff's poker bender started sometime in late
November 2003, just a few weeks before he was to fly to Amman, Jordan. Soon thereafter I received a call from him: "I'm at Commerce and
just won three grand playing $40-$80. Fuck it, I'm going to Vegas."

The Vegas card orgy ended less triumphantly. For the next six
days, Jeff's cell phone went straight to voice mail. This was not a
good sign. Finally I got a call from him asking for money. "I got in a
soft pot-limit game and couldn't hit a hand."

Now, some people would think it's a bad decision to risk all your money playing cards. Luckily for Jeff, I'm not one of them. We're also both suckers for people who gamble it all on a sketchy scheme or idea. We both love the grand gesture. Like once when our friend Bubba refinanced his Las Vegas home to play in the World Series of Poker. Most of our friends snickered and criticized him behind his back. We supported him, telling him it was the best thing he'd ever done, far and away. He got killed. Bubba was out the first day. Anyway, before Jeff was done in Vegas, he was tapped.

AND NOW, in Baghdad, our money was running down. With Jeff broke and our prepaid time at Sam's ending in a few days, we were in a bind. Had our luck run out? Where were we going to live? Could we get a paying job? Did we need to leave Iraq?

To the last question, the answer was no.

We were in limbo, and it started to take its toll. The money and housing pressure, along with the stress of Baghdad itself, was starting to eat at us. Maintaining a foothold of mental stability got harder by the day. The daily onslaught of Iraqis crying, screaming, or imploring us for help at the office, plus the about-daily destruction meted out by car bombs on the streets outside the GZ, was creating toxic sensory overload. A bus blows up down the street. Better go check it out. A car bomb explodes at the entrance to the Al Rasheed Gate. Well, we'll see it later. That's on the way home.

Witnessing continuing mass carnage takes a while to sink in. Wait . . . is that a bloody shoe in a pool of blood? Is that a torso? Chunks of scalp and hair? We still didn't know what to make of all the violence. Living with a growing insurgency, the contradictions were so inherent that the Iraqi "Inshallah" (God willing) attitude became contagious. It was in direct opposition to the CPA's all-American approach of self-direction and instant gratification, and the two were starting to clash inside everyone's mind. Like other Americans in the CPA who didn't always hide in the Green Zone, we had to adjust to the loss of control that had become life in Red Zone Iraq.

AS WE GREW more broke and desperate and the days ticked past, a house of cards was being erected on the Tigris. The new Iraqi state was to have eighteen new ministries. In keeping with a previously unmentioned CPA timetable, the new goal was to establish these ministries and transfer power to the Iraqis at the end of June. Suddenly everyone within the CPA was working toward the new buzzword-y goal of Transition of Sovereignty.

But things were far behind schedule, and there was no acknowledgment or attempt to change course. For instance, our office was supposed to be transferred to the Ministry of Planning and Development, but that ministry had no staff, furniture, office equipment, or computers. Ansam, the lady who was said to be taking over NGO Assistance for the ministry, never showed up for our scheduled meetings and didn't respond to phone calls or e-mails.

Hollow ministries like Planning and Development were one thing; they just didn't exist. Corrupt ministries were another thing altogether. The Iraqi Ministry of Defense, Ministry of Oil, Ministry of Finance, and Ministry of Education were all stealing money from the CPA. They would repaint buildings and facilities, then claim that the facilities were new, to specification, and ready for Iraqi inhabitation, though only a few cosmetic changes had been made. Corruption was infecting the whole CPA mission; there was no transparency, oversight, or accountability. In the interest of creating robust Iraqi ministries, American taxpayer dollars were being handed out by the billions. Much of that money has never been accounted for, and the list of those complicit in corruption grows longer by the day.

We could see that the story of Iraq under the CPA was just getting good, and we didn't want to lose our seats and miss anything, even if we had no money and were at risk of losing our sanity. The crash was coming, and we wanted to be on hand for the full who, what, when, and where of it. But being stuck in personal limbo as CPA Iraq was in national decline was a double shot of stress.

"Can you believe this place?" Jeff said one night in our room, as our time at Clowntown wound down.

"It's fucked. It's going to catch up to us. All this violence, the unpredictability."

"I think it already has. Or it's starting to. I feel different, kind of crazy. Sometimes everything seems to be in slow motion. Other times, I'll look down the street and everything'll be hyper-speed."

"You noticed I've been waking up in the middle of the night, yelling about nothing, right?"

"Nothing? You've been yelling about sex. Then you've been getting up and bumping into shit."

"Oh. Woops. Sorry about that. I think I'm losing a few marbles."

"Me, too. Time is going by so fast and then these moments happen, like the Assassin's Gate bombing or the mortar attack at the GZ Café, that seem to have occurred over the course of hours, not just second-long booms."

The drugs could've been contributing, too. Our Valium intake had risen to the point of excess. I was drinking a little more than Jeff, but he'd found an addictive painkiller to make up the difference: Tramadol.

"I've lost it before," I said to Jeff. "But this time feels different. Like last summer? I had the breakdown in Boston about the shirts. It was obvious what happened. I was under far too much stress commuting from New York. And the people surrounding me were, for the most part, losers. That time, though, it came on slow, then it boiled and that was it. I lost it, then left town. During that time I was depressed, tired all the time, and fried. Here, I'm never really depressed or tired. How can you be? Our situation is better than any Iraqi's. We can leave. There is little time for self-pity."

"You get too focused on living."

MORE AND MORE every day, the city surrounding the Green Zone crept closer to the brink of madness.

What made Iraq under the CPA such a crazed place? Living in constant need of food and clean water, without security or electricity, and perceiving no tangible future were just a few of the reasons people there were at the boiling point. Iraq's careening from totalitarianism to anarchy is another. The country wasn't just in anarchy, it was in free-market anarchy. At the Thieves Market, an open-air flea market in Tahrir Square just off Sadoun Street, you could buy a new stolen BMW for a few grand, just sitting there among the D batteries, bin Laden lighters, spark plugs, and other stolen, looted, or smuggled goods. Jeff was one of the few Westerners to be greeted by hugs and kisses whenever he entered the area. Satellite dish systems were being sold everywhere, sometimes it seemed on every street corner. Iraq had been closed off from the world for decades, but now the floodgates had opened, and the Iraqis wanted news and entertainment. No one knew where the country was going, or which way was up or down. Nobody could rely on anything.

The growing Iraqi opposition to the CPA was another major crazy-making factor. Military occupation is like living with your parents, except you don't know them, they don't like you, they speak a different language than you do, and they enforce their "belief systems" with big guns. It's humiliating. There were curfews and rules that made little sense; house-to-house raids by soldiers from another country were common day and night. Plus, there were the big Cecil B. DeMille-style predawn "extractions" using huge teams of soldiers, some of whom would surround a neighborhood with Hummers and APCs while others dropped out of Black Hawks onto neighborhood rooftops with cocked weapons. Then, searching for whatever it was they'd been tasked to find, they'd begin smashing up houses and tossing around concussion grenades, often in search of faked "terrorist objectives": people or things that had been leaked to the Army by a jealous Iraqi who'd only wanted to settle a score with a neighbor. Add to this Al Jazeera and Al Arabiya pumping in Palestine comparisons to Iraqi homes by satellite TV, and overlay it all with an armed resistance that preys on civilians and often spikes violently into public view through daily shootings and car bombings, and a sort of collective insanity sounds like the only obvious outcome. Occupation is a nasty business.

Everywhere we looked in Iraq, nothing was controlled—except information. The CPA and combined military forces tried to encourage the illusion that not even a sparrow could fall from the sky without their knowing. Unfortunately, this was a sham, since the Iraqis—who'd lived secretly for decades under Saddam—were more than up to the job of keeping areas of their culture and society, not to mention their growing resentment, a secret from the Westerners. All over Iraq, seemingly isolated destructive events—like reopened schools' getting bombed closed or oil pipelines and electrical generating plants' being sabotaged—were becoming commonplace. So to keep CPA and American spirits high, any Westerner in Iraq with authority and a mouthpiece began to torque the truth, ever so slightly, to put a gently more positive slant on the occupation's outlook. But as reality began to go sideways, even inside the Green Zone, most everyone could tell the CPA was starting to lose its grip in Iraq. The press knew it, but they couldn't get quotations or reliable facts from CPA officials to back it up for their editors. The Iraqis knew it, too.

Seeing the catastrophe that the occupation was becoming had a strange effect on Jeff and me. We were starting to believe our country had made a terrible mistake. We felt guilty about it, even though we'd been opposed to the invasion. But gloating self-righteously and saying "I told you so" doesn't work when people are dying. Instead, like most everyone working for the CPA, we found ourselves working even harder to make the CPA a success. More than anything, we wanted to see a safe and secure Iraq emerge from all that was starting to go wrong.

We tried looking for positives. And like so many others we knew in Baghdad—Heather Coyne, Jody, Charlie, and even the Duke—we were clinging to hope. But every day the promise of a peaceful and rebuilt Iraq flickered less brightly, and the CPA's goals—if the president held to the June 30 hand-off date—began to look like they might need to be reset to a slightly lower standard. It was hard to watch a group of people grow disillusioned while trying not to let it affect their work.

And, of course, for Jeff and me, we were still broke and soon would have nowhere to live.

.   .   .

THOSE DARK DAYS of early February were our low point in Iraq. With our future unsure, we realized how badly things were going for us and the CPA, and we began to ponder how many people—Iraqis and Westerners alike—were going to crawl out of the occupation intact. And yet, the war had its hooks in us. The magnitude of this American delusion was so big, and so in our faces, that we couldn't stop it from taking over our lives. Packing up and going home wasn't an option. So we waited, and hoped our luck would shift.

8

·

Shi'ite Happens

A ND THEN SADR CITY came into our lives.
It was our first day in the field on a humanitarian-aid mission.
Jeff had left early that morning and gone to Kerrada with another
NGO run by a woman named Halima, whose group changed its name
every week in hopes of getting more aid. This week it was called
"To Reverse Iraq." I went to Sadr City with an Iraqi we called "Mr.
Mustachio," who didn't speak English.

Mr. Mustachio, who was in his forties, had dark brown slivers for
eyes and enormous black bushes for brows. But it was that ebony
tsunami of sculpted Iraqi mustache that was his defining trait. Adams
had introduced him to us, after Mustachio had come to the Convention Center every day for a week trying to get a meeting with us, only
to be rebuffed by Ibty every time. So Mustachio found Adams, who
found us. Mustachio said he had an NGO that helped children in Sadr

City. Adams said he had a "very good feeling" about Mustachio, and around our office Adams's opinion was held in high esteem. So we figured anything brokered by a Kurdish transvestite—whose face on this day looked as if it had been glazed by blush—would work out just fine.

I went. We walked out to his car through the Al Rasheed Gate.

Mustachio drove a small white station wagon (a Toyota or Opel—they're Iraq's default vehicle and look virtually the same), and he had three friends waiting for him in the car. We traversed Baghdad in the morning sun. The capital's modern highways and cheesy shrines—the Martyr's Monument, just past the Oil Ministry, looks like two turquoise breasts—soon gave way to poverty: the Iraqi Shia way of life. Away from the GZ and central Baghdad, as one neighborhood delivered us to a still poorer neighborhood farther from downtown, dirty hustlers peddled gas in tin cans.

It took only a forty-minute drive from the Green Zone to see that the Iraq we'd been living in—palaces, forts, and middle- and upper-class neighborhoods—was not where the majority of Iraqis live. Sadr City was an utterly third-world slum that squeezed the population of Brooklyn, 2.5 million people, into an area of eight square miles, about one-tenth of Brooklyn's size.

WHEN WE ENTERED Sadr City, we were confronted by chaos. Dust choked the air and the sun felt hotter; it's an oppressive place. It bleeds an endless Pollock canvas of poverty. Donkeys munched piles of still-smoldering trash. Grids of foot trails and unpaved dirt roads doubled as open-air sewers, weaving between endless lines of mud-brick houses. Children wandered everywhere. Young men in stained athletic wear smoked cigarettes and stared at us. Women dressed head to foot in all-black abayas were orbited by swarms of children. Iraqi militiamen in black uniforms holding Kalashnikovs guarded mosque gates and patrolled the streets. There were no women between the ages of fourteen and forty. Every roadside shop sold something dirty, dusty, old, or rotten. The deeper we drove into Sadr City, the more it was the same. More dust. More trash. More sewage. More children. It just kept going. A skinny pony dragged a makeshift wooden cart behind it while its child driver puffed a cigarette. Minibuses and old trucks crammed with unwashed men hurtled past, trailing tall tails of dust. Water-pipe cafés proliferated at the same rate as everywhere else in Baghdad, providing even the poorest locals with a peanut gallery from which to ponder the world as it slipped past.

There was no sign of the U.S. Army or the new Iraqi Police (IP) in Sadr City. There are a lot of signs, posters actually, of black-turbaned Shi'ite clerics. The gray-bearded face of Iraq's most powerful man, Ayatollah Sistani, was ever-present. Still, the most popular poster was of a white-bearded man, Grand Ayatollah Mohammed Sadiq Al Sadr, the populist cleric who had been assassinated by Saddam in 1999. Another poster featured Mohammed Sadiq's son, the young, black-bearded Moqtada Al Sadr. Missing from the Day-Glo-looking posters were Sadr's real-life teeth. Rotten brown and fanglike, Sadr's grill looked as sinister as were his intentions.

Around Sadr City, though, Moqtada Al Sadr was emerging as the Shi'ite version of Che Guevara. And his defiant, iconoclastic attitude was striking a chord with the neighborhood's surplus of young, disenfranchised Shi'ite men. Already, his meteoric rise was becoming one of the wild cards of the occupation, and it could be linked directly to the country's demographics. Iraq is a nation of 25 million people. And as in so many Islamic or third-world countries, more than half of the population is less than twenty years old. In Sadr City, it's been estimated that 750,000 of its residents are poor and mostly unemployed males under age twenty-five. In the postwar power vacuum, Moqtada Al Sadr filled the paternal role of Saddam's collapsed state, and he began to cultivate a giant pool of followers awaiting direction and leadership. Using the Shia network of mosques and imams, Al Hawza, Sadr began to answer his followers' needs by providing various social and welfare services, including security.

This was Sadr's district. Postapocalyptic, end of the world, hell on earth: Call it what you will, Sadr City was a sea of needy humanity that had been crushed beneath both Saddam's heel and a decade of U.S. sanctions.

I had no translator and no clue what anyone was saying. Just Mr. Mustachio, who kept on driving. As he did, he'd tap me on the arm and point out another building or store; tapping and pointing, tapping and pointing. But most important, as he was giving me this tour of local landmarks in nonstop Arabic, he was smiling.

Mr. Mustachio's car stopped on the side of a bustling main street. A crowd of hundreds waited outside a building. In the sky, I saw minarets: a mosque. But it wasn't a freestanding mosque, it was built into a city block. Or maybe the mosque came first and the crumbling mud-brick houses started attaching themselves to its exterior like barnacles. The engine stopped and I moved to open the door. Mustachio motioned for me to stop. The crowd ringed the car.

A bullhorn sounded; a voice boomed. I popped three ten-milligram Valiums and washed them down with U.S. Army–supplied water.

Then, as the bullhorn quieted, the crowd began to queue at the mosque's doorstep. Those who didn't line up, mostly young boys, felt the wrath of a belt or a shoe as two sheikhs carved a path to the car to extract me. They kissed me on each cheek, shook my hands, called me "Habibi." Good friend. I breathed. It smelled like Manila, I was thinking. Children grabbed at me. Whack, they got a sandal to the head. Undeterred, they kept clawing. About then I remembered I was a hungover Jew who was now on drugs at a mosque in a place where the only law was Islam.

Mr. Mustachio and the sheikhs began to unload the aid boxes. I followed. We climbed a dark staircase, lined—packed, actually—with children. Old women, their faces and hands tattooed with henna, softly grabbed at me. I hoped the Valium would kick in soon. The stairway led to a dark, musty room lit by one naked bulb. Everyone was yelling. No one was listening. One of the sheikhs finally stepped up and became my bodyguard. I dropped back behind him.

The boxes were ripped open. A line formed. A Drew Bledsoe New England Patriots jersey was handed to a boy. Then a pair of shoes to a little girl, a pair of tiny jeans to another, and so on, all of it courtesy of the good people of Rhode Island. The crowd grew excited; borderline pandemonium broke out. Then a twisted mosh pit started. Children were struggling forward as old women and sheikhs whipped them with belts and plastic sandals until the crowd began to ebb and flow like the sea. I saw a little girl crying as she was crushed against a wall. Young boys were laughing.

A sheikh stood up on a desk, his head eclipsing the sole lightbulb. He shouted in Arabic. Calm resumed and everyone started laughing. The first box was empty.

The lull in activity and the laughing—just a few seconds, really— then dissipated and another mosh pit broke out. A baby girl, maybe two years old, was hoisted above the crowd. Wearing a dirty pink jumper, the baby's red-faced tantrum made her the strangest of crowd surfers. A woman's hennaed hands held the child up.

This went on for another twenty minutes until all the boxes were empty. By the end, I was fully adrenalized, even though the Valium I'd swallowed—enough to calm a person twice my size—was kicking in.

We exited as we'd come in, with a sheikh bouncer at the door creating a trail through the people to Mustachio's car. It was before noon, the sun was cutting straight down through the dusty air, and the frenzied crowd was cheering and saluting. Mr. Mustachio looked at me for approval. I nodded and smiled and we shook hands. "Habibi." Good friends. It was still before noon when we got back to the Green Zone.

BACK AT THE Convention Center I was abuzz. Jeff came back from his Kerrada run and was equally jolted.

"How was it?" I asked him.

"Great." I'd rarely seen Jeff this excited. "They were excellent, Halima was totally on-point." Halima was the woman running To Reverse Iraq. "It was a little staged. They seemed to have picked a few dirty kids off the street and put them in line with their kids. But I thought, hey, Halima has a good heart. I don't know if UNICEF would approve of the methods, but it was something."

"Doubt what I saw in Sadr City would fit into OXFAM's code of humanitarian ethics, either."

"Then again, at least we're doing something besides sitting at a hotel on our high horse with our thumb up our ass, like Philippe."

"You are not a true humanitarian," I said, mimicking Claudia's accent. Then I added, seriously, "You have to go to Sadr City. It is the only place I want to work."

My trip to Sadr City was supposed to help civil society building. But instead of helping civil society, I'd actually been aiding a mosque. Religion and aid work are often interwoven. A good example is Christian groups who do excellent work in Africa. But by giving aid directly to a mosque, we were helping to establish religious authority rather than a new civil one. I was inadvertently working against democracy and toward theocracy. Of course, in the afterglow of such an exciting day, this contradiction escaped me.

Nonetheless and even after we began to run things more appropriately, Mustachio remained a reliable Sadr City contact. Over time we noticed that most of his friends wore headdresses, while he stuck to a dirty gray suit. Of course, given that most Iraqis have three or four different jobs, the suit may have been undercover costume, and he could've been an agent of a mosque. But Mustachio never did anything to make us question his allegiances, he had great contacts across Sadr City, and we liked him. He remained an honest broker.

After only a few trips to Sadr City, we began lunching at his house, with his many babies. One afternoon, over piles of flat bread, succulent olives, and lamb, Mustachio told us his story through a translator. And like every Iraqi story we heard, it had its dark humor and crushing tragedy. In the 1980s five of his brothers had been killed in the war with Iran, since Saddam used Shi'ites from Sadr City as cannon fodder.

DURING OUR SHORT TIME inside the CPA, we were becoming schooled in the art of the government memo. Heather Coyne was a maestro of memos, having gotten her MA in international relations and economics at Johns Hopkins School of Advanced International Studies, where I imagine they have an Advanced Memo Writing class. Then she'd gone to work at the White House Office of Budget Management, where memo-ese is a required skill. After September 11, she joined the Army's Officer Candidate School. The Army and CPA were lucky to have her. Her e-mailed memos, sometimes just to one person, sometimes to a handful of people, sometimes to a hundred people, shaped workdays and weeks for many others. She must have been managing fifty to one hundred people's lives at any one time.

Our aid program needed supporters, so we took a cue from Heather and decided to send our drafted field reports out as e-mails. Of course, we understood that these field reports were more advertisements than factual documents, but the PR worked. Our first report generated positive e-mails from a bunch of CPA bosses and military brass. Naturally, it was a cause for celebration. We'd take any excuse.

ASIDE FROM JEFF AND ME, the NGO Assistance Office had become the stomping grounds of another American: Sergeant Shawn Jensen. An incredibly likable and honest thirty-year-old from the 2nd Armored Cavalry Regiment, Jensen somehow started working for the CPA on civil society building under Heather Coyne. He was technically AWOL from his unit, which was ending its tour and on the way back to Kuwait. It was odd; Jensen was going AWOL in order to continue fighting the war.

Hailing from North Carolina, Jensen was a southerner who understood the northern state of mind. Before joining the Army he'd studied religion at Gordon College in Beverly, Massachusetts, just a few miles from where I grew up. He understood the psychology of provincial, cynical, weather-beaten New England, and always took lighthearted jabs at me. "Yer Boston ass find anything to complain about yet today? I know you'll find somethin'," he'd say.

He also took his religion seriously, but in a love-thy-neighbor kind of way. Whatever religion he actually followed, it was a very appealing faith. Jeff and I pictured his daily ultimate moment as saying grace before tucking into a big slice of meatloaf. In the wake of 9/11, it was Jensen's faith that guided him to join the Army. As a student of religion, Jensen felt he could best understand what drove his enemy.

Jensen was a member of what we'd started calling the military's "9/11 generation." These soldiers were cut from a broad panorama of society, unlike the usual enlistees, who were mostly drawn from rural and urban poor and lower-middle-class areas or from families with a strong military tradition. Like Heather Coyne, Jensen probably wouldn't have become a soldier were it not for 9/11. It was an unseen consequence of 9/11's tragedy that would greatly benefit Iraq. People like Coyne and Jensen gave all of their energy, intelligence, and talents to helping Iraq. And many Iraqis (Coyne and Jensen had huge local followings) got to experience the benefits of their American spirit. To those who knew them, America's legacy in Iraq was more complex because no Iraqi could deny the selfless intentions of American soldiers like them.

With Jensen came his world. And what a strange band of followers he'd attracted. His focus was on rebuilding Iraq's educational sector, and his goals were huge: He supervised multimillion-dollar school rebuilding programs, plus his own NGO with Bob Dole's support, as well as the beginnings of an Iraqi Parent Teacher Association. Blond, fair-skinned, tall, and lanky, Jensen was the opposite of the dark-skinned, thick-bearded Iraqis he was meeting. His sunny attitude came with a sly sense of humor and a hokey laugh that often alerted us to his presence. Iraqis loved Jensen; they really believed in him. He never displayed the arrogance, ignorance, and cultural superiority that Iraqis too often associated with the U.S. Army.

Iraqis felt the United States was too paternalistic; they felt the Americans wanted to make Iraq into a mini-America. We Americans often get caught up in our own myth that we're the best society. Many Iraqis felt that America was just lucky. To them, we are a young nation, just three hundred years old. Many Iraqis pointed out that Baghdad was the New York of A.D. 1000: the greatest city on earth. They worried that it was American culture, with its loose standards, easy conveniences, and sex-mad commercialism, that would eventually distract the country from what was truly important.

Iraqis are not uneducated. Under Saddam, education was a state service, and most Iraqis are well educated, which doubled the insult of American paternalism to them. They would point out that many of the American troops in their country were undereducated and culturally inferior. The Arab press wasn't shy about touting the fact that many soldiers, especially the grunts patrolling the streets, lacked college degrees or any cultural or historical understanding of the Middle East.

Jensen, however, treated Iraqis as equals, and for that he gained their respect and trust. Jensen kept going on about his Iraqi buddies from Sadr City. After the invasion his unit had taken over an old cigarette factory, naming it Camp Marlboro. He saw and felt the plight of the Shi'ite slum, and with a heart the size of his, he had to take action. When a group of young locals had come to the base's gate to welcome them and offer support, Jensen and his unit befriended them. Together they built a dozen soccer fields across Sadr City.

"You guys are gonna love Hayder," Jensen told us the second week in February. "He and Abbad are great. You gotta meet these guys. I'll get them down here. They'll work with you guys on your program."

BUT DESPITE HIS GOOD INTENTIONS, Jensen could also be a flake. Every day he was overbooked, with more plans and meetings than were possible. But after he had promised us an introduction for days, a few days after I'd gone to Sadr City for the first time we finally stood face to face with Jensen's Sadr City buddies. Four of them showed up one afternoon.

"Guys, this is Hayder," Jensen said to us in the lobby of the Convention Center. We all shook hands.

They were all in their late twenties or early thirties, and all sporting the finest in butterfly-collar polyester shirts, none finer than the black and gray diagonal tiger print Hayder was wearing, plus Iraqi jeans and pants. If you didn't look at their faces, they looked just like Charlie. Hayder was the only one of them who spoke English. At thirty-one, he was short and stocky, with a perfect haircut and mustache. He was on his way to getting a Ph.D. in physical education. Abed—who had similarly perfect hair but no mustache and a more weathered face—was his right-hand man, and was obviously a smart, busy, resourceful guy, but he spoke no English. Nonetheless, Jeff and I realized after a few minutes of joking and talking with them that we'd found our Iraqi mirror images.

With Hayder came an insight into the youthful majority of Sadr City. Talking to him, you got the feeling the weight of his people was on his shoulders. When asked why he wasn't working harder to finish his degree, he'd say: "There are more important things right now. For the first time, we have a chance to make a better place to live.

We have an opportunity to help more than just our families, to help Sadr City."

Hayder saw the fall of Saddam as a new beginning. He also believed the Americans could help his people. And there was no one in Iraq who deserved a clean slate more than the Shi'ites of Sadr City. According to Hayder, many young Sadr City residents shared his hope for a new beginning. Few of them, however, had contact with Americans, and those who did often had a negative experience. Building soccer fields with Jensen, Hayder had seen firsthand the benefits of American support. Most of Hayder's peers had turned for their leadership to the mosque, which was turning increasingly anti-American, and especially to the followers of Moqtada Al Sadr. It didn't take long for Hayder to explain Sadr's pathway to us.

Even as Sadr worked with the Al Hawza network of mosques to give his followers more food, some medical care, and a security militia, there remained much Sadr couldn't provide. He needed to give the people of Baghdad's biggest, poorest, and most crowded neighborhood hope. And there had to be a reason that he and Al Hawza weren't succeeding: He needed a common enemy. As was becoming more and more obvious, that enemy was the United States.

Sadr began to speak out against the Americans just after the fall of Saddam. In mosques, on the radio, to the media, his rhetoric grew more venomous by the day. And as he grew more inflammatory, his groups of followers began to spread. Power was becoming Sadr's game, if only to offer disgruntled and hopeless Iraqis a different line than Ayatollah Sistani, Iraq's most revered cleric, who favored peace and generally supported the U.S. military presence. So in giving poor Iraqis an enemy, Sadr answered the question of why life under American occupation wasn't getting much better, even with the mighty and righteous network of Al Hawza and the mighty Sadr doing all they could. By invoking the American as the enemy Sadr was harnessing the disenfranchised young Shi'ites' energy and gaining their loyalty.

Problem was, the United States wasn't an enemy of the Shi'ites. If anything, the United States was trying to align itself with Shi'ites. But in a power vacuum, where intentions don't always link up with reality, that gulf between the two can be attractive to a man who has his own thirst for leadership, especially when that gulf is filled with hungry, tired, hopeless young men looking for a point to their lives.

THE DAY AFTER we met Hayder, he came back to our office with all of his NGO registration forms perfectly completed. Under the line that said "Name of NGO" was his new organization: Soccer Coaches.

"Jeff, are you ready to go to Sadr City?" Hayder asked.

"Can't wait."

JEFF'S FIRST TRIP to Sadr City was on February 10 with Hayder and the other Soccer Coaches (Abed and a guy we called "Turtleneck"). The day started in the Convention Center parking lot, where we split off: I went with Mustachio to another part of Sadr City while Jeff went with Hayder.

Just after I'd left on my field op, Jeff was still loading boxes into the car when an Iraqi man whom I'd double booked by accident came up to him yelling, "Mistah Ray! Mistah Ray!"

"I'm not Ray. Leave me alone," Jeff said after about the third time being called the wrong name.

"Mistah Ray! Mistah Ray!" the man kept yelling, shoving one of our aid distribution forms in Jeff's face.

Hayder told the guy to leave, and the group piled into two cars and headed off for a maternity ward on the outskirts of Sadr City, just past the Oil Ministry and Martyr's Monument. Because they were men going to a maternity ward—and with a non-Arab man to boot—Jeff and the Soccer Coaches handed over four or five boxes to a nurse, then walked back out of the ward's gate to the cars. Waiting there, and even more agitated, was the guy from the Convention Center parking lot. He was confronting Jeff about being brushed off. Again, Hayder told the man to leave, and he did.

The next stop was an orphanage, deeper in Sadr City, near Camp Marlboro, where Jensen had first met Hayder just after the invasion. The orphanage was a split building, one side for girls and one for boys. After a quick and surprisingly orderly distribution of clothes and school supplies, Jeff headed out to the courtyard and played soccer for a few minutes with a half dozen boys, ranging in age from about five to fifteen. Down the street from the orphanage there was a partially destroyed Baath Party building on the corner, which had been stripped of everything of value—even the windows and doors were gone—and it was covered in Arabic graffiti. It was so destroyed and strange looking that it kept dragging Jeff's attention away from the kids.

Then the screaming guy was back, yelling at Jeff in Arabic through the orphanage's gate.

"Fuck off!" Jeff finally yelled back at the guy, not that he'd been able to understand what the shouter was saying; he was just trying to get his own point across. With that, Hayder, Abed, and Turtleneck yelled at the man in Arabic, and the guy promptly took off in his car.

While driving through Sadr City, Hayder gave Jeff a great guided tour, pointing out the different-colored Shia flags on the buildings, denoting different tribes. On one small square on a main street was a huge billboard of Mohammed Al Sadr, the area's namesake, with a long white beard and airbrushed-looking horses behind him. Sadr, once the area's prominent imam, is more or less the hero of Shia. He became even more of a hero after Saddam executed him.

Jeff's third and final stop for the morning was a small clinic. Hayder pulled up on the sidewalk, and the other guys went inside to make sure it was safe for Jeff to enter, too.

Jeff was standing alone on the sidewalk, leaning against the car, when Screaming Guy showed up again.

Screaming Guy got right up in Jeff's face, shouting even louder than before, his face flushed bright red. Jeff was scared shitless, but he also knew Hayder and the guys were just inside, so he started yelling back. The guy took a few steps back to his car, opened its rear door, and pulled out an AK-47. He pointed it directly at Jeff.

Instinct told Jeff to lift his hands halfway into the air, then he just kind of shrugged his shoulders and put his head down. The guy kept yelling the same two or three words, which Jeff didn't understand, and each time he yelled them Screaming Guy stepped closer to Jeff, the rifle still pointed at his chest. Jeff didn't say anything back. All he could comprehend was Screaming Guy and the AK-47 coming closer and closer.

It seemed like forever, but finally Hayder and the crew came out and ran over, standing directly behind Jeff. Abed put his hand on Jeff's right shoulder, and as he did, Turtleneck and Abed pulled pistols out. Everyone was yelling, except Jeff, who was still scared to death. After another half minute of back-and-forth shouting, the guy backed off and drove away, still yelling at everyone from behind his rolled-up windows.

Hayder kept apologizing to Jeff, but it wasn't his fault. Not knowing what to say, Jeff just sat in the backseat of the car and looked out the window, holding everything back. They went to a little market and Hayder bought Jeff a Pepsi and a bootleg candy bar. Jeff could only stomach one bite. They sat on the hood of Turtleneck's car and talked for a while about everything from women to the war.

There's a fatalist undertone to everything in Iraq, and for good reason. At any given moment you could have a bunker-buster dropped on your house, a looter could rip off your whole family, you could get caught in a street battle on your way to school or the mosque, or some screaming guy could chase you around all day and pull out a machine gun. Jeff and I were already coming to have empathetic respect for the Iraqis. The fact that, in the face of decades of random persecution under Saddam, then years of American sanctions, then two American invasions and the hardships and dangers they brought, they could care about the welfare of others as they remained broke and starving was incredible.

LATER THAT NIGHT, after days of trying, we finally convinced Jensen to leave the Green Zone. Maybe he wanted to hear more about Jeff's little Sadr Experience. Maybe he just wanted to get outside the GZ. But on this night, when we suggested an evening's outing to Sergeant Shawn, he looked up and said, "Uh, sure."

It had just turned dark, maybe six o'clock, and our plan was to go to Fanar Chicken, then hit the Fanar Bar for a couple of drinks. When we met to leave, Jensen was wearing a brand-new PX outfit: still-creased Dockers khaki pants, a blue plaid shirt, and a Tennessee Titans hat that lit up with tiny flashing bulbs. Jeff and I cracked up laughing.

"You look like a redneck vato," I said. "The Hillbilly of East L.A."

"Or an East L.A. undercover cop—Shawn-ie Brasco," Jeff said. "Could you be any more obvious?"

"I had to buy some new clothes. All my civvies are too gross to wear in public."

"You can see your gun."

"Tried to conceal it best I could, man."

The second we left the Green Zone Jensen's eyes started darting back and forth. Jeff put up his arm to hail a taxi.

"You guys are nuts, hailing taxis like it's New York City," Jensen said. Baghdad is a city of gypsy cabs. Gas is subsidized to about ten cents, so driving comes with little overhead. We were picked up by an old VW. The driver was smoking a cigarette and wore a dishdasha.

Charlie was waiting for us at Fanar Chicken. Dinner was great, as usual. Surveying the scene after the meal, Jensen said, "This place is just asking to get bombed. All this glass would be perfect shrapnel."

It was true, Fanar Chicken's location made it an excellent target. Right across the street from the Sheraton-Palestine hotel compound checkpoint, the restaurant was unguarded and was heavily frequented by Westerners. Our ignorance of the rising insurgency led us to take Jensen's comments as paranoia.

"Ah, you can get killed anywhere in Iraq. Why waste time worrying," Jeff said.

We moved our party to the Fanar Bar, inside the cordon of concrete provided by the 1st Armored Division. The usual suspects were there: Michele, the French aid worker; Catalin, the hard-drinking Romanian radio reporter; intelligent American freelancer Andrew Butters; fake freelancer Ilya, who was wigged out on pills and left town shortly after; and the Duke, in his element, sitting at a bottle-strewn table of six.

Jensen tried to keep a stone face, but a glimmer of amazement twinkled in his eyes as he surveyed this collection of the war's B-list players.

The Duke pulled me aside and jokingly asked if Jensen was our own Secret Service detail.

"Someone's gotta look out for you assholes. Otherwise you'll end up dead," Jensen said. He'd found us a ride back to the Green Zone, provided by an Iraqi police officer in a brand-new truck.

9

.

Baghdad Central

ONE NIGHT at about seven o'clock, Jeff and I were sitting around our office and bitching about how we were spending our own money to get photos of our aid-distribution runs processed when Lieutenant Heather Coyne walked in. As always, she was dressed in her full BDU, but instead of her usual serious soldier's face, she was wearing an enormous grin. "OK, guys," she said. "I got you housing, and I got you badges. You can live in the palace. You'll be bunking with Jensen. And I got you authorized for full dining hall and mess privileges, too. You guys are official. Now why don't you come across with me to the Al Rasheed, where we're all having dinner. You should meet everybody."

"Thanks for saving us, Heather. We were almost dead broke," Jeff said, and then yelped in his best Beth Payne imitation, "You will not!" Heather looked confused. "When we registered with the consulate,

Beth Payne yelled at us: 'You will not get badges! You will not find housing!' And now we have both. Ha."

WITH THE HELP of her coworker, Lieutenant Colonel Joe Rice, Heather had solved all our problems. By setting us up with room and board in the Republican Palace, she'd pulled off an unlikely coup. Sure, there were some restrictions: We couldn't tell anyone where we were sleeping (Jensen was supposed to be living there by himself), but that was just fine.

Like no one else in the CPA, Heather Coyne was a master at success. She cut corners, pulled strings, and made phone calls that often turned lead into gold. She operated at a frantic pace. With a small frame and short blond hair, Heather always seemed like a mother whose child was late for school. She blitzed through the Green Zone cleaning up underlings' messes. By holding herself to the highest standards, she was forever letting herself down. To others, though, she was a maverick. She was the person we learned the most from in Iraq.

Her reach was incredible. Once while waiting in line for the buffet I spotted a stack of copies of *The Economist* magazine. Picking up a copy, I noticed the mailing address was to Heather Coyne. Another time, I noticed there was a library of books in a palace bathroom. Having read all the books I'd brought, I picked out five titles that interested me. Three of the five books had Heather's chicken-scrawl notes littering their margins from front to back.

Jeff and I joked that Heather was an all-seeing, all-knowing agent of Plato, sent to bestow a little liberalism upon the Kantian servants of the CPA and the Sun Tzu warriors of the military. A self-declared "Thomas Friedman liberal," she believed that American influence could transform the Middle East. She also felt that freedom was a universal human right. And as a quasi-feminist, nothing was more important than equal rights for Iraqi women, who she felt could easily end up disenfranchised by Islam's shackles.

WE LEFT THE Convention Center and followed Heather across Yafa Street to the Al Rasheed, with its secure KBR Dining Hall, off-limits to civilians. Heather flashed her badge and signed us in. Inside, a big group of Americans—some soldiers, some civilians, and a few Iraqi aides—was sitting around a long, rectangular table finishing their dinner. Heather introduced us around: Lieutenant Colonel Joe Rice; Leah Cato from the State Department; Colonel Bishop; Thanaa, Heather's assistant . . . we met everyone at the table, shaking hands with all ten or twelve of them.

After introductions were finished, Lieutenant Colonel Rice, a handsome, medium-tall guy in his midforties, pointed at us to get our attention. He smiled. "So, guys," he said. "I understand you need housing. Come on by the palace first thing in the morning, talk to Force Protection [the Marines at the palace gates], and tell them to call my office. I'll come down and we'll get you squared away." Then Heather said we could go through the buffet and eat all we wanted.

NEXT MORNING at about ten—after an evening of hash and political baiting with the Clowns—we showed up at the palace gate and asked the Force Protection guys to put a call into Colonel Rice.

Colonel Rice sent Jensen down. He led us just inside the palace gates, to the old guardhouse that had been converted into the Badge Office. Inside, a couple of attractive Eastern European women photographed us, took our signatures, and processed our CPA badges. There was no security check, no reading of any official rules, no signing of contracts, no issuing of manuals: nothing. Just a digital photo, a signature, and we were in.

Both Jeff and I got "Level O" CPA badges, which gave us full access to the many perks on offer inside the Green Zone. Jeff's badge even gave him permission to carry a weapon in the palace—though I still contend that was an administrative mistake. As the processing was finishing up, Jensen gave us the news that we were to live with him. "I'm not supposed to be sleeping here, either," he said. "But we all share some bunks down at the end of a hallway. There's another guy, too. I've blocked it, for a little privacy. But you gotta stay pretty quiet at night."

Once we had our badges, Jensen led us inside and showed us around. Our new home was a distant corner of a second-floor hallway of the palace's eastern wing. A few weeks earlier, we'd been backpackers with no jobs and no connections. Now we were living in CPA headquarters.

Our new home had two small pairs of bunk beds, which were separated from the hall by an office partition. Jensen had one of the bunks for himself, and his beds were covered in clothes, books, and a ton of other crap. He had a little nightstand next to his bed, made from an empty cardboard MRE box stood on its end. Nearby was a stack of care-package boxes from home, filled with an endless supply of beef jerky guaranteed to keep us farting.

Jensen said there weren't any sheets or blankets available for us, which was fine since Jeff and I had sleeping bags. We had a window that overlooked the palace's neoclassical/Islamic-corny facade. A few days before, the palace roof had been adorned with eight bronze Saddam heads that had since been removed following a party at which the heads had been doused with gasoline and set on fire. Digital cameras had recorded the event and images were being e-mailed all around the Green Zone and back home ("Hey, that's me with a beer and Saddam's burning head!").

The palace was a prime location: the center of it all. It had been the seat of Baath Party power during Saddam's rule and was now the CPA control center. Following the expiration of CPA power at the end of June, it was to morph into the U.S. Embassy.

Jagged chandeliers and fake-wood stairways gave way to colored tile hallways that led to epic ballrooms. Most of the rooms were too big for any practical purpose. The Hussein clan loved penises and fornication. Entire rooms seemed designed just for orgies. And it turned out the Republican Palace was the toned-down Hussein family orgy locale.

Saddam had the initials "SH" in Arabic placed pretty much everywhere, too. And like a Jewish mother, he had a love for teal, turquoise, and gold. Like the Jewish settlers of southeastern Florida, he had an enduring love of gaudy gold trim. The guy who sent Scuds into Tel Aviv and tried to nuke Israel had decorated his palace the same way my grandmother's friend Sookie did her condo in Pompano Beach.

TWO DAYS LATER our time expired at Clowntown, and we moved out of Sam's and into the Republican Palace.

"From Clowntown to a palace? How the fuck did we pull this off?" I said.

"You will *not*!"

"Six months ago I saw demons in my room while on mushrooms, slithering up bookshelves like weird shadows. We used to live in a haunted psychedelic loft. Now we live in Saddam's Palace. How does this happen?"

"I don't know, but we've effectively snuck into the government."

"Just two schmoes."

All thanks to Lieutenant Colonel Joe Rice, who had a lot more on his plate than just helping us. Rice oversaw Baghdad's municipal political structure, advising the city's interim mayor, as well as the city's various district and neighborhood councils. Rice had been receiving our field reports—Heather was forwarding them to him—and must have liked that we were getting results in a way that no formal CPA official could. We could travel around Iraq without the usual burdens of the CPA: official status and approved pretrip plans, Force Protection, armored vehicles, and private security. Because of the worsening security situation, all CPA officials leaving the Green Zone now had to be part of a multivehicle convoy. Being volunteers, or stupid, we had the freedom to leave the Green Zone with anyone we wanted. We were all trying to do the same thing—help Iraqis—and he'd do what he could to support us. Back home, Rice had been mayor of his town, Littleton, Colorado. He was a natural, with a manner that made you feel important and comfortable. We were fortunate to catch his attention.

THE CPA OFFICE we now slept next to, Baghdad Central, didn't seem to actually exist. Google it or mention it to a member of the press, or to anyone who lived and worked inside the Green Zone, and you'd get nothing. Yet there it was, on the first and second floors of the palace's east wing, a collection of offices that basically ran Baghdad province.

And the Baghdad Central office actually accomplished things. It set up a network of District Advisory Councils (DACs) and Neighborhood Advisory Councils (NACs), organized municipal elections, pushed through reconstruction projects, and even scheduled trash pickups. Baghdad Central's successes showed what could have happened had Iraq not hit the quicksand of guerrilla war.

Baghdad Central was staffed by a talented group of people. Right next to where we slept there were two smaller rooms filled with a few dozen desks, a mix of civilian and military, with a translator nearby for every staffer. Each district of Baghdad had a full-time advisor. For example, young Michael Cole was advisor to Adhamiyah. Leah Cato was Sadr City's advisor. Joe Rice advised the mayoral office. Heather was in charge of civil society building.

Occupying the last and largest office, right at the top of Baghdad Central's pyramid, was veteran diplomat Andy Morrison. In his midforties and looking like a day trader, Morrison pushed his job to the limit, sometimes working forty-eight hours straight. We knew this because his office was behind the wall where we slept. Few people at the CPA had as subtle an understanding of Islam as Morrison did. He'd been posted in Saudi Arabia for years, and could break into a detailed analysis of nineteenth-century Wahhabism or dissect Persian poetry. His ranking of FS-2 put him one step below an official ambassador. With that status, peons like us should've been pretty much off his radar screen. But Andy Morrison treated us with more respect than we probably deserved.

ONE AFTERNOON, not long after we'd moved into Baghdad Central, I returned to my bunk after a swim in Saddam's pool and a KBR buffet banquet of grilled cheese and Lucky Charms. As I walked past the office I saw that, up on a computer, was the website for Neiman

Marcus. Michael Cole, a medium-sized guy with short, wavy brown hair and brown eyes, was paging through some sweaters.

"Hey, what you looking at?" I asked.

"Just some clothes." He looked slightly embarrassed.

"Don't worry, I won't tell. Every girlfriend I've ever had has been a fashion Nazi. It has become my weakness. What designers do you like?"

"I like Ralph Lauren, Prada."

"I like Prada, too."

Glancing at his desk I saw a stack of books, including Samuel Huntington's *Clash of Civilizations,* and asked what he studied in school.

"Political science. Just like Miuccia Prada."

"Strange brew, Prada, Huntington, us, and that guy," I pointed behind us to Farouz, a young Iraqi who was Baghdad Central's best translator. He was blasting a live Bon Jovi concert DVD.

Cole rolled his eyes. "Farouz, why Bon Jovi?"

"Because Bon Jovi is great. I want go to America and live on a prayer, man. In New Jersey!" He sang along, "Whoooh-oooh, living on aaaa pray-yah! C'mon man, look at this."

"No you don't want to live on a prayer in New Jersey," I said. "Trust me. And Bon Jovi sucks." But the DVD he was watching made sense, especially if you were an Iraqi wanting American-style freedom, like Farouz. It was shot at Giants Stadium, with eighty thousand people singing and clapping along. Farouz wore Western clothes and had a goatee. He was fully invested in the work of bringing democracy to Iraq. He even referred to himself as part of "the Coalition."

Jon Bon Jovi was wearing the worst outfit Michael Cole or I'd ever seen. I added, "He looks worse than Bremer. Why do Iraqis love Bon Jovi?"

"If you don't like Bon Jovi, what rock 'n' roll do you like?"

"I like the Stones. You should see *Gimme Shelter.*" Farouz wrote it down.

Over time, Michael Cole, Jeff, and I would hang out together a lot. Like Jeff, Cole had grown up in D.C.'s Virginia suburbs. He loved cappuccino, and made great ones. At twenty-three, he was just out of Virginia's Radford University. He'd come to Baghdad to work for Halliburton's KBR unit, where his mother had worked as a VP. Michael was funny, urbane, and ethical, and he hated the corporate life of KBR. Crushed between the idealism of a political science undergrad degree and the corruption and org-chart structure of the world's leading war profiteer, Cole switched over: He left KBR and got a job in governance. Then he was moved to Baghdad Central.

Many of the Americans in the Green Zone were young. The CPA was top-heavy with young Republicans hired from the conservative think tank, the Heritage Foundation. Many of these kids wanted jobs on Capitol Hill, but ended up setting up the Iraqi stock exchange or something similar. At first, when Washington created the CPA, everyone figured that qualified American political professionals would jump at an opportunity to assist their country in the largest nation-building project since the end of World War II. But since security never improved, and in fact it got worse, few qualified professionals chose to earn a government salary while risking violent death in Iraq, especially when anyone with any real experience could work in Iraq in the private sector and make four or five times more money. Consequently, the CPA filled as many jobs as possible with kids who lacked experience, but who worked at a far lower pay grade.

ACTIVE COUNTERWEIGHT to all our youthful energy was Colonel Bishop, the office's security chief. Bishop was a man's man. Red-haired and freckle-skinned, with a deep Arkansas accent, he wore the insignia from the 101st Airborne—along with a Special Forces patch—on his sleeve. He spoke fast. He talked straight. He organized convoys, carried the cash, and omnivorously devoured all available intelligence about Iraq, its people, and its growing insurgency. Once, to make sure everyone was happy and could get where they needed to go on time, Bishop requisitioned a duffel full of crisp hundred-dollar bills, which he then used to buy thirty-two cars in Sadr City in a single day—mostly Opels and Hyundais—one for each DAC and NAC member.

Bishop also brought his own form of reveille to our hallway each morning, usually about five o'clock, on his way into the office. "*Wake up,* slackers!" he'd hee-haw at us as he stepped into the office, coffee mug in hand.

This soon became a running joke between Jensen, Jeff, and me, and we'd mimic Bishop's accent any time it was appropriate. Colonel Bishop was part Force Protection, part office manager, and mostly hard-ass. Still, we admired him, though sometimes we couldn't take him seriously when he was having an intense John Wayne moment.

Even early on during our stay at Baghdad Central, though, we could tell Colonel Bishop was meeting frustration. Creating democracy wasn't a military program, and the complications that arose from civil governance often drove him crazy. The "Eye-rakkis" didn't follow orders, which meant Bishop was constantly having his plans vaporized by events on streets beyond the Green Zone. So in an attempt to come to grips with Iraq's constantly shifting situation, Bishop turned to history. On his desk, used like a reference book, he kept a hallowed copy of *The Best and the Brightest,* David Halberstam's evisceration of America's policymakers during the Vietnam

War. Given the dramatic failure that it recounts of America's efforts to bolster a legitimate Vietnamese government, win the widespread support of the population, and check the Vietcong insurgency, it struck us as offering insight into what not to do, but scant guidance to what might actually work in Iraq.

10

•

A ROUND THIS TIME, Jensen and Charlie told us about a guy named Adam Davidson, who had his own mansion in Jadiriyah, across the 14th of July Bridge from the GZ. They'd both gone to a dinner party at his house, and he said he was a New Yorker and a reporter for National Public Radio (NPR), and that he was fond of poker. Adam sounded like our kind of guy, we told Jensen. We began demanding an introduction. Jensen promised us, but nothing happened.

The legend of Adam kept growing. All sorts of CPA people talked about him, his mansion, his roommates, and his team of funny, lazy Iraqi security guards. Jay, who was tasked to establish and run the Iraqi stock market, told us he'd been to "Adam's Baghdad Utopia." He said he ate a multicourse meal and learned about lemurs. Marla told us that her happiest days in Baghdad were sleeping on Adam's floor.

Grapes, wine, women, pasta, old copies of *Newsweek,* a WiFi network all across the compound—everybody knew this Adam guy but us.

Finally, we met Adam briefly outside the Press Center at the Convention Center just before the CPA's daily press conference, called the Gaggle. Jensen introduced us. Adam was tall and stocky, wearing glasses, jeans, and a button-down shirt. We told him we'd give him a grand tour of the Green Zone, using our badges to get into off-limits places. He suggested that we come over to his house. But so many people kept coming up and hugging Adam that we never actually made a plan. Then the Gaggle started.

"We're never going to get into Mistah Adam's house," I said to Jeff. He nodded, rocking his head sideways.

THE GAGGLE WAS the Baghdad version of the Five O'Clock Follies, Saigon's infamous press conferences during the Vietnam War. And since it was held just upstairs from our office, we'd attend from time to time.

Hosted by the camera-friendly Major General Mark Kimmet and Dan Senor, Bremer's spokesperson, the Gaggle was an exercise in relentless pro-CPA propaganda. Whatever the question, Senor's answer was that democracy was taking root in Iraq: Nothing could push him off this message. From Kimmet, the message was equally relentless: The United States was defeating the insurgency.

By representing Bremer and the CPA, Senor was supposed to be speaking for the Iraqi people. After all, the CPA was the interim government of Iraq. But instead of representing the Iraqi people, Senor was forever spinning news for the campaign trail back home. The Iraqis weren't blind to this. The American prevarications were yet another thing that turned Iraq against the CPA. All across Iraq, the Iraqi people saw Bremer and Senor as cleaner-cut versions of Baghdad Bob, Saddam's press minister during the invasion, who right up until American tanks were about to run him down contended on the international news that the Americans and their Coalition were being defeated. The feeling across the Red Zone's streets was that CPA deceptions had become another recruiting tool for the insurgency.

Of the two spokespeople, Senor was more disliked, by both the Iraqis and the Americans. Everything he said seemed to have been first run through the filter of presidential election-year politics. "The Iraqi people are standing up defiant to the insurgency forces," seemed to be his mantra. "Schools are reopening. Fresh water is being reestablished. The electrical power grid is nearly complete again across Iraq." None of these things was remotely true. But as Senor stood in front of a silhouette of Iraq—flanked by plasma-screen TVs and encircled with stars—nobody could see the reality of Iraq's streets outside. Senor was such a cocky, deceptive spinmeister that he made Kimmet's triumphalism sound something close to sincere.

It got to where Kimmet and Senor could say anything and expect it to be believed. During one later Gaggle, when it came out that a number of Iraqi women and children attending a wedding had been killed by Coalition forces, Kimmet acknowledged that American ground troops and aircraft had been the only forces present; then he smudged up Uncle Sam's complicity before hurling the subject into total ambiguity: "There were a number of women, a handful of women—I think the number was four to six—that were actually caught up in the engagement. They may have died from some of the fire that came from the aircraft. But no American soldiers shot women, no American soldiers involved in that operation shot children." This was technically true: They bombed them.

. . .

ONE MORNING AT THE CPA Press Center, we overheard Charlie saying he was going to Adam's later. Jeff and I decided to tail Charlie all day, forcing him to bring us to Adam's.

"Hey Charlie, what are you doing later?"

"I've got no plans."

"Want to get pizza?"

"Don't you guys have to work? And isn't it a little early for lunch? It's only ten-thirty."

"We're gonna call it a day. It's not very busy 'round here. Let's hoof it."

Jeff and I had been going to a smoke shop, called a diwan, after work. The owner had become our "habibi," as had his eight-year-old son, who worked as the shop's server. It had a dirty white-tiled floor, urine-yellow peeling walls, and a nasty bathroom without toilet paper. A soccer game was on TV, and we plopped down in the back. Three narghile pipes were ordered, double-apple flavor all around. Some of the locals, horny Arab males, had fallen for Jeff, earning him the nickname Heartbreaker. As we sat down, they started calling out to Jeff.

"Hey, Heartbreaker, your boyfriend isn't here," Charlie said, teasing. "Do you miss him? Want me to find out where he is? Need some loving?"

"Fuck you."

"Charlie, how's the journalism thing going?" I asked, trying to change the subject.

"Good. Starting this women's center story to report in a few days. Coming right up I've got an embed scheduled with the 82nd Airborne in Fallujah."

"For who?"

"*Raleigh News-Observer.* The 82nd is based at Fort Bragg, and their tour ends in a few weeks. Gonna see how things are going before they hand the city over to the Marines. It should be interesting; Fallujah is supposed to be getting hot."

"I saw an interview with a Marine commander about Fallujah," I said. " Sounds like they're gonna take a 'There's a new sheriff in town' approach. He seemed to think they're going to have more success than the 82nd. They're even asking the grunts to grow mustaches as a measure of cultural sensitivity."

"We'll see," Jeff said. "Fallujah has always been a violently independent place. It's where the uprising against the British started in 1920. It's like Iraq's Trenton. It's on the Euphrates and is a centuries-old trade city populated with a mix of all Islam's toughest breeds."

"Wow, nice briefing, Jeff," Charlie said, and we all chuckled. "All those CPA meetings are rubbing off."

"No shit. Heather Coyne can recite a dissertation on any subject in the world in ninety seconds or less. It would rub off on anyone."

Fallujah was turning into a powder keg. Things had been going downhill since the previous spring, when the 82nd Airborne fired on protesters there, killing unarmed citizens. The 82nd Airborne was an infantry unit, and foot patrols hadn't really worked in the hostile city of three hundred thousand. The 82nd lacked the mobility of, say, Jensen's 2nd Armored Cavalry Unit, which long ago traded their horses for jeeps, transport carriers, tanks, helicopters, APCs, and Humvees. The 82nd had pulled back to the city's perimeter, allowing Fallujah to turn into a cauldron of anti-American sentiment. Now, with the 1st Marines set to relieve the 82nd in mid-March, the dynamic in Fallujah was about to change. The question of Fallujah had to be addressed.

This intention was not lost on the people of Fallujah. Sitting as it does on an axis of trade along the Euphrates between the Sunni hotspots of Saudi Arabia, Jordan, and Syria, Fallujah is home to many of Islam's most fundamental strains, including the Saud-based Wahhabi sect and the Salafi sect. The city is like a border or port town, drawing the meanest and most rugged people around. These were people always ready for a fight. Even Saddam kept his distance.

In 1920, Fallujah had provided the spark in Iraq's nationwide uprising against the British, with the initial fighting costing five hundred British lives and six thousand Iraqi ones, prompting Arabist T. E. Lawrence to later write:

> *The people of England have been led in Mesopotamia into a trap . . . it will be hard to escape with dignity and honor. Things have been far worse than we have been told, our administration more bloody and inefficient than the public knows. It is a disgrace to our imperial record and may soon be too inflamed for any ordinary cure. We are today not far from a disaster. Our unfortunate troops . . . under hard conditions of climate and supply are policing an immense area, paying dearly every day in lives for the willfully wrong policy of the civil administration in Baghdad.*

Did America's leaders think she was exempt from history? And this happened sixty years before the United States had spent a decade arming Saddam to do its bidding against Iran. U.S. military planners and their computer-heavy National Ground Intelligence Center didn't factor Fallujah into the initial invasion plan; they skirted around it. For example, Fallujah is not even mentioned in the index of *The Iraq War: A Military History* or John Keegan's *The Iraq War.*

THE SMOKE SHOP OWNER's kid brought our water pipes, a tray of tea, and a deck of cards. We broke out the Bicycles and dug back into our never-ending rummy game. Charlie was winning, with eighteen hundred points.

The games flew by, with Charlie still grabbing the majority of the hands. Each of us had a narghile pipe at our feet. For one thousand dinars, or about seventy-five cents, you got an unlimited supply of double-apple flavored tobacco, roasted over hot coals and filtered through cool water on the way to your mouth and lungs. You breathed the smoke through the fitting on a small hose you held to your lips. The Arabs knew what they were doing. There is no better way to enjoy tobacco. A good cigar is hard to beat, but a good narghile does just that.

After an hour, we were getting hungry.

"Let's break for pizza," Jeff said.

Charlie and I agreed.

A few doors down from the diwan sat Napoli Pizza, home of Baghdad's best brick-oven pies. A portly Iraqi who'd learned the pizza-slinging trade while living in Italy ran the Napoli. He spoke English, and Jeff and I had quickly become chummy with him. Even though his shop windows were still blown out from the Assassin's Gate bombing that happened the day after we arrived, back on January 18, the Napoli's business was booming.

Located between two Green Zone checkpoints, the Rasheed Gate and Assassin's Gate, the pizzeria was in an ideal location to feed hungry Westerners. Some days, *Washington Post* bureau chief Rajiv

Chandrasekeran would pick up ten pies for his staff after the 5:00 P.M. press conference. The 82nd Airborne, which guarded the Rasheed Gate, often sent a runner to pick up a few dozen pizzas at the beginning of a night shift. Adam was a customer, too. Which by this time was not a shock, since apparently—like Allah and Fox News—he was everywhere in Baghdad at once.

"Do you know Mr. Adam? He is funny man. He tell me good jokes," the owner had asked us.

No, we said, we didn't really know Mr. Adam.

AFTER LUNCH, Charlie had plans to meet the Duke at the Al-Wiyah Club, next to the Sheraton-Palestine complex. The Al-Wiyah was established in 1924, and was a holdover from the British colonial days. You had to be a member to get in (we'd tried unsuccessfully a few weeks before), but Charlie said the Duke was a dues payer, so after our pizza we grabbed a cab there.

The Al-Wiyah was a relic of a time past. There were wood-paneled walls, tuxedo-clad barmen, paintings of foxhounds, whiskey galore, and a snooker room. It was all very proper and British, and T. E. Lawrence would have felt right at home. As usual, the Duke was holding court in grand fashion. Sitting on a couch with a triple Scotch, sweating profusely, the Duke and his table of three Iraqis were in a jolly mood, laughing, backslapping, and enjoying life.

"Just another afternoon of hard work?" Jeff asked following the announcement of our arrival. Everyone laughed, the Iraqis included.

"Gentlemen . . . welcome," the Duke said, wiping his brow with a handkerchief pulled from his sweat-darkened shirt's pocket. He introduced his party, which included the Al-Wiyah's owner and a lifelong member of the club.

We each ordered a Scotch, then sat back to enjoy the view. Aside from us, the club was empty. It was a sprawling place, complete with swimming pool (where political shysters Ahmed Chalabi and Ayad Allawi had swum as kids) and outdoor garden, but time and war had taken their toll, and the club was more than a little threadbare. Paint peeled and rust oxidized, the pool had been drained, the rugs were worn, and some of the mirrors were cracked. Unlike the Brits', the U.S. legacy in Iraq probably won't include monuments like the Al-Wiyah left seventy years from now. There are too many hundreds of tons of explosives in the hands of Iraqis who'd prefer to see all things American detonated.

The Duke told the owner we worked for the CPA in the Green Zone. "You are my government," the owner said, "you are just babies like my son." We laughed and apologized for the ad-hoc failure that was the CPA. "It's better than Saddam," he replied. "Bush is a good man."

"You don't mean that."

"I know. Bush is donkey, like Saddam." Everyone laughed. Iraqis tend to hate politics and politicians in any form.

The afternoon progressed, one Scotch at a time. "Anyone care for snooker?" Charlie suggested. Jeff, Charlie, and I moved into a dark room with three pool tables.

"Turn on the bright lights," Jeff said, referring to the lamps above each table.

Charlie was surprisingly good at pool. He told us he played a lot in the dive bars of Chicago. He beat us until it wasn't fun anymore.

The owner's son and his friend, both in their early twenties, showed up around 4:00 P.M. By then all of us were a little sloppy, the Duke and the owner included. The owner introduced Charlie, Jeff, and me to his son, Ali. "He likes the same things as you. He is my most

American son. Get him a job with George Bush. He loves freedom." We all introduced one another and hugged and habibi-ed.

The son went behind the bar and poured himself a huge glass of whiskey. He was dressed in an athletic Islamic disco outfit, including black nylon wind pants, white sneakers, and polyester butterfly-collar shirt. He was also sporting a close-cropped haircut. Arab men take their haircuts seriously. Barbershops are everywhere in Baghdad.

"The club is closing soon," the Duke said. "Do you gentlemen have plans for this evening? I know that Boris is having a dinner party at the Sheraton." None of us knew who Boris was, but the Duke was always dropping exotic names. Jeff and I waited for Charlie to answer.

"I think we have dinner plans with some folks," Charlie finally said.

"With who?" the Duke asked.

"Over in Jadiriyah, at Adam Davidson's house."

"Oh, really." The Duke's brow furrowed. He was very interested. "Adam Davidson, I've heard about him. He has a grand house and speaks Arabic, very funny, too, from what I've heard. How did you swing an invitation?"

"I've been before."

"Hmmm." It was as if a freshly grilled steak had been waved in front of the Duke during a hunger strike. He wanted an invite—and bad. But Charlie wouldn't bite. One could hear a Yoda-like voice in Charlie's head, a former professor maybe, saying, "Protect sources, always you must." The Duke kept staring at us, but we'd already started chatting with Ali.

"Do you want to see my car?" Ali asked.

"Sure," Jeff said, looking to escape the social standoff between our two friends.

Ali's car was the Iraqi version of a "pimped-out ride." It had shiny silver hubcaps, tinted windows, and a flashy license plate holder. Ali's friend, Hassan, was sitting in the passenger seat blasting rap's Elvis: Eminem. The stereo was custom, Ali said. "From best shop in Baghdad."

"Sweet ride, Ali," I said.

"You like, huh. Do you like Eminem?" he asked.

"Why not," Jeff said.

Charlie sauntered out Dukeless. The parking lot of the Al-Wiyah was big and empty. The day was overcast. Ali asked if we wanted to go for a ride. Of course we did. He pulled out a bottle of whiskey, swigged back a huge shot, and passed the bottle. We all took hits.

"What did you tell the Duke?"

"Nothing. He started talking to the owner about horse racing."

Ali revved the engine and peeled out, with us three white boys crammed in the back. He pulled right out to the square where the Saddam statue had been ripped down on world television. Driving at any time in Baghdad is pretty insane, especially at rush hour. Drunk driving in Baghdad at rush hour is absolutely nuts.

Heading toward Kerrada, Hassan put on 50 Cent and rapped along. The whiskey kept getting passed back and forth. Charlie started to look nervous and turned green. The car was whipping through traffic, zipping by Ali Baba Circle en route to Clowntown. There was a stopped knot of traffic ahead, and we came to a jerking halt. Charlie flew forward.

ALI WEAVED THROUGH the traffic and sped off again. He was a vicious driver, cutting off as many people as possible and honking his horn with fury. We tore past inner Kerrada's tight city blocks and made our way past the hotels of outer Kerrada. Outside, trim two-story buildings, their exteriors tiled in white with steel cages across the front windows, hurtled past. Tour buses galore were parked in front of the hotels.

The biggest Shi'ite holiday, Ashura, was approaching. Saddam had largely banned the holiday, and now, for the first time in decades, it would be celebrated publicly in the holy cities of Najaf and Karbala. Aside from the Iraqis celebrating, Iranian Shi'ites had been coming in, too. Shi'ites are the great majority of Iran's 70 million people, and this was the first time many of them had been able to make the holy pilgrimage to Karbala. Hotels from Baghdad to Basra were jammed with Iranians.

This area of Kerrada had seen a boom in new hotel development. Actually, all of downtown Baghdad had seen commercial growth. New stores dotted all of Baghdad's major thoroughfares. Our favorite store was Male Fashion, which had its sign written in a blood-dripping, spooky Charles Addams font.

We kept driving, streaking up streets, taking corners at dangerous speeds. The music kept blaring. The song "In da Club" came on. "Fuck this song. We have to write the book *Around the World on 50 Cent*," I told Jeff, laughing. "I've heard fucking 'In da Club' every-where from Cuba to Palestine to Amman to here."

"I fucking hate this song," Jeff shouted back. "What, you don't want to call it *Around the World on Eighty Shekels* anymore?"

That was our running joke for a book title, about traveling across the Muslim world and attempting to use only Israeli shekels to buy stuff from Jakarta to Algiers.

Ahead, Ali found some open road and wanted to show off. Hassan switched the CD to DMX's mediocre third album. Charlie suggested that the ride might now come to an end, but he found no takers. For another ten minutes we jammed through town, weaving and cutting across lanes at speeds up to eighty miles an hour.

Then the car screeched to a stop and Ali parked it. "Here you go. Baghdad's best music store, Ghost Music," he announced. We were in a very nice area, on Arasat Street, home to some of the capital's finest food and shopping.

We went inside. Ghost Music really was a good shop. Of course, Bon Jovi was the most celebrated artist there, but they also had a good selection of Oasis, Led Zeppelin, the Beatles, the Boss, the King, and even really bad U.S. pop like Good Charlotte. All of the CDs were bootlegs, of course. Ali and Hassan loved rap and kept asking for approval on their CD choices. "Do you like Nelly? The Snoop Dog?" They even bought us some CDs.

Ali put a new Eminem CD on in his car. He opened the doors and we stood around on the sidewalk talking about girls. "Do you lick the pussy?" Ali asked. "Does 50 Cent lick the pussy?" Hassan was laughing.

"White guys do more than black guys," I said. "Black guys hate licking pussy."

"Do you ever have the blow job?" Ali asked. I could tell they felt like they were smoking in the boys' room at school, or peeling out in a parking lot. We were all drunk and talked a little more about sex, sharing cigarettes and trying to stay on the ball.

"I have to wake up before dinner," Charlie said. "I'm too drunk."

I was tired, too. With respect to partying, Jeff had become Iraq's Iron Man. He could go for hours and hours.

ALI AND HASSAN dropped us off at Adam's just after dark. Standing out in front of Adam's house, Jeff and I were a little let down by its size. It was less a mansion than a Simi Valley porn set. We went in.

Adam was not the Duke. He played the role of host with modesty and without theatrics. "Beers are in the fridge," he said, pointing.

We were introduced to Adam's girlfriend, Jen Banbury, a novelist turned *Salon.com* reporter. Pale-skinned and in her midthirties, she had brown hair and a classically pretty face with strong features. She and Adam lived in New York. We had a lot in common. She knew about everything we knew about, except she knew more. Jen served as house matriarch and was heading the cooking effort, which tonight was pasta. Her slow, soft, nuanced tone was soothing, and unlike many journalists, she never talked about her own work.

Another couple, Jack Fairweather and Christina Asquith, also lived there. Jack was a twenty-five-year-old Brit, the same age as me and of similar build, but with short brown hair, scholarly glasses, and an Oxbridge affect. He worked for the *Daily Telegraph,* the U.K.'s largest daily paper. Christina was a little older and had gone to school at Boston University. Tall and blonde, with a cute smile, she was the prettiest girl in Baghdad. Finally, we were meeting some people in Baghdad who were normal, or at least normal to us.

Jack was quite the wild man. He was letting a buddy, this Swede named Jens, sleep on his floor, much to Adam's chagrin. Jack and Jens were a Euro version of Jeff and me, always getting into something stupid. They had recently taken a train from Mosul to Aleppo, Syria, watching the sun rise and set from the train's rooftop. Jens had just bought a moped to ride around Baghdad.

It was nice to be in a place where American civilians weren't playing war. Adam had filled his house with down-to-earth journalists; it was 180 degrees from the ego-driven media circus at the Sheraton.

Before sitting down to dinner I got a chance to talk with Jon Lee Anderson, another of Adam's roommates. Jon Lee is one of my favorite writers. He's been a correspondent for *The New Yorker* since I came of age, and he's had a profound influence on my life and travel. His books and articles had served as my guide to Latin America and Iraq. Talking to him was a highlight of my time in Iraq.

Two reporters from the *Washington Times,* Maya Alleruzzo and Willis Witter, were the strangest combo in the house. The *Times* is the paper of D.C.'s ultraright. The paper is owned by Korean billionaire Sun Yung Moon, who'd made his fortune by starting an eponymous religion that specializes in mass weddings. But Maya and Willis were the opposite of what you'd expect. Willis was a middleaged family guy who was emotionally attached to many of his stories. Maya was a D.C. postpunk-styled photographer. Neither seemed to care that they were working for the capital's right-wing mouthpiece.

DINNER WAS SERVED, and over bottles of Jordanian wine we broke bread and ate pasta. It was the nicest meal Jeff or I'd had in months. For the first time since we'd left the United States, we were in a room full of people that we felt in harmony with, both politically and in terms of lifestyle.

After dinner, talk turned to a postmeal visit to the Al-Hamra Hotel—yet another journalist stronghold—and a large group of us decided to go.

Unlike the Sheraton, which was guarded by the 1st Armored Division, the Hamra compound was protected by a team of bored Iraqis with Kalashnikovs. But it did have the same blast walls along its perimeter as every other Western-occupied zone in Baghdad. The Hamra itself is a ten-or-so-story, postmodern white concrete building; surely a fruit of the glory days of the seventies oil spikc. Inside there was a small lobby and space-age coffee shop, which give way to the larger restaurant and, beyond that, an outdoor pool. On this chilly winter night, people were huddled in the dark restaurant.

The Hamra was the LZ for Marla Ruzicka. In fact, she was the Duke of the Hamra: its most recognized tenant, hostess, party planner, and socialite. Everyone knew her, and everyone had an opinion about her. On this night, she was staining her teeth drinking bad red wine at a table next to a piano. As we walked through the restaurant's door, she greeted us like a jackrabbit, and introduced us to all the people she was sitting with. Then she ignored all of us for the rest of the night as she bounced from table to table.

Somehow we ended up talking to Mario Tama, a photographer from Getty Images. He was in his early thirties and lived in New York's East Village. He wanted a tour of the Green Zone—he'd spent no time in there since the invasion—and we agreed to do it with him the next day. Tama shared with us a love for a certain type of downtown Manhattan bar—the kind of place you miss the most when drinking in virtually womanless Baghdad. Anything goes in Baghdad, but it's not the same kind of anything that goes in New York.

As the night wore on, things got hazy. We met Phil O'Connor and J. B. Forbes of the *St. Louis Post-Dispatch*, both in their forties with graying hair and beards, but in good physical shape. Phil, the national security correspondent for the *Post-Dispatch*, was the kind of reporter who wore a nice trench coat. He had also seen the Grateful Dead over a hundred times. Almost immediately, Phil nicknamed me "Training Wheels," because I kept falling over into plants and things, thanks to a little help from my friend, El Señor Valium, who'd joined me at the Hamra. Phil was cracking me up, and eventually we all found ourselves gathered around the piano. A ponytailed Arab man wearing a fuzzy sweater was playing strange songs on the piano, while a British-accented guy filmed the scene. Drained beer cans were everywhere.

Phil told me he didn't sleep when on the big war assignments, like Iraq and Afghanistan. I asked him how long he was going to be in Iraq.

"Three weeks," he said.

"You're not going to sleep for three weeks?" I asked.

"Nope."

"Sleep is overrated. I like your style."

The Hamra had sucked Jeff and me in. We'd hang out at the Hamra with Phil for the next three weeks, sometimes sleeping on his couch. He never did sleep.

Sometime past late, Jeff turned to me and said, "Isn't there a chapter in that Friedman book called 'Hamra Rules'?" He thought he was referring to a chapter title in Thomas Friedman's *From Beirut to Jerusalem,* "Hama Rules."

"Yeah. You should go write that on the wall in the bathroom."

"No thanks."

And then it was Fade to Black. I woke up the next afternoon in a spare room at the Getty suite. Jeff was crashed on the couch. I woke him up, and we washed our faces, took the elevator downstairs, and began the several-mile walk through Baghdad's dusty afternoon sun to the Green Zone.

11

•

Good News
from Iraq

W E HAD A SLIGHT PROBLEM. Despite the fact that, in the eyes
of the Americans and Iraqis alike, Jeff's and my aid project
was succeeding, it still lacked a name—and this almost gave Heather
Coyne an aneurysm. How can something not have an acronym?
She e-mailed us and demanded we find a good acronym: immediately. So we came up with Humanitarian Aid Network of Distribution
(HAND); this way, we joked, we could have HAND jobs every day. I
know—we were under a lot of stress.

With a name out of the way and Jody now in Amman serving as,
among other more important things, our hype mouthpiece, HAND
could be used as a selling point for the CPA. We were hardly trying
to do PR for CPA, but if good publicity was a consequence of the job
we enjoyed, so be it. A TV crew from the United States contacted

Heather about trying to find the "Good News from Iraq." And Heather turned to us.

IF WE WERE the good news from Iraq, then the CPA had a problem. Here we were, two penniless idiots running a rag-tag program with zero funding and experience, and there was nothing better than us going on under the CPA?

The TV crew called to schedule a day to go out with us on a distribution run. We decided to make our field op in the middle-class Baghdad neighborhood of Kerrada, among the safest in the city. Jeff handled the logistics. His surrogate Iraqi mother, Halima, and her NGO—which had again changed its name—would take the lead.

One morning in early February, the TV guys arrived around ten and filmed me at the HACC, where I was busy packing, loading, and unloading boxes of clothes. The TV reporter gave me his card: He was Mark Hyman from the Sinclair Group. He was a tall, big-boned jock, and he asked me where the aid had come from.

"From the families of soldiers," I said.

He smiled. "Where is it going?" he asked.

"To Iraqi children."

He looked satisfied. I presumed this was the "good news."

Today's good news from Iraq: Twenty boxes of clothes donated by Americans are being handed out to Iraqi children in Kerrada. The bad news from Iraq: A car bomb killed twenty people just outside a police station near the Green Zone.

But this day was already on the rails, and away we went. Earlier that morning, Jeff and Halima had gone out to Kerrada, to make sure everything was ready for the TV crew. With the help of a few guys from the HACC, I loaded up several carloads and prepared to leave the Green Zone. The Sinclair Group folks donned their matching blue flak jackets, and together we all rode in a convoy with Heather Coyne and several other Army Public Affairs Officers (PAOs) out to Kerrada for the distribution.

A few minutes later, we pulled onto a middle-class street and up the driveway of Halima's NGO. The sight of TV cameras drove the local kids into a frenzy: They ran around the neat, grassy yard, playing with soccer balls; they climbed on a metal jungle gym; and they yelled and screamed anything on their minds to the cameras. It was a sunny day and the air was full of the sound of kids laughing.

Then Mark Hyman turned to me and said, "Uh, these kids are a little dirty."

"Well, this is one of the nicest neighborhoods in Iraq. It doesn't get much cleaner than this."

I walked off to find Jeff. "That asshole Hyman just said these kids are too dirty."

"What? Fuck him. Let's take him to Sadr City. They won't even have to get out of their armored SUV."

As we began to unpack a few of the aid boxes, Hyman came back over to us. He complained that the children were too rowdy while lining up for the distribution. This report he was making, he said, was to be aired in some thirty local broadcast markets across the United States.

Back at the Convention Center that afternoon, we looked on the Web and saw that the Sinclair Group was basically an exurb news provider. Of its sixty-two stations, none were in major markets. Nearly all the people who would see "Good News from Iraq" lived in Karl Rove's favorite landscapes, places defined by sprawl like suburban Florida, Las Vegas, and parts of Ohio. (In October 2004 the Sinclair Group came to national attention when the conglomerate announced it would air *Stolen Honor: Wounds That Never Heal,* an hour-long, blatantly biased anti–John Kerry documentary. Only after a national outcry and FCC complaints did Sinclair relent.)

12

•

Golden Sheikh,
and the Man Who
Could Do Anything

THERE WERE HAPPIER THINGS going on inside NGOAO, though. Hayder was now coming in to the Convention Center and working with us most every day. Much of the time, he would also bring Abed with him. When Hayder couldn't make it, Abed would come by himself or with another of the Soccer Coaches. Soon, they not only knew how HAND was organized and worked, they had an advantage over us, as they all spoke both Arabic and English. One day, when Jeff and I asked Hayder if he'd like to run the aid program after we left Iraq, he was shocked.

"Yes, of course," he said. From then on, we started preparing him to be our successor.

Across late February and into March, HAND was picking up steam; we were making distribution runs nearly every day—sometimes twice a day—with Jeff, Hayder, Abed, and myself splitting the work.

Some days, the four of us would venture out separately to four different distribution sites. Other days, all four of us would travel together.
As a matter of policy, we tried to go out with every approved NGO
applicant, just to make sure that we had a paper trail follow-up
through written reports. These adventures were never boring, and
they were sometimes frightening.

One Tuesday, at the weekly NGO meeting, Hayder introduced me
to Sheikh Raad, a tall, broad-shouldered man in his fifties who wore
his gold-rimmed aviator sunglasses even when indoors, a dishdasha
in the best Iraqi tradition, and a red-and-white kaffiyeh over the top
of his head. Sheikh Raad had a thing for gold jewelry, wearing
bracelets, rings, and necklaces like a rapper. But he also carried with
him a photo album filled with pictures of himself, usually shaking
hands with U.S. military officers.

"Is that fucking Bishop?" Jeff asked as he flipped through the album. It was indeed a photo of Colonel Bishop, enmeshed in a grip-
and-grin with the golden sheikh. A few pages on we saw Lieutenant
Colonel Joe Rice smiling with Sheikh Raad.

The sheikh spoke no English, but I still agreed to go out to Sadr
City with him and see his NGO in action. If he was good enough for
Bishop, he was good enough for me.

One morning, the sheikh and I loaded five boxes into his old
black Mercedes sedan. Then the two of us drove directly to his house
in Sadr City and he gave all five boxes to his children. He had essentially stolen the aid. I kept lifting my hands up, palms to the sky,
essentially gesturing to him: What the fuck are you doing? But I had
no translator, so couldn't really ask what he was doing. Plus, the
guy was six-three and weighed about 230 pounds. He'd also probably killed a few hundred Iranians, as most Sadr City men his age had
been conscripted by Saddam in the 1980s to fight against the Irani-

ans, and were either killed or returned home as hardened combat veterans.

The sheikh kept forcing cigarettes on me and a kid, who was no older than fourteen. With the aid "delivered," we now stood in front of his house smoking. It was a nice house for Sadr City, with a five-foot wooden fence encircling the yard and glass doors. From behind a curtain on one of the glass doors, a teenage girl kept peeking at me. She wore a black headdress, but her face was uncovered.

Growling at us across the street was a wild dog with dangling teats and a clumpy, cow-print coat. My fourteen-year-old smoking partner was angered by the dog; he ran over and kicked it, in the process losing his sandal, which landed in a putrid brown puddle. The kid started yelling at the dog, blaming it for wetting his sandal. Picking up a rock, the kid chased the dog down the street. Now, admittedly, third-world dogs are nasty creatures, rabid megarats. And, like all Arabs, the Iraqis believe dogs are dirty and the lowest of life forms. But it was still hard to watch even a third-world dog be beaten. I winced when the rock landed with a mushy thud against the dog's back, eliciting a squeal of pain. The sheikh was laughing. The kid somehow kept his cigarette intact and was puffing it proudly as he walked back. The sheikh turned to me and said, "Good, Mistah Ray."

I let out a nervous laugh and got back to my cigarette, which was giving me a headache.

After another round of smokes, Sheikh Raad ushered me back into his Mercedes. He then took me on a tour of his various businesses. In an hour's time, we stopped at a half dozen Sadr City auto body shops, each dirtier than the last. There were thousands of auto body shops in Baghdad, usually just tiny storefronts overflowing with mufflers, tires, and grease-covered Iraqis smoking cigarettes while squatting.

Every time the sheikh pulled up to one of his shops, a similar scenario unfolded. He would screech to a halt and all the Iraqis inside would busy themselves by faking work. We would end up in some dingy back room where he picked through stacks of papers and files. In a few minutes, one of the greasy shop boys would serve us tea, or offer us cigarettes, or bring a plate of falafel salad. It was like he was showing me off.

Pushing on, my tour found its way to where Sadr City melts into the rest of Baghdad. We stopped at a car dealership. Almost every license plate was from another country: Deutschland, Turkey, Dubai, Qatar, Jordan, and so on. Aside from stealing humanitarian aid, he also ran a stolen-car lot. He offered me more tea, bread, and vegetables. I shook my head and pointed to a blue Opel with Turkish plates. "Good, Mistah Ray," he chuckled.

The tour continued. We hit an Internet café where he knew all five people inside. He made me play a war video game and laughed every time I shot someone, saying, "Good, Mistah Ray."

Back at the Convention Center I complained to Hayder, "That Sheikh Raad stole five boxes from me. Fuck him."

"Shhh," Hayder said. "He is a very powerful man. His tribe is one of the most powerful in Sadr City. He is very trustworthy. He wanted to show Sadr City that he had American friends."

"Trustworthy? The guy just stole from us. Having American friends is a death sentence. That guy is fucking crazy. He was beating up dogs and shit."

"Maybe he thought the boxes were a gift?"

Maybe he did.

TURNS OUT, Sheikh Raad did think the boxes were a gift. In his mind, I was giving his family a gift in return for his connections and protection. At least three-quarters of Iraqis are members of a tribe. Sheikh Raad's was one of the most influential in Iraq. And, as I learned over time, becoming his friend meant I had access to his reach. Sure enough, Sheikh Raad came in a few days later with a fellow tribesman, an armless sheikh from Sadr City, who lost his arms fighting Iran and had them replaced by wood. Raad and Armless told Hayder about a "polio" clinic Armless ran.

Hayder told Jeff and me that we should go there and check it out. "Those guys are full of shit," I said. "There's no polio in Iraq."

"Nah, let's go check it out," Jeff said. "I missed your big adventure with Raad. It sounded pretty incredible." So we piled into Hayder's mini-SUV and followed Sheikh Raad's Mercedes back to Sadr City.

Armless Sheikh, in his forties, wore a dirty, dark gray dishdasha and coiled a kaffiyeh over his head and around his wizened, tough-looking face. We pulled up to his house and there was a crowd at his door, including a half dozen children in wheelchairs. Inside, over flat-bread and tea, we talked, with Hayder translating. "When I lost my arms I was a young man and very sad," Armless said. "But I decided, if I can learn how to drive a car again, I can do anything. Since then, I have become a famous man in Sadr City. That man has no arms and drives a car, people say. Now I help children and everyone knows me as the man who can do anything."

From his mud-brick house, Armless Sheikh ran a clinic for handicapped and deformed children, some of whom he claimed suffered from polio. A cardboard sign reading "Polio Club" in both English and Arabic hung above his doorway. The kids we saw were definitely suffering from something terrible. Jeff and I know little about diseases and birth defects, but the Polio Club was filled with a wide spectrum of heart-crushing cases, playing games, cooking meals, and providing comfort for the most desperate children in Iraq's most desperate place. Armless brought these poor kids together and tried to bring some hope and joy into their lives.

Supposedly, polio had been eradicated from the globe, except in pockets of India and Nigeria. Whenever a case is confirmed, it becomes an international news story. A few weeks later Jeff and I arranged for a doctor, plus a reporter and a photographer, to see Armless Sheikh's Polio Club. But on the morning of our planned visit, the doctor was nowhere to be found, and the reporter had just stumbled onto a bigger story. We ended up going with only a photographer, our friend Daniel Pepper. Pepper said he doubted that the Polio Club actually had any incidents of polio, but we never found out.

BUT WE DID FIND out more about Sheikh Raad and Armless Sheikh. One night, Hayder invited us to dinner at his house. And when we began to turn on to his street, we saw this huge crowd of people, mostly children, closing the road and mingling in front of Hayder's house. It looked like a block party. Confused, Hayder jumped out to see what was happening.

He began moving through the crowd, asking questions. After a few minutes, he returned to the car. "It turns out this is my doing," he said, shaking his head slightly. "I told my little brother that you guys were coming to eat, and he told everyone that my American friends were coming. The whole neighborhood wants to meet you guys." Not wanting to cause a scene, we postponed dinner and drove back toward the Green Zone. Hayder knew as well as we did that hosting Americans in your house was never a good thing to be advertising.

As we rode back toward the GZ, we started telling Hayder about Raad and Armless. "Hayder, I love those sheikhs," I said.

"See. I told you. They like us, too, it seems. Sheikh Raad wants you to come back tomorrow."

Hayder began to explain the change he was seeing in Sadr City. Divisions between generations were opening up. Arguments broke out between older and younger men about the Americans, the insurgency, the occupation, and Iraq's future. A generation gap was widening.

Armless and Raad, he said, represented the old guard of Sadr City. They were both veterans of the Iran-Iraq War. Saddam had used their generation, poor Shi'ites from Saddam City, as his shock troops against Iran, in a war in which a million died, creating a gap between males and females.

Charlie would later point out that if there has ever been an argument for Islamic polygamy, it was in Sadr City after the war with Iran. There were many more women than men, often widows with children, fatherless families that couldn't possibly get by without a man's help. Women did not have equal rights, and raising a family without a male breadwinner was not an option, while polygamy was.

Men like the sheikhs were survivors, and they had returned and become pillars of the Sadr City community. They were responsible for not just their own families, but for the families of fallen brothers, cousins, friends, and fellow tribesmen. And what they had achieved, they had done without assistance from Saddam. They had been through so many hardships and seen so much bloodshed that fatalism took over. To them, this American war was just another struggle in their history of endless war, yet another chapter that followed Iran, Kuwait, the Gulf War, and sanctions. Nothing was going to really change, they reasoned. Sadr City would remain a poor ghetto. Still, when they saw Americans, like Jeff and me, who were willing to help, they also weren't above reaching out to us. After all, they recognized that Sadr City's people needed all the help they could get.

But the older generation was losing in Sadr City. The sudden fall of Saddam had created a vacuum that infected the younger majority of Sadr City with a newfound feeling of relevance and vibrancy. According to Hayder, it had awakened a religious nationalism. "They really love Iraq, almost as much as they do the mosque. Sadr City's future belongs to the mosque. Al Hawza and Moqtada Al Sadr want to solve the problems Saddam and the Americans couldn't."

This youthful awakening was confusing to the old guard, like our sheikh friends, who'd always treated the younger Sadr with ambivalence. Nonetheless, Sadr was gaining influence and followers in Sadr City. As February ended, his threats were increasingly hostile. Aside from his followers, few were taking Sadr's threats of a coming confrontation with the Americans seriously. But in fact, Sadr City, a place we had grown to care deeply about, was moving toward violence faster than anyone knew.

13

·

Operation
Enduring Bender

ONE AFTERNOON, an Army private walked into our office and introduced himself. His friends all called him Ski, he told us. He spoke in a slow, low, mumbly monotone. After a little small talk—he was from Phoenix, and only wanted to go home and work a civil-service job like his dad—he got to the point.

"All the people in my unit suck," he said. "I hate the Army. Do you guys have access to any drugs?"

"Huh?" It was a bold question.

"Drugs . . . you guys look like you might have some."

We did? Well, we did.

"Uh, we don't really have any good drugs," Jeff said. "Just a little Valium, some weird painkillers, but we could get hash in a couple of days, I guess."

"I'm a straight Candy-Raver."

We didn't know that was still popular.

"Out West," Ski went on, "there's still these crazy raves. Popping pills in the desert under the stars with my girl. That's my shit." Hmm.

Being the losers we were, the trail of Baghdad's drug trade was one we'd successfully negotiated. There were some drugs around, we told Ski, but only the pharmacies were a sure thing. We liked this guy, though. His honesty was refreshing, and he seemed totally helpless. His bunk was about fifty yards down the hall, in a closet behind the Royal Jordanian Airlines desk. Medium tall and thin, with dirty blond hair and an innocent-looking baby face, Ski was a normal kid who'd joined the Army for career reasons and ended up going nuts. He hated the structure of the military, with its power-hungry NCOs bossing him around. He was the only unfat white person in his communications unit, so of course he stuck out. With his build, he looked like he belonged in the infantry. But he wasn't in the Army to kill anybody, he wanted to learn a trade as his father had before him.

Jeff gave him some painkillers. I gave him a sheet of Valium. Jeff took him across the street and introduced him to Dr. Hair, an Iraqi barber at the Al Rasheed Hotel, who could get just about anything. That was Day One. By Day Three, Ski was a full-fledged member of our crew. In return for the drug hookup, he took us for huge meals at the Rasheed Restaurant, one of Baghdad's finest private dining rooms, just across the lobby from the KBR cafeteria buffet at the Al Rasheed Hotel. There the waiters would serve him beers in a hidden corner booth so no officers would see him. Sometimes he'd blow his whole paycheck on beer and food there.

Like us, Ski hung out at malls in high school. We bonded over appreciating the great Phoenix-area malls. Jeff and I had been through

Phoenix several times on band tours and to play poker at Casino Arizona.

"Guess I'm the only cool soldier around, huh?" Ski asked Jeff after meeting Dr. Hair.

"Well, definitely the only one to just walk up and ask for drugs."

FACT IS, we were meeting an amazing cross section of soldiers in Baghdad, from Marine Corps officers to Civil Affairs reservists, airborne troops to infantry recruits. The most impressive soldiers, by far, were the elite fighting forces, like the 82nd Airborne company guarding the Convention Center, fresh off a tour in Afghanistan and commanded by our man Lieutenant Mikey. These 82nd guys would look right through most of the rest of the soldiers when they passed each other in the hallways, not even acknowledging their existence.

At the opposite end of the spectrum from the 82nd in Iraq was Ski's signal unit, which was responsible for communications within the Convention Center and much of the Green Zone. Mostly, Ski's unit staked out the chow line at the Al Rasheed messhall. They were a motley mix of overweight and out-of-shape minorities, plus a few fat white girls tossed in for diversity. We were never quite sure what all of them did, but three times a day they watched for the start of the messhall lines like vultures. Once the buffet's doors were opened, they piled inside and ate as if they were starving.

Unlike the airborne troops, Ski's NCOs were complete losers. One young sergeant, no more than twenty-one years old, was a steroid user who loved his new command as much as his physique. He was always yelling at his soldiers, making them perform menial tasks while leaning forward to flex his shoulders and upper arms. Most nights, this guy could be found amusing himself with fantasy role-playing video games in the unit's bunkroom.

Ski's lot in life was a trailer behind the Convention Center: It was barely large enough to stand inside, and was choked and overflowing with radio equipment. Basically, Ski was a radiotelephone switch-board operator.

"This place sucks," Ski said as he gave us a tour of his trailer one night. "People just call in and yell at me."

"Sounds great. How'd you pull this shitty job?" Jeff asked.

"My whole unit hates me. You guys are my only friends."

We took turns trying on Ski's body armor and taking pictures of ourselves holding his M-16. I e-mailed one of these photos to friends and titled it "Operation Enduring Bender." It seemed like a fitting name for our time in Iraq.

We both felt awful for Ski. He'd just gotten to Iraq, which meant he had at least a year more of this existence. It seemed every couple of days Ski was running out of pills and looking for more. This soon turned into a desire for steroids, after he became friends with a few of the guys in his unit who were juicing.

"I need steroids," Ski said one night over dinner, in his blunt fashion. "One of my NCOs has been getting huge. He's power-lifting and doing cycles of Deca. Can you guys get some for me?"

"Did you talk to Doc Hair?"

"Not yet. I will. That dude is a sketchball, man. He's the worst barber on Earth. I saw him practically stab a guy last time I was in there."

We'd never bought steroids before, since we had little interest in shrinking our dicks and wrestling with each other in front of a mirror, but we knew that buying steroids in Iraq was easy. All it took was

walking into a pharmacy and saying "Deca? Muscle? Ameri-kee soldier?" while flexing your arm.

SKI HOOKED UP WITH Dr. Hair. It didn't take long before he started
bulking up. As his muscles began to grow, he seemed to become a little prouder of being a soldier. Still, it didn't stop him from regularly
drinking half-liter bottles of homemade Arab Tom Collins while on
duty. One night he was found passed out on the ground outside his
trailer while on duty, having left his loaded M-16 inside. His NCO
jumped all over the opportunity to flex his authority.

"This asshole is making me carry my weapon everywhere I go for
the next two weeks," Ski said. "I gotta take it with me to the latrine."
He even had it with him when the three of us would sneak up to the
Convention Center roof to smoke a little Clown Hash. Occasionally,
Ski started going off on tangents, spouting Army rhetoric about how
many rounds per second his weapon could fire. Ski was losing his
mind. When we pointed out to him that he was starting to change
and seemed to be going crazy, he agreed with us.

"I was under psychological observation back in the U.S.," he said.
"I told the Army shrink at Fort Hood that I wanted to kill myself and
other soldiers, and that I didn't want to go to Iraq."

"Jesus. What did he say?"

"He called me a pussy and said: 'You're going to Iraq, soldier.'"

THE ARMY HAS NEVER exactly been known for its compassion, and
hanging out with Ski only reinforced this observation. So as time
went on and Ski kept sliding further and further down, Jeff and I

started to think of ways to get Ski transferred from his unit. Maybe, we thought, we could get him into the Iraqi Assistance Center with a Civil Affairs unit. Ski's father worked at a post office in Phoenix, and he'd agreed to set up a clothing drive similar to Sergeant Grimley's in Rhode Island.

Ski suddenly had motivation. He got his dad aboard by e-mail, then began generating and drafting plans for ways to set everything up at home and on the ground in Baghdad. He wanted to call it "The Soldier's Foundation." A lot of people in the IAC thought this was a great idea, too, a way to get even more donations into the country for Iraqi kids. But this hope was squashed in late February by the IAC's newly arrived Lieutenant Colonel Weaver, who, just like Ski's NCO, was eager to wield authority. With one quick "no," all of Ski's work and plans were destroyed.

"Fuck Weaver, man. The old bastard is worthless. Gotta love that chain of command."

"What's the guy's problem? I'd do more good working with you guys than sitting in that fucking trailer," Ski said. He was crushed.

But then, who were we to try to get a soldier transferred from his unit? Among the American soldiers and civilians, we had been made to understand just how little pull we had in the CPA.

To FURTHER CONTRIBUTE to Ski's mental breakdown, he began getting into Instant Messenger fights with his sixteen-year-old girlfriend, who was back home in Phoenix and cheating on him. Almost nightly she'd come clean to Ski about yet another round of cocaine- and Ecstasy-induced infidelity. These exchanges would sometimes go on for hours as she asked for forgiveness while, basically, he pleaded for her to stay and endured hearing her tell him how she fucked yet

another guy in Phoenix. When these marathon sessions would be finished, with no real resolution having been made, Ski was always completely wrung out: His arms would hang slack and his shoulders
would slump, his usually pale face would be ashen, his eyes dead, his
expression a bruised mix of terror and confusion. The guy was desperate. He was lost. With each of these confessionals, he felt more
and more alone.

We tried to console Ski as best we could, but he was quickly pushing his mind over the edge with the help of a never-ending bender of
pills, booze, and 'roids; no thanks to us. After a few weeks we began
to feel terrible about our part in what Ski was doing to himself. But
we also knew that he no longer needed our help—with money, luck,
and a connection or two, you could get pretty much anything you
wanted in CPA-occupied Baghdad.

14

•

Palace Life (Other Aspects Of), the Ascendance of the White Sheikh, and the Battle for the Balkans at Uday's Pleasure Club

ABOUT THE TIME our aid-distribution program was really finding its legs in Baghdad and beyond—we were now sending out several drops a day—another assistance operation, called Operation Starfish, also started getting under way. Starfish was the brainchild of Sergeant Van Dent. He was the bodyguard for a guy named Chaplain Fred Vicciellio, an Army minister based in the palace (chaplains can't carry weapons, which is why, like all chaplains, he had a personal security soldier with him at all times). Dent was famous for being one of the few chaplain bodyguards anyone ever knew to have shot anyone, when an Arab hopped over a wall near Vicciellio. At Heather Coyne's urging, we met with the sergeant and the chaplain one morning to see if we could work together.

Vicciellio's office was on the second floor of the palace, right above the office for Strategic Command in Iraq (STRATCOMM). The Starfish digs were small, underfurnished, and paneled with wood. Vicciellio and Dent were both somewhere in the borderland of their late thirties or early forties, but, aside from their similar ages, they couldn't have been more different. Vicciellio was a laid-back Zen surfer from San Diego, with a golden tan and a tattoo of a turtle on his leg. Dent was a wisecracking American Indian from a small tribe in Arkansas whose coloring was dark, if not the old Indian red. The two made a great duo: Dent the foul-mouthed gunslinging Indian and Vicciellio the laid-back SoCal Man of God.

As we talked over coffee, they couldn't believe our story. Given Jeff's and my approach to life, it was strange to hear a pastor of all people heaping praise and encouragement on us. "You guys just have to come speak at my Sunday service," Vicciellio said.

"Sure," Jeff said. "Any time you want us."

THE IDEA FOR Operation Starfish had come to Dent after interacting with some Iraqi kids who hung out at the Green Zone PX. The PX was stocked like a Wal-Mart, though it was only the size of a 7-Eleven, with its across-the-board, Army-subsidized prices, soldiers could buy everything from nonalcoholic beer to sanitized versions of the latest rap CDs to candy and fitness magazines. Outside, Iraqi kids sold bootleg DVDs that leaned heavily on porn. Dent used to give the kids candy. He soon became attached to "this one little bugger" and decided to help him out. The plan was to solicit goods for children through military religious networks in Iraq and at home. But once the stuff was collected, the program still needed somebody to distribute it in Iraq. After listening to the Starfish plan, we said we could get Starfish's stuff to the Iraqis.

Dent was ecstatic about prospects for his new program. Within days, he'd written a full-page article for *Stars and Stripes,* started a website, and gone on an e-mail spree. Vicciellio was in touch with fellow chaplains, pastors, priests, and members of his congregation. The project picked up momentum quickly. Vicciellio invited Jeff and me to speak at his next five-o'clock Sunday service, which took place right below where we slept at the palace.

Just minutes before 5:00 P.M., we arrived at the service and were surprised to see Chaplain Vicciellio in shorts and a loose-fitting white linen shirt. He was sitting on a stool with an acoustic guitar—surrounded by a semicircle of about fifty congregants—and he looked like nothing so much as some cruise-ship folk crooner. The palace's de facto house of worship was a room that, when you entered it, looked upside down, like an M. C. Escher drawing. An unsupported stairway climbed down from the ceiling into the middle of the room, and heavy golden lanterns dangled everywhere. Because it was intended to be multi-denominational, half the room was partitioned off as a carpeted prayer area for Muslims.

Vicciellio banged out a few chords, tuned up, then began an acoustic set of the Lord's most up-tempo tunes. Jeff and I grabbed lyric sheets and sang along. People were getting down: singing and grooving, clapping and waving their arms in the air and smiling, then pausing to cry and reflect. This concert passed for church? It was like nothing I'd ever seen. Jeff spotted Dent in the back of the room practically sleeping. "Look how bored Dent looks," he said.

About half an hour into the service, Vicciellio called us up on stage. We were greeted by modest applause. We went straight into a quick speech about the dire humanitarian situation in Iraq. We talked about Sadr City and the world beyond the GZ. We talked about the enormous faith the Iraqi people had placed in the Americans and everyone working inside the Green Zone. An off-key chorus of amens from the crowd dotted our speech patterns. When we concluded, our statements were met by quick applause and we sat back down. We felt strangely legitimate, almost baptized.

WE LEFT THE CHAPEL and climbed back upstairs to our hallway bunkroom. The hallway was also home to the office of Black-water USA, one of the largest private-security outfits in Iraq. The office's door was open. Music was on. Inside sat two mercenaries wearing top-of-the-line outdoor gear, with a wall of M-4 automatic rifles behind them. Blasting from Blackwater's office was Slayer's heavy-metal classic "Angel of Death." It was just past 6:00 P.M. on a Sunday.

Jeff and I looked at each other in disgust, shaking our heads. "Satanic metal. . . . What else could it be?"

The private security contractors are the darkest side to Iraq's occupation. Fighting for a flag is an honorable act of patriotism. Fighting for money is murder.

At that time, Blackwater USA—along with two other companies, DynCorp and Custer Battles—accounted for the majority of subcontracted security details in Iraq. Though no official numbers have ever been made available to the public, it's estimated by *The New York Times* that there are at least twenty-five thousand American security contractors in Iraq. All of them provide "Force Protection" and other "security-related" tasks, such as guarding high-level U.S. officials, like Bremer.

After the U.S. military forces, these private companies make up the second-largest fighting force in Iraq today, with the British Army coming in third, at around eight thousand troops. About two hundred have been killed, giving them Iraq's second-largest figure for Coalition casualties, as well. The number of Iraqis they have killed has not been recorded.

The contractors are paid up to one thousand dollars a day, tax-free, to guard some people and kill others without consequences, should it come to that. This lack of accountability—not to mention the disparity in pay—was starting to cause tension between the contractors and the men and women of the U.S. military, who often had to go in after a cowboy mission went bad to clean up the mess. And the U.S. troops had to do it for a fraction of the contractor's salary.

The overwhelming majority of contractors carried themselves with an air of great physical menace, and a look that included sunglasses, worked-out biceps always showing, and a taut-mouthed glower meant to imply they were bulletproof. Sharing a hallway with them was depressing.

Jeff and I sat slumped in our bunk area, which smelled like a sweaty sock. A pile of discarded MREs—brown cardboard boxes and ripped-open PVC bags that held the food—lay next to a few stacks of books and old magazines. Both our backpacks looked like fish that had been stepped on, with dirty clothes strewn about like guts. Our bunkhouse felt desolate, especially with the Slayer soundtrack thundering around the hard hallway walls all around us.

After fifteen minutes of our silence and Blackwater's heavy metal Jeff said, "I'm starting to think the palace makes the Red Zone look normal."

"We have to find a new way of living."

The palace had burned us out. The Green Zone was too big a contradiction to live in without approaching breakdown. Rocking out to Jesus or Satan wasn't our thing. If it weren't for our roommate Sergeant Jensen and his eternal optimism, chances are we would have packed our bags somewhere around the end of February.

At the end of our ropes financially and mentally, a big box showed up addressed to Jeff one day, via Heather's APO address. His sister had put together a collection of medical supplies for distribution, some books we had requested, and some cash to get us by.

"Fuck yeah, man, along with new shampoo and some books, my sis sent some cash! Let's hit up the smoke shop." We were saved, for the time being.

AROUND THE GREEN ZONE, Jensen was still up to his usual politicking, even earning himself a new nickname: the White Sheikh.

With such a big heart, Jensen could listen to others' problems for hours, as he did for us on numerous occasions. Now the White Sheikh was constantly mediating Iraqis' problems, too. Iraqi sheikhs began treating Jensen as if he were the spiritual leader of the CPA tribe. American journalists, especially at the NPR house, treated Jensen like the only true human in the Green Zone's zoo. A combination of soft-spoken candor and a tendency to drop bread crumbs of information had made Jensen a bona-fide source.

Jensen the White Sheikh lured more than just Iraqis and American journalists into his fold. A couple of Lebanese guys were soon regularly coming into the NGO Assistance Office, too. They were Jensen's buddies Georges and Nick, from Montreal and Huntington Beach,

California, respectively. Jensen had started an NGO called ALIVE with his family and friends back in the States. Georges and Nick were working on a school-rebuilding contract that ALIVE was trying to secure. These two Lebanese businessmen had honed their craft under fire during their home country's own sixteen-year civil war. In Iraq, Georges and Nick occupied that gray area between war profiteering and the slightly more altruistic world of "reconstruction," a conceptual seam we knew well.

Georges was a smooth guy. He wore fine suits and a Rolex Sub Mariner. He was a true operative who knew Baghdad very well. Georges had cousins, connections, and friends from Dubai to Mosul to Paris. Georges was the second person after Beth Payne at the U.S. Consulate to tell us how stupid we were. "You guys are going to get killed. You have no security. Even when I travel, and I'm Arab, remember, I only stay in one place for ten minutes. You guys are riding around like two wild men. . . ."

Seeing Jensen, the lanky good soldier, hanging out with smooth Georges made Jeff and me laugh. Only in Baghdad could you find a good ol' boy from North Carolina sitting across the table from a Lebanese-Canadian businessman who looked like a gangster. Stranger still, Georges and Jensen would remain close friends. (In summer 2005, Jensen would marry his college sweetheart. At the wedding Georges was at one of the tables closest to the bride and groom. Jeff, Charlie, and I were relegated to sitting with the organ player at the farthest table in the room.)

FRIDAY IS THE DAY of worship for Muslims worldwide, so Thursday night was each week's Big Party Night inside the Green Zone. It was the only night that Uday Hussein's old disco, on the Al Rasheed Hotel's second floor, was opened up to the CPA minions. Back in Iraq's Baath Party days, Uday was said to bring his pet tigers and a fist-sized pile of cocaine up to the disco, where he would then rape women and feed them to the tigers. During the CPA rule, the disco was the one place where the khaki-clad, God-fearing GOP set could dance to rap and retro disco with mercenaries and Iraqi translators.

One day, Jensen came back to our hallway bunkhouse saying he was going to the disco with Georges and Nick later that night—did we want to come along? "You can ride in Georges's red Mercedes," Jensen said, as if he needed to sell us on the idea. But that evening, Jeff and I couldn't find Jensen or Georges and his red Mercedes. Instead, Jeff said, we should call Inigo. This was the British journalist and filmmaker Inigo Gilmore. He was a sharp Londoner transplanted to Tel Aviv, with piercing green eyes and impeccable dark brown hair. We'd met him a few weeks earlier, when he'd come to the Green Zone with the Getty Images guys to take the "Ray and Jeff War Disneyland Tour." We'd since intersected with him at several other points around the Baghdad social circle. We liked Inigo's style: the foreign correspondent cum Brit-pop superstar. We phoned Inigo and asked him to join us for a night of disco dancing. He met us outside the Convention Center just before ten. Jeff agreed to sneak a small video camera of Inigo's into the disco, since he was badgeless and had to be searched more thoroughly than us Level 0 types.

The disco was packed to capacity, with at least three hundred men and upward of twenty women. A crowd five deep surged around two tuxedoed Iraqi barmen. "These guys are probably the best-paid people in Iraq," Jeff said, pointing to their tip jar, which overflowed with cash. "Look at all those USDs."

The Bee Gees' song "Tragedy" came on. An Arab DJ was bobbing behind two turntables on a stage with red carpeting that looked very strip club–ish. A full-fledged light show was going on. A flashing light in the shape of the Baath Party star covered the dance floor. Inigo would later include the disco scenes in a film he made for the U.K.'s Channel 4, his voice overdubbed saying, "And yes, they really are play-ing 'Tragedy.'"

Aside from being the place where GZers got smashed, the disco also doubled as Baghdad's unofficial Mustache Olympiad; seemingly every male—Iraqi or Western—had his own version of finely sculpted lip hair, including Jensen, who had recently grown some peach fuzz. Unfortunately there was no mustache repellent available for the few women who dared dance. As we watched, a handful of borderline-looking Balkan women, who worked for the CPA in ser-vice capacities, became disco mustache high-value targets. Drunken mercenaries aren't very subtle, which meant the Balkan girls were being treated in the manner of Thai hookers.

Thank God Inigo was with us. He was from a similar world: a Londoner with ties to the music and club scene. Not that Jeff and I were clubbers, but we got the joke that was the Al Rasheed Disco. It was a parallel universe: a futuristic Wild West saloon in the middle of a modern-day Crusade that was being led by a male cheerleader from Andover who now acted like a cowboy. The post-9/11 world was a strange place: a seventies-style Arab disco could be home to mercenaries and diplomats buying one another strong drink while hoping to get lucky with the few women drawn to Iraq from a third country by the allure of the salary . . . all paid for with American tax dollars.

Some of the people from Baghdad Central were on the floor danc-ing and we joined them. I was shuffling alongside Coyne, Cole, and even Colonel Bishop, who was doing a strange Delta boogie. Dancing behind me was a big black mercenary wearing an XXXL "Operation Camel Toe" T-shirt and a baseball hat with a bandanna under it. The guy was in the process of stealing a Balkan girl from a big cowboy mercenary wearing a brown ten-gallon hat and also wearing an "Operation Camel Toe" T-shirt, though this second guy's was skin-tight.

Well, my arrival moved the packed dance floor's arrangement just enough that the cowboy suddenly thought I'd stolen his Balkan. So the cowboy grabbed me by the neck, and we began to scuffle, though mainly it felt like I was trying to run away from a six-foot-four-inch side of beef.

"Hey, you little pussy," he said as he began to crush my throat.

About halfway to my demise, the cowboy realized that his Balkan had now started dancing with the black guy—which was far worse than losing a girl to a "little pussy." Suddenly, fists were flying everywhere, and a real old-school donnybrook broke out between the cowboy and his posse and the black mercenary and his gang. It was race war. Fortunately, there were plenty of other big muscles in the room to break up the fight. (Later that week there was news of a drive-by shooting between two rival mercenary teams, crews widely believed to have been those from the disco beef.)

AFTER I'D HAD a minute to settle down, Jeff grabbed me and pointed across the dance floor. It was Charlie, standing around with still another bunch of mercenaries.

"What the fuck's Chucky doing here?" Jeff said. "Maybe he knows the guy who was trying to kill you."

We regrouped on Charlie's side of the disco. Charlie and his group of contractors seemed to be enjoying themselves.

"I'm going to Fallujah again," Charlie said.

According to his blog, the last time Charlie had told us he was going to Fallujah we had said, "Can we come?"—which we didn't recall. So this time we said, "Can we come?"

"Can't you assholes get to Fallujah through a CPA hookup?"

"Does anyone in this room look like they could do anything? They're all dancing to Michael Jackson!"

"I'll see," Charlie said.

Then, just behind Charlie and his contractor buddies, we spotted the White Sheikh and his Lebanese buddies. Georges and Nick had a bottle of 1800 Tequila.

"Hey, just like Puffy," I said to Jeff (1800 is P. Diddy's favorite drink).

We joined them and Georges pulled out Cuban cigars for all of us.

Inigo was still filming away. I grabbed the camera and took it over to the bar, hoping to get film of the tip jar. A big fellow wearing a vest grabbed me and pulled me into the kitchen.

"I'm Security here," he said. He grabbed the camera from me and informed me I was a dickhead. "You can't be filming in here. Who are you?"

"I'm an NGO coordinator for the CPA. I work across the street. Sorry, I was just having some fun."

"You smell like tequila. Where did you get it? Man, you stink."

"My friend has a bottle." The security guy was watching Inigo's footage on the small screen; all of it was too dark to make out.

He handed me the camera and said, "I could take this, you know. But just get me some tequila and we're even."

As soon as the guard left, Inigo turned to me: "You're an idiot. Stop being such a moron. That camera cost a lot of money."

"Sorry."

"Did you at least get any good footage?"

"No."

"Idiot."

15

·

Women
for Women

MORE THAN ANYTHING ELSE Heather Coyne did, her heart lay
with the cause of establishing women's rights in the New
Iraq. Iraqi women were invisible citizens, often kept indoors from
puberty until menopause, and then shielded from the world by
abayas that curtained them off from head to toe, and Heather worked
tirelessly to get them something close to equality with men across
the country. Her program's goals had been set by Heather and her
colleagues, as well as the newly returned Iraqi female expatriates
from IRDC (Iraq Reconstruction and Development Committee).

To support this effort, one of Heather's major focuses was to set up
a network of women's centers all across Iraq, facilities backed by
Women for Women International, an NGO run by women from around
the globe. These centers would underwrite Internet cafés, clothing

swaps, microloans for new women's businesses, meeting rooms, and libraries, among many other things. Though Women for Women enjoyed tacit support from the CPA, such as ribbon-cutting ceremonies attended by Bremer, they were more or less on their own in trying to build up a women's rights support system in Iraq.

Opening women's centers in Iraq was a noble undertaking, but it was also one that may have come too early in the reconstruction of Iraq. The CPA was focused on bringing Western ideals to a newly "liberated" society, one deeply rooted in Islamic tradition. And in overwhelmingly poor, needy, and Islamic Iraq—where men traditionally controlled all of society—the culture was wary of making room for women's lib. This would prove to be very dangerous for Iraqis and Americans alike.

While a small women's center had been quietly opened in the Iraqi city of Hilla, south and west of Baghdad, the prototype center was to open in mid-February in Baghdad's upscale Mansour district, a sophisticated neighborhood of worldly Sunnis just a couple of miles west of the Green Zone. For weeks on end, Heather had been pulling all-nighters at the office. She was a one-woman powerhouse pushing to make the center open on time, no matter what. But already there were threats.

FINALLY, on the morning of the Mansour Women's Center's grand opening, Heather was totally focused. You couldn't get a word in with her. It was a big day for her and she had a million things to do. In late morning, she took off from her office to set everything up in Mansour, but not before reminding everyone that she expected our presence at the opening.

People were excited for Heather. She and Women for Women were doing something unprecedented in Iraq. With this prototype women's center in Mansour, Heather was helping Iraqi women take a huge step forward for their equal rights. We all felt this was the first day of modern Iraq's new sexual-equality movement.

Heather had arranged a ride for Jeff and me, in a convoy with Air Force PAO Captain Paula Kurtz and Leslie "Cap" Dean, a senior diplomat who ran Baghdad Central. We followed Paula downstairs from Baghdad Central to Cap Dean's office to pick him up, along with his assistant. Also in the office were a couple of Blackwater USA guys, who were armed to the teeth. They were to give us a security briefing about the ride over to the center.

"Our primary concern is Mr. Dean's safety," one of these guys told us. "If anything happens, we'll try to help you out as well, but we can't promise anything." The guy talking was heavily muscled, wearing Oakley Blades and sporting a thick mustache. Jeff and I looked at each other and laughed.

"If we take small-arms fire, exit the opposite side of the vehicle and get behind the wheel well," the mercenary went on. "If that's not an option, head for the nearest building and stay put."

With that, we set off down the halls of the palace to a waiting convoy of three black Chevy Suburbans, sandwiched by armored MP Humvees at the front and rear of the convoy. We got into the middle Suburban with Dean and Kurtz. Cap Dean was wedged on the front seat's bench between two huge Blackwater guys in full body armor, their weapons locked and loaded. Kurtz, Jeff, and I sat directly behind them. We were the only ones in the entire convoy who weren't suited up in body armor; in fact, we were in our usual clothes: flip-flops, jeans, and T-shirts. (We dubbed our look "the Anti-

Bremer," in protest of those who took their fashion tips from Lord Bremer.)

We'd never been in a convoy before, and we got to see the inner workings of a military/contractor joint operation. A shooter was in the passenger seat, and we were nose-to-tailed by two other Suburbans, which would take turns in the lead at high speeds. We exited the GZ, and a few minutes later we pulled up to the women's center. When we got out, Jen Banbury from *Salon.com,* Maya Alleruzzo from the *Washington Times,* and Charlie were standing at the entrance, gawking at the spectacle, surprised to see us emerge from the Suburbans, carried out of the vehicles on a seeming torrent of guns and muscle. They all got a good laugh out of it.

"What the hell are you guys doing?" Maya asked.

"You know how we roll!" Jeff said.

We all laughed for a minute, then walked inside and through to the back courtyard where festivities were well under way. Bremer had already come and cut the women's center ribbon, officially opening it. His officiating done, he was off to his next Imperial Event.

Heather walked over to us. "Glad to see you guys could make it," she said. "I was going to kill you if you didn't show." She knew there was no way we'd miss this.

All attention now turned to Cap Dean, who had arrived shortly after Bremer left. Like a true politician, he was handed a slip of paper and began to speak to the sparse crowd. He spoke some Arabic to try to get some laughs, which worked.

Off to one side, I pointed out the always-quotable Colonel Bishop to Charlie, who was working diligently on a spec story about women's rights in Iraq. Charlie introduced himself to Bishop and asked for a few comments. The questions quickly turned to the subject of the legitimacy of the war we were waging in Iraq, and if he felt it was right.

Bishop thought for a moment. "If we do not find weapons of mass destruction in Iraq, and no clear regime ties to Al Qaeda, then I do not think we should have come here," Bishop said in his stern and commanding voice.

That was a pretty bold statement, one we all agreed with.

Over the next forty minutes or so, we toured Heather's first step toward Iraqi women's equality. The building was small, but it was clean and freshly painted. Inside there was an Internet café and meeting rooms, plus a small kitchen and a seating area. Behind the building was a small backyard and a bedouin-style tent with pillows and rugs on the ground. It was obvious that Heather had been spending all her energies on making sure the women who would use this center were both completely comfortable and securely confident that this place—with its Internet and telephones and privacy for women—was theirs.

We all left the Mansour center around the same time. Maya and Jen went off on assignments in Baghdad, and Charlie, Jeff, and I went back to the Convention Center.

Nights and weekends were often the best times for Jeff and me to get office work done, since Ibty and her crew weren't there wasting everyone's time on our computers. In only a few weeks, our office computers had become a nonstop battle zone between us and most of the Iraqis in the office, especially since Ibty seemed to bring a new friend or cousin into the office every day to perform some meaningless job online and take up space. Sawsan continued to work hard, entering the new NGOs that trickled in every day and translating the NGO database from Arabic to English. Between the stress on the streets and the workload, Sawsan was so high-strung it seemed as if she were having mild nervous breakdowns every other day or so, and

Jeff became her shoulder to cry on. She would complain about Ibty to Jeff and me in private, saying that she never did anything and was a bullying presence, though she would never say anything about it.

Jeff and I actually enjoyed working long hours in the office, as long as no one else was around. During the workweek, beyond the battle for computers, the endless distractions in the office were almost unbearable: from screaming Iraqis looking for lost relatives in the cubicle behind us to Army officers from the IAC spouting orders at anyone with ears. Now, on quiet nights or weekends, we could get our e-mails taken care of, or finish our own preparations for our aid program.

THE BAD NEWS got to Jeff and me a day or two later.

A few hours after Heather's grand opening, a U.S. military unit made the women's center part of its nightly security rounds, stopping there every few hours to deter any Iraqis who thought Heather's project was a bad idea and wanted to stop it.

Since she knew the military was stretched so thin, though, Heather had hedged her bets, hiring a local security team to guard the women's center. This group was made up of a few older Iraqi men who needed the money and who—like most Iraqis—legally owned an AK-47 for their own use. On that first night, as one of the local guards dozed in a chair outside the women's center, his throat was cut and he bled to death.

When news of the killing broke, the Army came back, making a big show of Humvee and foot patrols around the women's center. For some time, they moved through the area in the dark, making their presence unambiguously known. Shortly after the soldiers wrapped up their perimeter check and climbed back into their Hummers to head for the night's next circuit stop, the women's center was at-tacked with hand grenades, blowing out some windows and damag-ing the buildings.

The grenade attack in Mansour had said it all. Soon after, the women's centers in Mansour and Hilla were closed. It became a huge emotional setback for Heather. It never really made much sense to us why anyone expected the women's centers to succeed. To average Iraqis, an American-backed building for women, guarded by U.S. troops, looked like a place to steal and corrupt their women.

THE MT. LEBANON HOTEL BOMBING

(© *Spencer Platt, courtesy of Getty Images*)

BOOK ★ THREE

Worlds Collide

16

.

A CROSS IRAQ, March started on a violent note, as a succession of suicide bombings killed two hundred Shi'ites in Karbala and Baghdad. The bombers struck on March 2, the second day of Ashura, the largest annual holiday on the Shi'ite calendar. Tens of thousands of Shia pilgrims from Iraq, Iran, and beyond had descended on Karbala and Baghdad's Kadhimiya neighborhood by the busload when the bombs started going off.

What made the Ashura bombings new was their sectarian nature and utter brutality. Other bombings may have targeted Shi'ites, but none before or since have been as deadly. Ashura commemorates the martyrdom of Imam Husayn, the grandson of Prophet Muhammad, the event that birthed the Sunni-Shia schism that has endured for more than thirteen hundred years and given it the quality of a blood feud.

Few Westerners understood the significance of the Ashura bombings. We certainly didn't. The Hamra was still hosting its share of blowouts. Baghdad's tepid winter was winding down and the press corps was ushering in spring on a flowing river of drinks.

On Saturday, March 6, there was a big pool party at the Hamra's bar, a Marla event. About fifty people milled about poolside, listening to music on an iPod plugged into a boom box. The music was too low to dance to, and even if it were loud enough, guys outnumbered women at the party ten to one.

As I was into my second drink, Marla walked up. We chatted for a few minutes before, out of nowhere, she started yelling at me. She said I was an asshole and had a bad attitude. She dug in deeper until I told her to fuck off and walked away. Sure, Marla was drunker than usual, but there was no need for the tone. I walked off to Jeff to complain.

"Who the fuck does she think she is?" I asked.

"Yeah, well, she's no different than you, except she gets drunker."

Jeff was sitting with Phil O'Connor and J. B. Forbes from the *St. Louis Post-Dispatch,* Inigo Gilmore, Maya, the *Washington Times* photographer from Adam's house, and now me. Jeff and Maya were giving each other puppy-dog eyes and showing off their tattoos. "I got this one when I was sixteen," I heard Jeff say. Jeff's sensitive-yet-rough-around-the-edges act was succeeding.

I turned to Inigo and said, "Maya's biting like a shark to a tuna."

"He's in there." Inigo wore an open suit jacket with a black *Time Out* T-shirt underneath, jeans, and loafers without socks. His hair, as usual, was perfectly messy.

Inigo was making a follow-up to his film *Searching for Saddam,* which was shot right after the fall of Baghdad. In it Inigo drove up to Tikrit, the Hussein clan's hometown, stopping people and asking,

"Have you seen Saddam?" The film ends with him getting chased out of town by a tinted-out Mercedes sedan. He thought Jeff and I could help with the sequel.

"God, there really are no women here," Inigo said. "It's depressing."

"Except Marla."

"I love her, but she's crazy."

"No shit. And crazy trumps pretty every time. She just completely lost it on me and told me off."

"What'd she say?"

"That I was an asshole."

"It's true."

"I know." We laughed. "What's Marla's deal?"

"She's been here too long. It takes its toll. She gets really drunk and is depressed—which the drinking doesn't help. But she's right about this thing. Her cause is real and important. I love her."

"I hate her."

"She's a good kid. With a big mouth."

MARLA GREW UP in a small Northern California town, the daughter of a flight attendant and a businessman. After high school she started helping at an HIV/AIDS clinic in San Francisco. During college she found herself in Africa, where she married a Zimbabwean musician. She became involved in left-wing politics and went to Afghanistan. In Kabul, she became Bubbles, the tireless humanitarian worker with a gregarious, party-down streak. In any war, that's a rare and welcomed convergence.

Before the Iraq War, Marla became aligned with Code Pink, a feminist peace organization that practices nonviolent direct action. Marla traveled to Baghdad with Code Pink as a human shield. Code

Pink had become a major player in the peace movement, and Marla made a great poster girl.

Then she started her own NGO called CIVIC. The U.S. military "doesn't do body counts" but that didn't mean the U.S. military wasn't killing a lot of people. According to CIVIC's mission statement:

> *CIVIC seeks to mitigate the impact of war and its aftermath by ensuring that timely and effective assistance is provided to unintended victims of conflict. Our goal is to see that such assistance be a permanent part of the U.S. and other governments' approach to armed conflict.*

With CIVIC, Marla provided a voice for the innocent victims of war's collateral damage. Her days would be spent zooming around Iraq, in and out of the Green Zone, trying to get confirmations and then compensation for civilians killed or injured by the U.S. military.

How many Iraqi civilians had been killed or injured by the U.S. military? The question was moral and relevant. If the war is being waged on the dime of American taxpayers, it seems within our rights to ask how much blood is on our hands. Marla was the only American we met in Iraq working solely on this question. Here was a twenty-seven-year-old scatterbrained California blonde with a slight drinking problem and no formal training asking the biggest of all questions. U.S. Army colonels respected her. U.S. senators were her buddies.

Marla defined moral bravery: She was going house to house, neighborhood to neighborhood, trying to get a handle on just how many Iraqis had died at the hands of the American-led Coalition. She didn't just waste time crying about the injustice of the occupation.

The ideal was one thing. Then there was the way the world could be: The United States could have a better Iraq policy, one that took civilian casualties into account during the occupation. Marla was all about tangible results: This was a world that could be improved and changed, maybe not to the ideal level, but to a place where at minimum the U.S. military acknowledged the people it killed. She found helping the victims of conflict more important than wearing pink and holding up slogan signs like "Bush Lies People Die: End the Occupation of Iraq."

At first she did it all by herself. Then she began to get help. At Marla's (no doubt forceful and relentless) urging, Senator Patrick Leahy (Democrat, Vermont) secured $30 million in congressional funds for civilian casualties in Iraq and Afghanistan, an unprecedented acknowledgment of U.S. responsibility for civilian damage as a result of battle and occupation.

One of the reasons Marla was so successful with CIVIC was that she didn't become fully invested in the unilateral peacenik-jihadist rhetoric. The peace movement is guilty of the same love of oversimplistic, black-and-white dualities that drove George W. Bush before the war, with his good and evil rhetoric.

THE NEXT DAY I found Ski in his usual spot behind the Convention Center, under a palm tree next to his radio Humvee. He was doing push-ups. I greeted him and he popped up, red-faced, and exhaled.

"I did a thousand yesterday," he said. "Look at this." He flexed his right arm and it rippled. A zit goatee was starting to cluster around his chin and mouth. "I already put on ten pounds of muscle." I regretted ever helping him get steroids.

Ski's NCO had finally lifted the "weapon at all times" punishment, and his unit might soon be moving somewhere outside the Green Zone, he told me. He was having trouble making eye contact. "So I'm marrying my girl. What do you think?" Ski spat on the ground.

"Umm. Well, just remember how young you are. There are a lot of girls out there."

"I don't feel young."

"You're nineteen. She's sixteen. That's young."

We moved around to the side of the Convention Center, where a series of empty fountains ringed by palm trees formed a deserted garden. Sitting on a slate bench we made small talk—the weather, how much Kuwait sucks, could I try and score him some hash, how his unit was always the first in line for meals at the Rasheed buffet.

"Those fat fuckers love to eat," Ski said.

"Remember when you passed out back here?"

We both laughed. "Fuck," he said. "I woke up to my NCO kicking me in the ribs."

"Same shit happened to me last night. I passed out at a party at the Hamra. They call me Training Wheels now."

"Training Wheels . . . that's great. Fuck, man. I just want to kick back in my parents' basement, smoke a bowl, put on a DVD, and just space out. Or drive out to the desert, looking at the stars and holding my girl. This is the worst decision I ever made. You know how some people are just not supposed to be in the Army? Just aren't cut out for it?"

"Yeah, like me."

"Well, that's me a hundred percent, too, man. But it was too late once I realized it. Some of my buddies from Fort Hood got out."

"How?"

"They were crazy and out of shape; they pulled the psycho card and got sprung. Some went AWOL before Iraq. There's so much about the

Army that sucks." Despite his mental instability, Ski was now a perfect physical specimen for the Army: a muscular kid who, through exercise and discipline (and the wonders of pharmaceuticals), was now in perfect fighting shape. Compared to the rest of his unit—a pudgy budget-radio crew—Ski was Achilles. The Army couldn't afford to let him go.

"No one back home sees this side of the war, or any war, really," I said. "You know that."

"What side of war?"

"The despair of soldiers like yourself fighting a war that you don't want to fight. An honest account of how you feel about the Army and the war. Americans are entitled to understand the personalities of the soldiers that we're asking to die. Especially the side you're on, the ones who aren't hoo-rah and gung-ho about war."

"I'll talk to anyone and tell them how much this sucks."

That was that. Later that day, Jeff called Inigo to film the interview. We began calling it "The Emancipation of Ski."

THAT NIGHT, Jeff and I joined Inigo for a drink at the Hamra. We talked about Inigo's film. "I've filmed this American military DJ," he told us. "A young girl, quite cute, named Niki Cage, but that's not her real name. It's her stage name. The station is called Freedom Radio."

"We love Freedom Radio. They play some good stuff. I even heard 'Immigrant Song' the other day."

"It's a hilarious operation; you have to see the footage." Later we would see it, and it was fantastic. Niki Cage was a cute soldier with a tan, a brown ponytail, and a crooked smile. The station may have been called Freedom Radio, but she wasn't allowed to pick the songs. That duty fell on her commanding officer, who applied cultural sensitivity to the selections. Sometimes there were flubs, like the time they played the Gap Band song with the chorus: "You dropped the bomb on me, baby." Angry Iraqis called and said, "You play song about dropping bomb on my baby."

The station was broadcast across the capital. Occasionally, Jeff and I would jump into a cab that was blasting a Justin Timberlake song or some southern rap. Older Iraqis who'd lived through the freewheelin' seventies tended to like American R&B. Once when we were in a car with an Iraqi driver from the NPR house and R. Kelly's "Ignition (Remix)" came on Freedom Radio, the driver said: "I like this music. Remind me of when I was a young man, back when I went to disco and had sex with my wife. Now America brings AIDEZ. No more disco." A popular Iraqi rumor was that AIDS was the American disease. Saddam had made foreigners take an AIDS test before they were allowed to enter his country. Since the letters d and s never go together in Arabic, AIDS was pronounced AIDEZ.

Bored with the Hamra, we decided to go out on the town. "I've already paid a driver for the full day so we have a car," Inigo said. "Let's go to Clowntown." He'd filmed the clowns in action and was a big fan of Jo. "She's really got it, man. You know, she's really a bright one. Back in the U.K. she is quite a well-known activist."

"She's a nutty peacenik," Jeff said.

A few minutes later, we pulled up to Clowntown—where the security guards were watching porno with a pile of cocaine in front of them and a stack of Kalashnikovs behind them. Upstairs, Clowntown was unchanged: Peat, Jo, Luis, and Sam sat on mattresses in their tiny room, their makeshift bong on the floor. If anything, the room had gotten messier and more strewn with empty bottles. Peat looked to have lost some weight and was complaining about a stomach ailment. Inigo told his favorite joke: "Looks like you've really been clowning around."

Jeff and I plopped down on a mattress and Inigo pulled out his camera. Soon a heated debate broke out with Jo. She was tough and sharp but was also into conspiracy theories. My favorite was that the U.S. military used Mexican immigrants on the front lines during the battle for Baghdad International Airport in order to keep casualties hidden from the public.

Jo did make a semivalid point about how the CPA was ripping off the Iraqi staff. Most Iraqis working in the Green Zone were hired as translators employed by Titan, no matter what they actually did. The pay was a measly fifteen dollars a day. Meanwhile, private security contractors or mercenaries were pulling down as much as one thousand dollars a day.

The clowns hated the U.S. military with a passion. Most young Brits we'd met in the Middle East felt that the U.S. military was the enemy. We agreed that Bush-era civilian policymakers at the Pentagon were corrupted by power and emboldened by September 11. We agreed that generals often placed their careers ahead of truth, sanity, and the lives of civilians. But we disagreed vehemently with the Clowns' hatred for the U.S. ground troops.

"You Americans are afraid to criticize your military," Inigo said.

"No. We criticize the decision makers," Jeff said. "But we can't criticize the kids fighting. I mean, I grew up the son of a Marine. It would be like selling out my family."

IT WAS THE DAY of the Ski interview, and Inigo was running late. Ski, Jeff, and I sat slouched in orange leather chairs in the Convention Center. Ski's night shift was coming up. Jeff's cell phone kept ringing with a frantic Inigo on the other end, "Stuck in traffic, mate. Be there in a hurry."

Rumpled and anxious, Inigo finally burst upon us, a whirlwind of boom mikes, tripods, and lighting schemes. We retreated from the Convention Center and made our way to the Parade Grounds. Aside from Black Hawks and Kiowa OH-58 helicopters moving across the hazy late-afternoon horizon, the Parade Grounds were at peace. The whole area, which includes the old zoo, might be the most relaxed place in Baghdad. A Humvee would pull up for a photo op every so often, or a jogger might cruise through, but it was a good place to interview Ski in peace and quiet. American soldiers in Iraq aren't supposed to give interviews without a Public Affairs Officer (PAO) present, and we didn't want to call attention to ourselves. Ski gave an impassioned hour-long interview, albeit one riddled with outlandish statements like, "I'd say fifty percent of the Army uses marijuana, thirty percent cocaine." He talked about how he wanted to go home; how the Army had duped him and kept him in as a kind of volunteer slave; how he was in hell in a half dozen different ways. Cradling his M-4 carbine, Ski told the camera, "I told the shrink I wanted to kill myself and others."

Later, Jeff and I watched the footage and my stomach dropped. "And he still has twelve more months to go," Jeff said.

17

•

Not Love,
Just Rockets

C OLLARD GREENS, watermelon, and fried chicken . . . these were
the highlights from the KBR "Black History Month" buffet
menu, which was posted around all Green Zone dining halls during
late February 2004. We still can't figure out how they got away with
such racist smack.

Most of our meals were eaten at KBR's lunch and dinner buffets
because we were still broke. We usually ate at the main palace, the
Wolfpack Staging Area (which had a great Wednesday taco night), or
the Al Rasheed Hotel, which was across Yafa Street from our NGO Assistance Office in the Convention Center. No matter where we went,
though, the line for the buffet would start piling up thirty to forty
minutes before the doors opened and the meals were ready. The food
was served by a hodgepodge of workers from the Philippines, Nepal,
Indonesia, and pretty much every other South Asian country. KBR

didn't care where their service workers came from—as long as they weren't Muslim. The servers were usually really friendly guys, but if you started chatting with them, a fat, white American KBR overseer would step up behind them, saying something like, "You guys finished here?" in a less than friendly tone, to squash fraternization. As time went on, the service workers became less afraid of the KBR bosses.

One night in early March, the seventh to be exact, we'd decided to pull a night work session with Jensen at our office in the Convention Center. Charlie was there, too, in the background. He was busy using "Ray & Jeff's Freelancer's Internet Café." At about 7:30 P.M., we walked across the road to the Rasheed for the last half hour of dinner, Charlie staying behind to finish some e-mails. Over dinner, Jensen told us stories from the invasion for the first time.

"Most of the time, those stupid fuckers would forget to pull the pins on their RPGs," Jensen told us in his slight southern drawl. "Which meant the rockets would hit the truck but not explode. One night, we were driving through Sadr City, and all of a sudden, RPGs started bouncing off the hoods of our Humvees. It was crazy, man."

We knew Jensen's unit had taken control of Saddam International Airport, allowing American troops, weapons, and supplies to fly into Baghdad, and that they'd also rolled through Sadr City and had set up Camp Marlboro in an abandoned bootleg Iraqi cigarette factory outside town. We knew he'd lost several good friends in the early days of the war—he'd made a few allusions to it, but had yet to give us details.

"So, what kind of weapons were you using most of the time?" I asked, hoping to lighten the conversation and keep his thoughts moving.

"Anything from M-16s to—"

Just then, a long screech—followed by a loud BOOOM—abruptly

ended our conversation. The building shook. A rocket had hit the face of the Rasheed, several floors up.

"Everybody, get the fuck *down!*" an Army officer yelled as he ran in a crouch through the messhall.

There were more screeches and explosions; through the floor, we could feel the building shake with each impact. We scrambled across the floor to get away from the wall of windows right behind us.

Light gray smoke began pouring in through the dining hall's front doors. A Marine and two soldiers from the 2nd ACR came into the hall from their Al Rasheed guardposts out front and shouted: "Everyone get downstairs to the bomb shelter. Now! Move, move, mooovvvee!"

Once downstairs, we instantly felt like we were crashing somebody else's party. The "Bomb Shelter" signs led down a flight of stairs to "the Bunker," which was a sports bar being tended by a large southern woman whose patrons on that night were British and Australian rugby fans happily watching a match on a projection screen TV.

"What the hell is this?" Jensen said in a pissed-off voice.

Over the protests of the rugby fans, the channel was turned to CNN. On the screen was the Rasheed. Blurry orange flames licked out of upper-story windows. The voiceover was along the lines of "What you're looking at now is what appears to be some sort of attack on the Green Zone and the Al Rasheed Hotel."

"Nice fucking view, man," Jeff said.

After a few minutes, as the flames died down on TV, the channel was changed back to the rugby game. We had to wait for the "all clear" to leave the Bunker, which we knew could take hours, so we set up in a booth and stretched out to try to sleep off the rocket attack. Our old buddy Beth Payne was a few booths over, having drinks with a handful of men in civilian clothes; she didn't seem bothered by the night's turn of events at all. Adding to our shitty feeling was the thought of Charlie walking across the road to meet us, or Ski in his hot box, or Lieutenant Mikey and the 82nd guys sitting right out in the middle of it all.

In a world fed by instant news worldwide, what the rocket attack also meant was that we'd have to e-mail our families and friends to let them know we were OK. A couple of hours later, we left the Bunker at the "all clear" and headed out to catch a shuttle back to the palace.

Turns out, the rocket assault had been a full cocktail of ordnance: Several different types and sizes of rockets and mortars had hit the hotel and dropped into the courtyard. All of them had been fired from the bed of a pickup truck at the edge of the Green Zone.

The Rasheed rocket attack tipped the insurgency's hand. This strike to the heart of the occupation was the most brazen assault on the Green Zone since we'd arrived in Iraq. From that night on the Green Zone remained under constant siege. Mortar attacks, which had been a weekly or twice-weekly affair, started dropping on the palace nightly. And if the area just outside the Green Zone couldn't be controlled, we began to wonder, what was going on across the rest of the city? And the rest of Iraq?

18

•

Rocket Man

S AMIN WAS AN IRAQI from Kirkuk, probably in his midforties. Jeff and I knew him from our Tuesday NGO meetings at the Convention Center. He always sat up front and asked the majority of questions. Samin had tried to get us to go to Kirkuk with him and grand open an "NGO Center" that had been set up by him and his buddies. In early March, we finally agreed to go with him. We were a little tired of Baghdad, Sadr City, and Kerrada, and excited at the idea of seeing a new part of Iraq, its Kurdish-occupied northeast.

A couple of days later, on March 9, Samin showed up at our office in a navy blue panel truck built like a tiny U-Haul, with a pull-down door in the back and a wall separating the cab and the storage area. Jeff and I both immediately realized there was no room for everyone, at least not comfortably.

The road to Kirkuk from Baghdad is a fairly straight shot north

through the city of Baquba, where the road veers off to the east a little and keeps going north. Jeff ended up lying on the floorboards of
the van, and I was half on Samin's lap and half on the lap of the
truck's toothless, smiling seventy-year-old driver. Just a few miles outside Baghdad, we were stopped at a U.S. Army checkpoint and told
to exit the vehicle.

Two or three times more as we got farther and farther from Baghdad we were stopped by Iraqi Civil Defense Corps roadblocks. About
halfway along, a couple of hours into the trip, our little traveling circus stopped at a roadside restaurant just past Baquba. Samin went inside and bought us all Pepsis. We sat at a table in the stand's covered
open-air dining area and finished the drinks. Then Samin gave us little glass cups, and we drank chai with him and the driver. A minute
later, a platter arrived with the usual Arab fare: rice, beans, and bread.
We also got plenty of uncomfortable stares from the locals. Samin
spoke no English at all, and neither did the driver—who, it had become clear, didn't know Samin at all.

We got back into the truck and drove now to the northeast. As we
cruised into Kurdish northern Iraq, the air cooled and grew more
pleasant. We'd left the flat, gray-brown Tigris and Euphrates flood-
plains behind and the landscape had become hilly and lushly green,
much like the front range of the Colorado Rockies. Tumbling streams
flowed out of the mountains, crossing fields of crops below.

Several more militia checkpoints and a few stretch breaks later,
we reached Kirkuk at dusk. The van pulled up in front of our hotel
around the corner from an old Baath Party Headquarters building.

We got our driver to help us find a few pharmacies, where we
could grab our usual evening cocktail ingredients of Xanax, Valium,
and Klonopin. The hotel was your standard Iraqi midrange option:

the obligatory satellite television in the lobby, three or four shady-looking men with pistols and AK-47s standing around smoking cigarettes and drinking chai, a few dead potted plants, and your basic decor of benches and plastic chairs. We realized we'd need to find our own entertainment in Kirkuk.

Once in the room—a white-painted cell with two twin-sized beds and purple curtains framing the window—we discussed going out to wander around Kirkuk. It was only 7:00 or 8:00 P.M. at this point, and we were both still pretty restless from the ride up. We toyed with the idea of sightseeing about thirty seconds before deciding to follow our instincts and stay in. We dipped into our stash of antianxiety drugs and talked ourselves to sleep.

Only the roar of jet engines directly overhead could have dragged us from our pharmaceutical slumber that night. Which actually happened sometime in the middle of the night, when we were jolted out of sleep by fighter jets directly over the roof of our hotel, followed by the detonation of their payload a few miles away.

Jeff opened the curtains. In the direction of the explosions, we were shocked to see what can only be described as a pitched battle: In the darkness, two huge areas of the outlying city seemed to be aflame—the fires went forty or fifty feet into the air, illuminating the city's low, flat rooftops—and the two areas were separated by about a half mile of total blackness. Between the two flaming areas, red tracer bullets streaked across the black, and every few minutes artillery and RPG explosions threw fragments of flame. The fighter aircraft, obviously American, were bombing both sides.

Jeff and I just stood there, watching the battle unfold through the window. Jeff pulled out his camera and took some shots. The fighting went on for hours, occasionally waking us from pill comas. We later found out that the two combatants were the PUK (Patriotic Union of Kurdistan) and the KDP (Kurdish Democratic Party), the two main Kurdish political parties.

THE NEXT MORNING, Samin came for us in a car—an Opel or Corolla—with his twelve-year-old son behind the wheel. One of the guys in the car reached out his hand to shake ours: "Hello, Americans," he said. "I speak English, though not so very good."

The NGO center we were driven to was an old Baath Party building with a fresh coat of off-white paint. A few long tables and white plastic chairs were set up out front to greet us. As we got out of the car, a Kurdish television crew ran toward us for a quick interview, although nobody from their side spoke English. We were laughing a lot at each other during the interview. Apparently, the TV crew had been led to believe this Grand Opening was a state-level meeting between the Kurds and their new friends, the liberating Americans.

Samin was also well aware of our "no tolerance" regarding bogus NGOs. We'd made it a perfectly clear point at the beginning of each weekly meeting back in Baghdad, just to let anyone with an NGO scam know it wouldn't be tolerated. We'd generated a fake blacklist—filled with fake NGOs—that we'd flash as a prop to discourage scammers from trying to pull fast ones. Samin had obviously made it a point to have this operation look as legitimate as possible. Everyone in line to receive aid had to sign several forms, all written in Arabic, which could have said anything. They also had to show some sort of ID card.

As the aid-distribution queue was being set up, we returned to the car. It turned out Samin's English-speaking buddy had been a colonel in Saddam's air force, where he'd been a design engineer for air-to-surface missile systems. In the late 1980s, he'd traveled to China and Portugal for missile-design conferences. His English was pretty good, but we could tell he was nervous when talking to us, as if he half feared we were going to rat him out for something. Trying to loosen him up, we began calling him "Rocket Man." For fun, I asked him where in Kirkuk we could buy a Scud missile and how much one might cost. I pulled out my wallet. Rocket Man looked confused. His eyes darted around the car, and he offered no reply.

A few minutes later, when I got out of the car, Rocket Man turned to Jeff. "Why does that man ask me this?" Rocket Man demanded. "What does he want these . . . these rockets for?"

Jeff told him that I was only kidding, but he didn't believe Jeff. "Tell him you're kidding about the Scuds," Jeff yelled to me from the car window. I did.

Finally, after more than an hour, Samin and Rocket Man began to open boxes and distribute clothes. Almost immediately, Samin began complaining about the clothes' being previously worn—"But these clothes are not new," Rocket Man told us, translating. "These clothes have all been used!"—until we finally had to tell Samin to shut up. And anyway, Jeff and I were wearing dirty jeans with gaping holes all over them while Samin, in his pressed clothes, was pissing and moaning. Annoyed as Jeff and I might be with Samin over his griping about the quality of our aid clothing, we were also very glad we came. As we packed up to leave, everyone said they hoped we'd return again, and shook our hands and hugged us and thanked us.

IRAQ'S KURDS have been trampled on for decades. Even before Saddam, Sunni Iraqis were sent up north to govern them while extracting all the oil, food, and natural resources possible from their lands at the point of a gun. Saddam's vision of a Sunni Babylon for Iraq had no place in it for the Kurds. A United Nations report concluded that the atrocities committed against Iraq's Kurds by Saddam's regime were "so grave and . . . of such a massive nature that since the Second World War few parallels can be found." On March 16, 1988, the Iraqi Kurd town of Halabja was nearly destroyed by Iraqi artillery and air force bombs, then targeted with sarin and other poison gases. In 1989, using bombs and bulldozers, Saddam leveled several Iraqi Kurdish cities, including Qalat Dizah, displacing seventy thousand people in that one city alone. All told, human rights organizations estimate as many as three hundred thousand Iraqi Kurds were exterminated by Saddam in the 1980s.

The Kurdish national motto states the point succinctly: "The Kurds have no friends."

Our drive to Baghdad later that afternoon was uneventful, and we arrived back at the GZ that evening just in time for the tail end of the Rasheed buffet. We told Jensen and a few journalists we ran into about the battle we'd seen, but no one believed us.

19

·

"A" or "The"

THE NEXT MORNING, we caught the whiff of a political storm that was brewing over Iraq's interim constitution: the Transitional Authorities Law, or TAL. It was the scheduled day of signing, March 10, and the news media had already infested the Convention Center. The TAL signing was supposed to start at 5:00 P.M. Iraqi time, late enough in the day to be carried live back in the States. But at the last second, the whole event was abruptly canceled. Supposedly, the Shi'ites had a problem with some language in the draft. As the day wound down, the media slowly dissipated until nobody but Charlie, Jensen, and us remained. We walked into the Convention Center's main foyer, where the TAL signature ceremony was to have taken place. It looked like a stage set, complete with a prop table and golden pens. Charlie, Jeff, and I took the opportunity to pose a fake signing for souvenir photos.

"Hey," Jensen said in his coastal twang as he lifted the camera, "ya'll act like you're putting your John Hancocks on that."

THE CPA TRIED to pretend the aborted TAL signing was no big deal. In fact, it was a big deal. The problem came down to a matter of a single word: Was Islam "a" or "the" source of law under the TAL? Ayatollah Sistani, the Shi'ite megacleric of Najaf, had demanded the word be "the," while the Americans and secular Iraqis wanted it to be "a." Declaring Iraq to be a theocracy under Sharia, or Islamic law, didn't exactly sit well with the American mission to bring Western-style secular democracy to the Middle East.

But Sistani was arguably Iraq's most powerful civic and religious leader, and what he said was virtually law anyway, in the form of religious decrees, or fatwas. Now, seizing his moment, Sistani threatened fatwa on the TAL, claiming it was "unfriendly to Islam." In a bind, the Americans and Iraqis worked in the first of two all-night sessions to fix their "a/the problem." As a compromise, the language was changed to make Islam "a major source" for the rule of law in Iraq, and the TAL was reluctantly agreed to and prepared for signing a few days later.

IN AN IMPORTANT SENSE the TAL was a sham. Other major obstacles to creating a unified, democratic Iraq had also been shunted aside or left to simmer until after the U.S. presidential elections in November. The issue of federalism, so important to the Kurds, was placed on a back burner, right next to the Islamic law questions. Also placed to one side was the fate of Kirkuk. The Kurds wanted Kirkuk to be their regional capital. But Kirkuk and the Kurds sit directly over Iraq's second-largest oil field, and nobody else wanted it ceded to a people who might treat it as a down payment on the cost of independence. Complicating matters, Iraq's north also has a large population of Turkomen, whose long-running dislike for the Kurds predates even the British creation of Iraq, and who view the prospect of increased Kurdish power very darkly.

Meanwhile, the CPA and the Governing Council *did* find time to include an article in the TAL that retained all Bremer Orders as rules of law. Among other things, this protected and kept tax-free all CPA-approved business interests in Iraq (Order 37), and codified that the Americans retained the power to appoint Iraq's ministers of Defense, Foreign Affairs, and Intelligence to five-year terms—Orders 67, 68, and 69.

Sistani had been calling for democratic elections since Saddam had been ousted. It took the CPA nine months, until January 2004, to set a date for Iraqi elections. Iraqis would have to wait another year, until January 2005, before being allowed to participate in the democratic process. The CPA claimed it needed to establish the ministries, begin large-scale Iraqi reconstruction, and support increased Iraqi cultural stability. But none of that was happening. The CPA was failing Iraq, and was further endangering all U.S. troops there, not to mention all of the Westerners working there. Things seemed backward to us. Sistani was calling for democratic elections, and the CPA and White House, which claimed to want democracy in Iraq, were delaying them.

But the CPA was continuing to do one thing effectively: It was protecting the president. Had the United States listened to Sistani and held elections early on, the CPA risked having all the problems it kept hidden from view jump to the surface, grabbing Bush's re-election chances by the throat. Nothing looks so bad as liberating a nation only to preside over its speedy collapse into bloody tribal and civil war; that kind of good news gets nobody re-elected.

20

.

Free Birds

B Y THE SECOND WEEK in March, we were working hard seven days a week—often for twelve to sixteen hours at a stretch— but we also remained almost existentially unattached to any larger CPA agenda. It was field ops followed by more field ops, then back to the office to write them up as reports.

Every time we went out to Sadr City and other areas to distribute aid, we would travel unescorted and with Iraqi NGOs. That had always been the point: Iraqis helping Iraqis. On March 15, we agreed to take Phil O'Connor and J. B. Forbes of the *St. Louis Post-Dispatch* along to report on the process.

We had a lot of aid boxes that had come into the KBR post office behind the palace, so Jensen did us a huge favor and signed out a big, shiny, white GMC pickup with U.S. government plates. The truck was to be used strictly inside the Green Zone, to move boxes of clothes from the palace out to Hayder's car just outside the blast walls. It was a nice gesture on Jensen's part, and he even helped us load several of the heaviest boxes into the truck's bed. Moving these boxes one by one on the shuttle would have taken days.

"So just don't crash this thing, all right?" Jensen said in a fatherly tone.

"Come on, man, you know you can trust us, it'll be fine," Jeff said as he took the keys and climbed into the driver's seat. "We just need it for a couple of hours."

Jeff fired up the truck and we headed for the Convention Center to grab Hayder, Phil, and J.B. and transfer all the boxes over to Hayder's cars, which were to be waiting outside the Al Rasheed Gate. Windows down, Freedom Radio up. Niki Cage, the DJ for Freedom Radio, was actually playing some decent music that morning. As we passed the last checkpoint on the road to the Convention Center, Lynyrd Skynyrd's "Freebird" came on, and we cranked the stereo all the way up.

"Don't wreck this bitch," I shouted.

We rolled slowly past a bus stop queue of CPA staffers, in an effort to offend them with the music and our freedom. Then, as Jeff coolly began to slip the truck into a diagonal Convention Center parking space at a good clip . . . fuck. Right in the middle of the "Freebird" guitar solo, we heard a thud, followed by a scraping sound. We'd creased the passenger side of the truck on another CPA vehicle's bumper. Jeff and I jumped out to observe the damage. In our defense, the other truck had a huge steel cattle-guard rear bumper.

The damage wasn't too bad. Still, we were worried about what Jensen would say if he saw it. Except for some white paint on it, the other truck's bumper was fine.

"Fuck it, man, let's pull down a few spots further. No one will notice."

We parked and headed into our office, the usual chaotic scene. Our computers had been commandeered by Ibty's cousins and friends, all IM-ing each other while sitting in the same room.

Hayder was nowhere to be seen. It was the first time in our now dozens of trips out with him that he hadn't shown up when he said he would. We were effectively screwed. Our buddies from the *Post-Dispatch* were hanging around, waiting to go. It was embarrassing. Almost every night at the Hamra, we'd been telling stories about what we'd done that day in the field, and we'd promised Phil and J.B. several times that we'd take them out.

"We've got the truck, and we both know how to get to Sadr City. Let's just do it," I said. "It'll be a cowboy mission."

"All right, man, should we take the other Hayder with us?" There was now another guy named Hayder from Sadr City, whom Jensen was paying from his own pocket to do manual labor around the NGOAO and IAC offices.

Phil and J.B. didn't think twice about joining us. "Is it cool if we still come?" Phil asked.

"Of course."

We lied and told Ibty that our usual Hayder and his guys were waiting outside, and we were off. Jeff jumped behind the wheel with J.B. in the cab, while Phil, Hayder, and I sat in back with a couple of dozen boxes. We drove through the Green Zone to the nearest vehicle exit, the Rasheed Gate. It was Jeff's first time driving in Baghdad traffic. We went over the Jumhuriyah Bridge, past his favorite hangout, the Thieves Market, and out on the road that passes the Oil Ministry. As we got to the outskirts of Sadr City, Jeff got in the back and I jumped behind the wheel.

"I'm stopping at the first soccer field I see," I told everyone.

Jensen's Hayder was trying to help out by pointing down streets, but I knew Sadr City well enough by now and needed no direction. We stopped a mile or so inside the city's slums, next to a barren soccer field hemmed in by one- and two-story slab homes. I got into a soccer game with a few kids who were already playing. Hayder and Jeff began to open boxes of clothing. It only took a minute for Jeff and Hayder to be surrounded by excited, screaming kids. Hayder made a feeble attempt at forming a line, but soon the field erupted into a near riot. We unloaded all of the clothes from five or six boxes and had to get back into the truck.

I drove to the opposite end of the soccer field, where another large group of kids was gathering in an alleyway. We all jumped out, and the truck was immediately surrounded by dozens, then well over a hundred people . . . we weren't going anywhere. Understandably, J.B. and Phil were a little freaked out by this, and stood up on the roof of the cab, Phil taking notes, J.B. shooting photos. I mingled in the crowd as Jeff threw clothes out over his shoulder.

Soon the crowd was crushing in on the truck, which once again was being rocked. "The boxes are empty," Jeff yelled. "We need to get the fuck outta here!"

I got back behind the wheel, but we were totally surrounded. A few old men began yelling, pushing, and hitting kids with switches, to clear a path for us to get out.

This is from what Phil wrote for the following Sunday's edition of the *Post-Dispatch*:

> *Many adults joined the crowd, which became unruly*
> *as people pushed forward and grabbed at boxes still in*
> *the truck. As they pulled away, a boy on a small motor*

scooter followed the truck for blocks in hopes of receiving something. Neumann tossed a pair of trousers and the young boy stopped and picked them up.

A second stop in a narrow alley proved even more uncomfortable. People grabbed, pushed and pulled each other to get at the goods. At times, the crowd seemed about to turn into an angry mob.

LeMoine began to back up to get out of the area, but found his route blocked by a pushcart and several small children. Finally, he pulled forward around a pile of rubble, turned right around a corner and accelerated down a narrow alley. After several blocks he stopped to check on his passengers and the condition of the truck. Puff Daddy boomed on the truck's stereo.

"That was a little hairy," he said. "At least it's getting to the kids in the street."

. . . Neumann and LeMoine don't apologize for their methods. They're trying to make a difference any way they can, they say.

They do see many problems with American efforts here; out of the $87 billion the U.S. is spending in Iraq, only $50 million, or less than one-tenth of one percent, is directed to meet the basic needs such as education, primary health care, food and nutrition, according to the U.S. Agency for International Development. . . .

"Kids come up to us with bloody feet, walking through a foot of raw sewage. They had a typhoid outbreak up there. They had a hepatitis outbreak up there and no one cares," Neumann says.

Both are angry at the level of bureaucracy, ques-
tion the use and potential conflict of so many highly
paid contractors and wonder about corruption. They
are frustrated that current reconstruction isn't mak-
ing life much easier for Iraqis.

After a field op of such intensity, we all agreed that a tailgate party was in order, so we headed back to the GZ after a stop at Napoli Pizza and the liquor store down the block. We bought enough booze for a frat party, then got back into the truck and drove through the Rasheed Gate. The next stop was our favorite private party spot, Saddam's Parade Grounds, a huge deserted paved road right under those big swords. Bottles of arrack were consumed, and snapshots were taken. Then we climbed into the truck headed back out across the 14th of July Bridge to take Phil and J.B. home to the Hamra.

As our reasoning went, we'd already made it in and out of Sadr City, so we might as well test our luck and head back out into the Red Zone driving a huge, white target. We returned the truck to the lot across from the palace, where we'd picked it up hours before, only slightly the worse for wear.

Jensen was at his desk in Baghdad Central when we handed him the keys. We thanked him profusely for signing the truck out for us. "We couldn't find you to return the keys this morning, so we left it parked at the Convention Center while we were in Sadr City," we told him. "Thanks, man."

Later that week, Phil's article debuted at number eleven on the *Early Bird Wire,* the DoD's collection of all new Iraq-related news articles. Luckily no one of major importance saw it, Jensen included. We'd squeaked through, again, but we could feel the door closing.

21

·

The Orders

J EN AND ADAM had slowly become our favorite people in Baghdad. Whether we were theirs is another matter. Jeff, at least, was
dating one of their roommates, Maya. But sometimes Jeff invited me
over to their house without asking anyone, and when I'd show up
with Inigo or somebody, I was stared at as if I'd broken in and pissed
on the carpet. After one such particularly embarrassing night I re-
solved just to stay away, but my resolve failed me. The place was pow-
erfully seductive. Among other things, you never knew who was
going to turn up there.

One night, when I was actually invited for dinner by Jen and
Adam, a pretty young woman sat at the head of the table on my left.
She had auburn hair and wore a black outfit. Slightly drunk, I started
telling her how the CPA was a big scam, then launched into a few an-

ecdotes about Lieutenant Colonel Weaver—that grandpa stress ther-
apist from Florida now in charge of the Iraqi Assistance Center—and
how he was always counseling us on our stress levels.

"Hey, Iraq is headed down the shitter . . . you should be stressed,
too," I told her I had counseled Colonel Weaver. In fact, I didn't say
that, as alcohol plus a woman equals lying to impress. I told her how
Order 45 was helping to turn Iraq into a humanitarian catastrophe.

Then she began talking. The young woman knew about the Orders. In fact, she was working on a story that had something to do
with the Orders.

I said, "They're more radical than anything postcommunist. Fuck
the Orders."

"No one in the press reports on them, either. There is very little
attention paid to them."

"CPA keeps it like a secret."

After the meal, I found out the woman's name was Naomi Klein.
She is among the world's most visible critics of globalization. I'd seen
her best-selling book *No Logo* in nearly every country I've ever been
to. She's also a columnist for *The Guardian,* the *Toronto Globe and
Mail,* and *The Nation.*

Over the next few weeks, Jeff and I would see Naomi around,
mainly at the Convention Center or NPR house. She was working on
a piece for *Harper's Magazine,* and was frustrated about the virtually
hermetic information seal surrounding the CPA. A couple of after-
noons, Naomi stopped by the NGOAO to chat. I gave her as much
gossip and info as possible, but usually I was useless.

Naomi was another of those women, like Jen, Heather Coyne, Jo
the Clown, Maya, and Jody, who seemed better adapted to wartime in
Baghdad than were most men. With cool confidence and a razor-

sharp mind, she offered more proof that testosterone makes war possible but doesn't necessarily improve a person's thinking. Maybe estrogen was the missing ingredient in our pharma-cocktails. Confident, strong, individualist women like Naomi certainly weren't present in excessive numbers.

Naomi's piece finally appeared in *Harper's* in July 2004. Called "Baghdad: Year Zero," it was the first story to dissect the underlying philosophical thrust of the CPA, which she did by examining the Bremer Orders. No one else has written about the Orders in such detail. So with apologies, we'll use her story as a springboard for our own stump speech.

By March 2004, Bremer had inked sixty-seven Orders. By the time the CPA dissolved at the end of June 2004, that number had increased to one hundred and reached into all aspects of Iraqi society. Socially the Bremer Orders blocked the establishment of civil society. Politically they ensured U.S. appointees in many high-level positions of Iraqi governance. Most sweepingly, they made Iraq the world's most open market for commerce.

Bremer's Orders were the invisible Iraqi constitution, the one not celebrated with a press conference and talked about in Bush's campaign speeches. The Orders were the operating system for everything in Iraq and Baghdad. They remain in public view on the CPA's website: www.cpa-iraq.org.

Order 12, for instance, the Trade Liberalization Policy, lifted all taxes for any import or export goods leaving or entering Iraq by land, sea, or air. Order 37, the CPA's tax strategy, freed any foreign corporations approved to do business in Iraq by the CPA from any and all forms of taxation. Order 11 privatized the Iraqi telecommunications industry (strange that this would be important in a country that didn't have a functioning electrical grid). Order 39 supported Foreign Direct Investment (FDI) to "develop infrastructure, foster the growth of Iraqi business, create jobs, raise capital." Order 39 added that a "foreign investment may take place with respect to all economic sectors of Iraq"—except the Iraqi oil industry. These four orders meant that Iraq's economy—excepting its petroleum sector—was for sale to any qualified foreign investor, who could then dismantle it, sell it, and remove the profits from Iraq without taxation.

Recent history shows that the economic shock therapy Bremer and his CPA cronies prescribed for the new Iraq—opening up markets from a standing start in what was formally a centrally planned economy—is, to say the least, problematic. After the fall of communism free markets didn't lead to freedom in Russia; instead they led to a stratospheric rise in organized crime and a police-state-style crackdown by the government. (Freedom House, a prodemocracy NGO that tracks the world's governments, has recently labeled Russia "not free.") But in Iraq, regardless of the teachings of recent economic history, Bush, Bremer, and the CPA were clearly making the bet that their new Iraq would set the standard for what a bottom-up free market could deliver.

Making Iraq the Delaware of the Middle East was a happy thought, but numerous problems stood in the way of the opening of Baghdad branches of the Olive Garden, Bed Bath & Beyond, and Citibank. The two largest impediments were Iraq's longtime state corruption and a fast-growing insurgency that increasingly was targeting and destroying Western-supported infrastructure. The Iraqis Jeff and I met weren't saying, "If only they would open a Chili's, everything would be perfect." Instead they were asking: "Where is the electricity? Where is the security?"

In a category by itself was Bremer's Order 1: de-Baathification. This called for the ousting of all traces of Saddam's old Baath Party, which controlled virtually every aspect of Iraqi life. Order 1 stripped the Iraqi state of any functioning government, military, or social programs. Certainly, top-level Baathists deserved expulsion from the CPA's new Iraq. But cutting out Saddam's huge national bureaucracy meant that any newly erected ministry beneath the CPA would likely be filled with incompetents who lacked even the most basic practical experience.

How Washington expected to keep Iraq secure and functioning after Saddam's defeat is still a mystery, and one that has never been publicly addressed. New York City, for example, has thirty thousand police officers to keep order among its eight million people. In Iraq under Saddam, the army had always been charged with keeping the peace. With Order 2, the army was disbanded. How did the CPA expect to fire Iraq's 300,000-man army—letting them keep their weapons, incidentally—while bringing in only 150,000 of our own troops to take military control and enforce security? The planners of postwar Iraq needed to look no further from our shores than Haiti to find a shining example of how out-of-work armies grasp for power in broken states. In Haiti, the former military has been the wellhead for a half dozen coups in the past two decades. To a majority of Iraq policy critics, disbanding the army is the single biggest mistake of the occupation.

There were other options. Why not employ a truth commission and try reintegration for nonoffenders? This would have kept the national payroll flowing, the governmental and social services helping those who needed it, and the militaristic quarters of society happy. Why not keep the army intact, except for high-level purges? International transitional justice over the past twenty years has had a number of precedents that could have offered practical guidance for the CPA: Poland, East Germany, Argentina, South Africa, Sierra Leone, and even Rwanda. All of these have dealt with fallen regimes in more modern and enlightened ways than the CPA did in Iraq. State deconstruction on the scale of Iraq has not been seen since postwar Germany, and due to economic crises there in the years after World War II, some ex-Nazis were eventually brought back into the system owing to their institutional memory. Washington and the Green Zone willfully shattered every aspect of Saddam's old Iraq, and in doing so created a monster.

After firing the army and all mid- to high-level Baathists in the government, the CPA also took control of all the ministries and their buildings and all assets and property "controlled by the Baath Party, its officials and members, and all residences occupied by officials and members" (Order 4).

As we've already said about the GZ, much of the CPA-confiscated land was the finest in Iraq. With the fall of Saddam, it was reoccupied by the CPA or Coalition military, and then turned into a fortress. To the average Iraqi, these actions were interpreted as one cruel regime replacing another.

Other Bremer Orders protected American political interests in the future Iraq. As we've seen, Orders 67–69 define a five-year term for the American-appointed (and non-Iraqi-elected) head of Iraqi Defense, Intelligence, and Foreign ministries. Inside these ministries, despite the alleged CPA oversight, the corruption of the old Iraq has been juiced up by the almost untraceable torrent of American taxpayer dollars flowing through the CPA. According to the *Washington Post* and the Government Accounting Office, Hazim al-Shaalan, Iraq's post-CPA-appointed defense minister, disappeared from Baghdad with roughly a billion American dollars sluiced from the new Iraq's coffers. The allegations describe a flight to Lebanon on which Shaalan was carrying $300 million in cash.

IN THE END, by completely obliterating Saddam's Iraqi state, Bremer and the CPA planted the seeds for the shattered, sectarian Iraq of today and the foreseeable future. By destroying even the functioning areas of the Iraqi government and deposing all those in power, the CPA created its own instant Sunni Arab opposition. Not only are the Sunnis the wealthiest of the Iraqis, they're also the country's best-educated population.

Instead of considering the religious and cultural dynamics of liberated Iraq, and working to avoid its further fracture while addressing the welfare of Iraq's people, the free-market-minded CPA, its leader Paul Bremer, and the unilateral enforcement of the one hundred Bremer Orders didn't simply encourage the new Iraq's splintering, they set it into motion.

22

·

Jeff's New Leg

I T WAS JUST PAST sunset on March 17, 2004, and Charlie and I were standing inside a pharmacy in Baghdad's middle-class Kerrada neighborhood, waiting for Jeff. As usual, we were gearing up for a party at the Hamra. Charlie's cell phone rang. It was Jeff. He was running late. When the pharmacist saw we weren't leaving, he began to try to sell us more drugs. He bent behind the counter, then lifted a huge carton of Viagra: "You'll get addicted to this, but—OK—I sell to you by the box. . . . You want some chai?" he continued. "Viagra? Kebab? What you want to buy? I get anything for you, misters."

Charlie and I spent a few more minutes joking with the pharmacist, but eventually we got fed up and decided to leave. Just as we reached the door, we felt a sudden pop in our ears—a quick pressure burst—immediately followed by an ear-splitting explosion.

A bomb had exploded nearby, closer than I'd ever experienced.

The explosion was followed instantly by the chime of splintering glass tinkling at the edges of the rumbling blast. We ran into the street. Sparks were spewing into the air and smoke was tumbling skyward. It was only a few blocks away. Iraqis were running toward the site. We followed. The only sounds were yelling Iraqis and glass from shattered windows crunching beneath hundreds of running shoes.

The explosion site was a wall of flames. An entire four-story hotel, the Mt. Lebanon, had its face ripped off and was burning. The street was totally dark, with only a thirty-foot ring of fire to illuminate a square block of total destruction. A man sat atop a pile of rubble, blood streaming from his head and blotching and running down his legs in streams, his pants shredded. The two houses that sat directly across the street from the Mt. Lebanon had been reduced to rubble. Cars up and down the street were burning and smashed and flipped.

We approached the crater. Frenzied Iraqis wept and yelled. Some of the older men started digging feverishly through piles of bricks and debris in search of survivors or casualties. Unfortunately, there was such poor lighting that the bricks and chunks of concrete they were throwing from the hotel rubble kept hitting bystanders, often women and children. The crowd was in the dozens and growing, many trying to help the effort, but a small number simply enraged.

About fifteen minutes after the blast, the 1st Armored Division arrived, teamed with a squadron of recently trained Iraqi Police (IP). A quarter hour earlier, this had been a typical commercial street in Baghdad, with cinder-block and plaster hotels, restaurants, shops, and apartment compounds. Then, in a split second, there had come fire, blood, screaming, and destruction. The 1st Armored Division soldiers rolled in with their guns up. They jumped out of the Hummers and APCs shouting in English: "Back the fuck up! Back the fuck up!" though the Iraqis didn't understand. Using the flashlights that clip to the barrels of their rifles, they were pointing their weapons at everyone, trying to illuminate people's faces.

The more they did in attempting to restore order and create a cordon around the bomb scene, the more the dozen or so U.S. soldiers and a roughly similar number of their IP colleagues lost control of the situation. Now there were hundreds of Iraqis in the streets. They were panicked and, with the arrival of the Americans with their guns and flashlights, becoming fiercely angry.

This was Kerrada, Baghdad's most cosmopolitan neighborhood—a place that had been touched little by terrorism to this point. And it was night. Suicide bombers rarely struck at night. All of this combined to make a hellish scene filled with angry civilians and confused soldiers.

An elderly Iraqi woman clawed and screamed at a young American soldier. With a baffled expression, the soldier kept yelling "Back the fuck up!" at her in English, a language the woman clearly didn't understand. Faced with such chaos, the soldiers were acting professionally. I saw Sanchez, a guy I knew from the 1st Armored security in front of the Sheraton, trying to act like the cool Miami kid he was. But the Iraqis were furious in a way I'd never seen them before, and there were no translators.

Just minutes after the Humvees arrived, the ambulances and Iraqi fire trucks began to pull up, too. These were shiny new Volvo fire trucks, bought with American tax dollars and manned by amateur, out-of-shape Iraqi firemen. They rushed toward the flaming panorama of carnage and destruction with hoses.

Charlie and I pushed a little closer. A sunken crater in the pavement was the eye of the firestorm. It was about five feet deep and ten wide. Soon the blue flak jackets of the Western broadcast media made their appearance just as the bright spotlights of CNN further lit the scene. Photographers climbed and scrambled over the rubble. Hamra regular Spencer Platt from Getty Images ended up with a front-page *New York Times* shot of a dazed Iraqi in front of the burning shell of a house.

An hour after the bombing, the area had become a circus, almost literally: The Clowns were there videotaping. Tension between the Iraqis and the soldiers continued to escalate. Face-to-face Arabic and English yelling matches were occurring all around the cordon, and the Iraqi Police, who couldn't speak English either, could do nothing to help. Up and down the cordon, the two sides were shouting— faces inches away from one another.

Then, as Charlie would later write on his blog, "The adrenaline wore off, I started to feel morbid, and when Ray suggested we split I agreed."

JEFF AND MAYA WERE on their version of a Baghdad date, eating at their favorite falafel stand next to Clowntown in Kerrada, when the Mt. Lebanon was hit by the car bomb. As they hurried to the scene on foot, TVs at outdoor cafés and in storefronts in Kerrada were already showing scenes from the hotel: flames pouring out of the remaining windows and panicking Iraqis moving around in a frenzy behind U.S. Army security cordons.

When Jeff and Maya arrived, the area had already been sealed off by soldiers from the 1st Armored Division, but Jeff flashed his CPA badge. They ran into Sam the Clown, who held a video camera. "You don't wanna go in there, mate," he said. "It's a bloody mess. And people are pissed off."

They continued, past the explosion crater and to the front of the now faceless, burning hotel. Maya and Jeff kept bumping into journalists they knew, like Jon Lee Anderson, who'd been inside his spare room at the Palestine Hotel just a few blocks away when the blast hit. He'd been knocked out of his chair by the explosion.

Jeff and Maya drifted toward a house whose owner, an Iraqi man, was standing on the roof, screaming and holding a huge piece of shredded sheet metal with both hands above his head, gesturing and bellowing angrily down at the crowd. A squad of 1st Armored Division soldiers showed up in front of his house and pulled the guy down. A minute later, they'd stuffed him into a Humvee.

Another Iraqi man in a flowing dishdasha came toward Jeff. In the dark, it took him a second to see the man was covered in blood. He handed Jeff a black plastic trash bag, yelling in a high-pitched, Arab-accented voice, "The meat! The meat!" Then the man handed Maya a torn and unraveled length of seatbelt. Taking a deep breath, Jeff grabbed the bag—which was really heavy—and looked at Maya, who returned his distressed expression.

Inside were the remains of a human thigh, blood-soaked and hairy. It was meat and hair and shattered bone, sitting in a pool of blood so deep it made the corners of the plastic bag stand out fully. A blinding glare hit Jeff holding his new leg. It was a spotlight from an Al Arabiya TV news crew. Jeff carefully laid the bag on the ground, spread open the top, and quietly walked away.

Farther down the road, a group of women was gathered in a pack. Maya started taking their picture, which really upset them. They chased after Jeff and Maya, throwing rocks and screaming in Arabic. After Jeff and Maya got around a corner and were able to lose the mob, they gathered their wits and decided to get out of there.

Jeff had a cell phone on him, and he finally got through to me and learned that Charlie and I had been the first Westerners on the scene. Maya and Jeff hopped into Letta Taylor's car, and with most of the

NPR house they headed to the hospital to scout for more photos of the bombing's aftermath.

At the hospital, nobody would let them in. Jeff flashed his CPA badge again, this time to no avail. In fact, it actually backfired. The guards at the hospital made him stand farther away than the journalists. They retreated to the Hamra.

23

•

It was March 23, and our Tuesday NGO meeting had been canceled for the third time in a month. First week there was a bomb threat. Second week: bomb threat. Third week: meeting. Fourth week: something called a "bomb catch." Just after lunch, while Jeff and I were waiting in line to re-enter the Convention Center, an explosion pounded the earth. Looking toward the Rasheed Gate, we spotted an automobile tire flying eighty feet into the air.

"Controlled explosion! *Yooo-weeee!*" yelled a soldier from the 82nd standing nearby.

Each time we'd faced a Tuesday bomb scare, Jeff and I asked Heather if she thought the insurgents were targeting our meeting. No, she said, it's just a coincidence.

Violent disruptions had compromised our work. The momentum we'd built up, and the Iraqi goodwill we'd cultivated, was being lost.

Because of the increased attacks and threats, the Rasheed Gate was now closed every couple of days due to security concerns. When that happened, the Iraqis we worked with couldn't enter the GZ, leaving Jeff and me with nothing to do.

At the sole Tuesday NGO meeting that did go off during March, we were informed by Heather that the meetings were slowly to be taken over and directed by the Iraq Reconstruction and Development Committee (IRDC). Led by Iraqi exiles—two Iraqi men, Kamal and Mr. Nouri, and a woman, Bushra—the IRDC was a Pentagon-supported program created at the war's outset. We applauded the change: The IRDC was a first step toward Iraqi self-governance.

During the meeting, Jeff announced that Hayder would be taking over HAND. In front of four hundred Iraqis sitting in a large auditorium, Hayder stood at a microphone and gave a quick speech, publicly associating himself with HAND.

THE INCREASED ATTACKS on the Green Zone made it difficult to go on aid runs, so Jeff and I repositioned our work. We focused on creating robust NGOs in the educational, medical, and environmental spheres. There was this one young Iraqi who believed in cleaning up the Tigris River at its run-down parks. Another group was working on a public arts council. A group of rich old men from Mansour, Baghdad's most affluent enclave, was setting up a national NGO conference.

MORE AND MORE, I was working by myself. Jeff had been spending most evenings and nights with Maya at Adam's house or at the Hamra, leaving me to my own devices, which usually meant solitude. Jensen the White Sheikh was still working Herculean hours around

Baghdad Central, but he was also in the process of moving from our hallway bunkhouse into a cushy CPA housing trailer outside the palace, deserting me to sleep in the hall alone.

Each night in late March, the palace was attacked from outside the GZ walls. The mortars weren't the problem; they were just a few loud booms and rarely struck anything. But I came to dread the rising wail of the palace air raid siren, since it signaled a mandatory visit to the palace bomb shelter—a trip I soon grew to hate. Climbing out of bed and shuffling down to the palace basement at 2:00 A.M. with a Valium hangover, looking like a bum in dirty clothes, I felt degraded and invisible at the same time. And being in this condition while the Bremer Youth chattered all around me, jacked up on caffeine and power, made the experience all the more horrible.

After a string of late-March nights alone in the palace, sleeping in a hallway, the Blackwater boys blasting their heavy metal, I realized I needed to get out. I didn't have enough work to do. The inequity of my life started eating at me and a mixture of guilt, anger, and depression began to take hold. I felt like an intruder at the palace. Sure, no one knew that I was the palace's official drifter cum squatter, but I sure did. Every day, I woke up not knowing if I was going to work or not, if Jeff would be around or not, if the Iraqis in the office could make it through the Rasheed Gate or not. I needed some air. I had to get away from Baghdad for a while.

FORTUNATELY, about then Jeff and I found an excuse to leave. A friend of ours, Eric "Rusty" Ferentz, a fellow Boston T-shirt entrepreneur, was coming to the Middle East. Rusty had been in Vietnam drunk-driving a motorcycle through the jungle for a few months and e-mailed to us that he was bored with Asia and Asians, who, he claimed, kept ripping him off. Jeff and I would take a break from Baghdad in the first week of April and go meet Rusty in Egypt for some R&R. We wanted to do some scuba diving in the Red Sea, gamble in Cairo, ride camels, check out El Alamein, tame the Nile . . . anything that took our minds off Iraq for a few weeks. Also, Egypt had commercial banks, so Jeff and I could access some cash and buy some clothes. I'd been reduced to buying a pair of Levi's "Cowboy Cut" that fit like sandpaper from the PX inside the Green Zone.

As I WAITED for my moment to jump to Cairo, Michael Cole kept me sane. Cole had a brain of his own and his company was both inspiring and calming. Among other things, he hated the Bremer Look, the khaki pants with desert combat boots, and he rebelled by wearing fine Gucci loafers everywhere in Iraq. Never in my life would I have expected to associate Gucci loafers with rebellion and individualism, but thanks to Cole, now I do. I now associate the Gucci loafer with those who dared question the pernicious CPA groupthink that had started sinking Iraq.

One night, bored with the palace, Cole and I walked over the 14th of July Bridge, the Green Zone checkpoint that led to Kerrada and Jadiriyah. The bridge, a green suspension span, was covered by a myriad of armed positions, including a Bradley fighting vehicle. On the bridge's far side, Baghdad teemed with people and cars. As we walked, I was reminded of an incident that had taken place on the bridge a week before.

"The other day Jeff and I were trying to drive through this very checkpoint with Inigo, and we got busted by the MPs for having bomb dust on us," I said. "Inigo's driver was this fucking maniac. We didn't trust him for shit. We thought we were going to Abu Ghraib.

The MPs had these three-hundred-thousand-dollar GE bomb-sniffing machines out, and we kept turning up positive for explosives. I thought the driver must have had guns hidden in the car or something."

"Really?"

"Yeah, we were held up for an hour. They tore the car apart and shut down all entrances to the GZ. Then, after a few more searches, a soldier said, 'Sorry. These machines keep fucking up. What a waste of three hundred g's.' And we just drove right in. I was ready to throw Inigo's driver off the bridge. He had all these fucked-up stories. He said he was a tank commander during the Iran war. He said: 'I shoot and the Iranians go flying in the air. They were stupid to run straight at tank. Like poof! I shoot them.' Then he'd start dying of laughter. Inigo was like, 'Uh, that's not funny. Killing people isn't funny.' But the driver thought killing Iranians was the funniest thing he'd ever done."

Cole and I kept walking, cruising along the Tigris riverbank. A decrepit playground led us to an outdoor diwan: an al fresco hookah den. There was a handful of people there, mostly old men in head-dresses, sitting and smoking, playing cards, and drinking tea. In the growing dark, it was peaceful. We sat and ordered a pipe with apple-flavored tobacco.

Cole had his own stories of Baghdad's madness. "The other day, I was jogging in the Green Zone along the Tigris, just down the river a little, and I got shot at," he told me. "I was running, and I heard this distant gunfire and thought: That's nothing unusual, this is Baghdad. Then I saw dust being kicked up all around me, and I realized *I* was getting shot at! I ran for cover. Shooting at me while on a run? How *uncivilized*!"

We both laughed. In Iraq, strange experiences could happen at any time, but in the last few weeks the velocity seemed to be really speeding up.

ONE NIGHT A WEEK or so before we were to go to Egypt, Jeff and I were sitting around the Baghdad Central office, doing e-mails and shooting the shit, when Morgan, the assistant to Baghdad Central's high official, Andy Morrison, stopped to chat.

Morgan was in his thirties, a clean-cut Beltway type who valued knowledge more than rank and honesty over politics. He started talking to us about the Foreign Service. He was telling us we should consider it as a career. "You guys are really good at this stuff," he said.

"I wish we could go into the Foreign Service," Jeff said. "But I've probably been arrested too many times for doing stupid things. We're both pretty screwed by that, I think."

Morgan chuckled and said that, well, being unable to join the Foreign Service might actually be a blessing, since, in his case anyway, being in Iraq was hard on his family. "But I guess that's part of the deal," he said. He shrugged.

After a few minutes, Morgan asked, "You guys are out there on the streets every day. You see more of Iraq than about anybody. What do you guys think is going to happen here?"

"Civil war," I said.

"Yup," Jeff agreed.

Morgan winced. "Me, too," he said.

24

.

Disco Inferno

A DAM LOVED POKER almost as much as we did, and since we'd come to know him, many of our conversations eventually gravitated toward our mutual affection for cards and gambling. We'd always talked a big game, as poker players usually do. You know: the countless Vegas trips, Paris and London poker tournaments, the casino gaming floors we liked best, which casino-hotels were the easiest touches for free comp rooms on cross-country gambling excursions.

One Thursday night, while we were all hanging out at the NPR house, Adam got a call from Karl Vick of the *Washington Post*, inviting him to a poker game at the *Post* suite in the Sheraton. He said sure, and asked both Karl and us if we might come along, too. Being dead-ass broke, Jeff and I had to turn it down, almost with tears in our eyes.

"I'll bankroll you pussies, come on!"

"Well, I guess, man. But, uh, you know, we don't know . . . we can't really do that, you're our friend." Even as we said this, we fully understood we'd be taking up Adam's offer.

"We're leaving in twenty minutes," Adam said, allowing no room for further refusals.

I was a little torn about it for another reason. Jeff was already sort of with Maya, but there happened to be a very cute girl named Alana at Adam and Jen's house, who was in Baghdad writing for *U.S. News and World Report.* Given the right amount of good pasta, Jordanian red wine, and funny conversation, she might have become sold on my charms. Instead, Adam and I hustled Alana and her translator into driving us to the Sheraton, which, she said, wasn't a problem since she was going to meet a friend at the Palestine Hotel anyway. We all packed into her tinted-out black BMW. Jen, Jack, and Christina were planning to meet up with us later at the Rasheed's "CPA Disco Night," where they had a friend from the British Embassy who was willing to sign them in.

We arrived at the *Post*'s suite at the Sheraton and were introduced to Sewell Chan, fresh from D.C. and on the first leg of a year-long assignment covering the fledgling Iraqi government. We also met Anthony Shadid, a reporter who in our book was right up there with John F. Burns of *The New York Times* for doing the best newspaper reporting in Iraq. A photographer for *Time,* Stefan, came in shortly after us, and soon the cards were dealt.

Jeff and I both made a little money, but soon enough the game became secondary to the conversation and hanging out. Shadid would regularly get calls on his cell phone, which he'd answer as he stood up from the game. Then he'd pace around the suite's buffet table, speaking in rapid-fire Arabic. The game would resume each time Shadid hung up. At one point Shadid said that this week things in Iraq had started feeling different and strange to him. He didn't think it was a positive sign. He said he'd even started to sense hostility when he'd go into the mosques.

About 10:00 P.M., Alana called to say she was coming by to pick us up. It was time to disco. To my dismay, an older, more experienced reporter had talked Alana out of going to the disco by saying, "Don't be stupid, this a war zone."

Inside the Rasheed's second-floor disco, we met up with most of the NPR house. Like any club, the CPA disco was loud, hot, and sweaty. We greeted friends from the Convention Center, Baghdad Central, the buffet, and the pool. Tensions were especially high this Thursday, largely due to the escalating violence just a few hundred yards away, over the blast walls and Hesco Barriers in the Red Zone.

It was also another typical Thursday in that every woman who entered the Rasheed was quickly eyed and accosted by a sea of horny men. The dance floor resembled a third-world cockfighting ring. Shoulder to shoulder, standing at the base of the slightly elevated dance floor, crews of guys decked out in new PX clothing panted and heaved like animals in heat. Many of the men were straitlaced CPA/State Department types, or off-duty soldiers enjoying some down time. But there was also a dark element that seeped into the party every week, private security contractors who tended to act as if they owned the place. Whenever there was a problem at the disco, you usually only had to look to the nearest mercenary steroid meatball in the room.

The major security firms, Blackwater USA, DynCorp, and Custer Battles, all had offices in the GZ. Those companies were divided along racial lines. The white guys were predominantly southern, products of NASCAR/NFL culture, and big into cowboy hats and ice-washed dungarees. On the opposite end were the black guys, who generally played up the "gangsta" vibe. Angry men on steroids, more men on steroids, booze, and a ridiculously high ratio of men to women are never a good mix in close quarters.

Upon arriving, we got the news that Heather, Dent, and Chaplain Vicciellio had been taken "off line," and were possibly facing an Article 32—or court-martial—for soliciting money, something soldiers are not allowed to do. The other week, in an article in *Stars and Stripes* about Operation Starfish, Dent had been talking about making donations of clothing and goods, and without even thinking about it, he'd suggested that anyone interested could also make a cash donation. Since Heather's APO address was listed as the contact for Starfish, she was implicated as well.

This put a damper on our evening. It was absurd: Starfish was solely concerned with giving humanitarian aid to children. In the midst of the biggest, most corrupt fire sale in history, the Army's most visibly humanitarian chaplain was going to be tried in a military court for soliciting humanitarian donations? With that news, neither Jeff nor I felt much like partying. And before we knew it, we were standing around the parking lot in front of the Rasheed. Jeff said he was going to ride back to the NPR house with everyone so he could see Maya. I was going to take the KBR shuttle to the palace, alone. So much for wine, women, and song.

As we stood out front chatting with Charlie, waiting for the stragglers to file out, a scuffle broke out between two groups of mercenaries, one of whom Charlie had just been sitting with inside. Punches flew, and before long both sides had drawn weapons. Then bursts of gunfire broke out—warning shots, more or less—that sent everyone diving for cover. Women in skirts and high heels were hugging the earth alongside neatly dressed Bremer Youth. Jeff and the NPR house crew were piled into Jack's driver's white station wagon, hunched over beneath the car's windows in search of cover. They sped off for the 14th of July Bridge exit.

On the way back to Adam and Jen's, Jeff spilled the news on the Article 32 charges to a car full of journalists hungry for stories about the absurdity of the CPA. As Jeff retired to a warm bed with a warm woman, I headed down to the late-night buffet in the palace, solo.

25

•

Hayder Gets a Visa

ONE AFTERNOON near the end of March, we got some great news. Hayder and his NGO, Friends of Sadr City (the rechristened Soccer Coaches), had been selected to be among the few dozen Iraqi humanitarian groups to attend an international aid conference in Beirut. The State Department's development arm, USAID, was funding the trip. USAID had asked Heather Coyne to get a list of Iraqi groups together for the conference, and she'd sent them to NGOAO and had tapped Jensen to coordinate everything. Jensen had wanted his favorite NGOs to go. Of course, Hayder and Friends of Sadr City made the list. For all Hayder's hard work—for his friendship and professionalism, for his outlook on life, for his dedication to his community—a working vacation to Lebanon seemed like a modest reward. Jeff and I worked to get Abed on the junket, too.

Hayder was shocked by the news. "How will I get there?"

"By airplane."

"I've never left Baghdad."

"Well then, get ready, Beirut is very different. It's called the Paris of the Middle East."

"Where will I stay? I have no money."

"Just the nicest hotel in town: the Movenpick," Jeff said. "And don't worry about money. It's all been paid for already. It's free."

"Yeah, tear up the minibar, the trip's on Bush," I added.

"Bar? I don't drink."

"There's other stuff in a hotel minibar. Cokes. Pretzels. Potato chips. All very expensive. So eat up."

A FEW DAYS LATER, Jeff met Hayder and Abed in front of the Convention Center and escorted them across the GZ to the palace, a place inside their own country that they, like most Iraqis, had never dreamed of being granted access to. As soon as they were inside, Hayder and Abed began to stare at the gaudy, opulent decorations, the blue tile walls and enormous arched doorways and multistory ceilings. The three of them climbed the palace's central stairway and walked down the hall to Baghdad Central, where I was waiting for them. "Baghdad province is run from this room," Jeff said.

Hayder stared around the office. "This place looks like it was built for giants," Hayder said. Tears welled up in his eyes. Having grown up in Sadr City's slums, Hayder was seeing Baath Party opulence for the first time, with its marble floors and gold-crusted lamps and fixtures. It was crushing. "Damn you, Saddam," he said. "Damn you."

We brought Hayder and Abed to the visa office, which was on the palace's second floor, just above Bremer's suite. We helped Hayder and Abed fill out the applications, and then sat outside the office for more than an hour, overlooked by the clerks inside, who were busy doing absolutely nothing. Jeff's and my tempers were rising when, as if like a genie, the Duke appeared.

"I've been searching for you guys," the Duke said as he walked up, smiling and sweating as usual.

"Duuuuuke!" Jeff and I both shouted.

"Hey, I got a badge." The Duke proudly flashed the coveted plastic card that dangled by a lanyard around his neck. Now he could bring his wheeling and dealing inside the Green Zone, where the real action was. It was a moment of triumph for him, and we basked in our friend's obvious happiness.

Hayder shook hands with the Duke, and the two immediately began exploring potential joint ventures. The Duke could make a deal with anyone. He was telling Hayder about an opportunity in Babil involving trash removal and scrap metal. Another fifteen minutes passed as we waited outside the visa office. Finally, after about ninety minutes of waiting, the visa clerks took Hayder's and Abed's applications and disappeared back behind their little partition.

Jeff had told Hayder and Abed to bring swimwear. Our afternoon's work done, we hit the pool. The Duke said he'd come along. The pool area was pretty much deserted. An Irish soldier lay passed out on a lawn chair, surrounded by a dozen empty beer cans. Jeff and I pointed out the changing rooms to Hayder and Abed, then pulled off our clothes, climbed the high-dive tower, and jumped into the pool. When we surfaced, Hayder and Abed were still standing there.

"Hayder! Abed!" I shouted. "Go change into your swimming stuff!"

They remained standing there, staring at the pool complex.

Sensing swimming was not going to be the afternoon's activity, we climbed out of the pool, dripped dry, and chatted with the Duke.

"You guys should come with me to the CNN Orgy Room tonight," the Duke said. "It'll be a good time."

"What orgy room?"

"Room 1136 at the Palestine."

"But CNN is at the Sheraton," Jeff said.

"That's precisely the point."

"What?" I asked.

"It's an orgy room, at the Palestine. Room 1136."

"Who told you about this?"

"A Romanian senator. He said it was surreal."

"OK," Jeff said. "I'm picturing Anderson Cooper surrounded by 360-degree mirrors with an Iraqi hooker dancing a jig on his testes with high heels. Or Wolf Blitzer under a haze of *sheesha* smoke in bed with two billy goats, a tub of Vaseline, and an empty bottle of Scotch as a naked Iraqi boy at his bedside feeds him olives."

"Stop, stop . . ." the Duke said. "Those images are hurting my libido."

Once more, we tried to cajole Hayder into changing for a swim.

"I don't know," Hayder said. He glanced over toward a black American woman who ran the pool for KBR. Arab men are very sensitive about showing skin, especially in public—and even more so in front of women. We understood. Hayder and Abed weren't in the mood to violate cultural customs, so we left, leading Hayder, Abed, and the Duke past Lord Bremer's chamber on our way out to the palace's front steps, where we commemorated the visit with a photo.

A few days later Hayder and Abed both got their visas, but due to space restrictions, we were informed by Jensen, only Hayder would be going to Beirut.

26

·

O N THE MORNING of Saturday, March 27, Jeff and I awoke at the
NPR house with searing hangovers from a night of booze and
pills. As I remembered it, it had been quite an evening. It had ended
for me when I'd gone outside to throw up on Adam and Jen's lawn,
then fallen asleep on the metal two-person swing, the one I was still
lying on as the sun slowly warmed me and drove what felt like a hardened shard of its pale light deep into my brain.

The night before had been spent in Baghdad's best Chinese
restaurant, eating, drinking, and attempting Team Karaoke. No matter
where you go on earth, the Chinese are already there and working. In
Baghdad, they were succeeding gloriously—too well, in fact. In a few
days, the restaurant we'd visited would get the ultimate stamp of
business success in Iraq: Insurgents would threaten to bomb them
for serving the occupying infidels.

Jeff joined me outside. As we were laughing about the night before, Willis Witter, a reporter from the *Washington Times,* strolled out onto the porch, dressed in only a T-shirt and boxer shorts. "Hey," Willis said, "what do you guys know about this court-martial for Dent?" Willis had heard about the court-martial, and he found it offensive, especially after Dent had done so many things to try to help the Iraqis. We agreed that court-martialing a guy for trying to help war-affected children was absurd, but we'd also sworn to protect Dent, and our great concern was that if the story about all he'd done got out— about the way he'd made Starfish succeed by soliciting help from churches in Iraq and beyond—then he might get slapped with even harsher charges. We worried that this would then trickle down to Vicciellio, and then to Heather, too.

Willis didn't care about that, he said. He felt the Starfish story got at all that was misguided with the Army's management of Iraq, and he was intent upon printing it, no matter what. Within minutes, the three of us were yelling at each other about the rights to a free and honest press versus a reporter who, by not considering the consequences of his reporting, does pointless extra damage to people who don't deserve it. We told Willis we'd been talking to him as a friend, not as a journalist, and now he'd crossed the line and was selling us out. Our argument reached a boil, and Willis shouted, "Fucking kill me, then. This is my job! So if you want to stop me, go ahead and fucking kill me! Go ahead! Kill me!"

Clearly, everyone was under a little stress. Cue our exit: Jeff and I were angry, but we weren't about to kill anybody.

We left Adam's house on foot and went straight to work. As soon as we were inside the Convention Center, the first people we saw were Hayder and Abed, sitting in the orange leather chairs outside the Iraqi

Assistance Center. Hayder could tell we were upset, so we told him why. After we had recounted the story of Willis, the *Washington Times* article, Dent, and the damage being done by Article 32—leaving out the part about Willis and his death wish—Hayder thought for a minute. "Do you want me to kill this man?" he asked.

"That's funny," Jeff said. "The last thing Willis said to us before we stormed off was that we should kill him."

"Well, I will kill him . . . though I like Willis."

"We don't want to kill anyone. We don't want you to kill anyone. We like Willis, too."

"Oh, OK then," Hayder said. Hayder was playing with the line between dark humor and Iraq's deadly seriousness. I went to the bathroom to wash up. When I came back Hayder was in the middle of a detailed explanation of Shi'ite tribal justice. "Suppose my cousin hurt a person from another tribe. Both tribes sit down together and negotiate. They say: 'We want you to kill your cousin.' Then my tribe will talk about it for some time among ourselves, like we're really thinking about that, weighing it . . . but not."

"A delay tactic?"

"Yes. Then we go back to them and say: 'Killing is too much, don't you think? But we will offer you ten goats in exchange for his life.' Then they go back and pretend to think and say: 'No, that is not enough. We want one hundred goats.' And we go off, talk among ourselves, as if we are truly considering that, and we return and say: 'One hundred goats? But that is too many, don't you think?' But now we are negotiating, and we are off of the discussion of killing the cousin and onto the subject of money for what happened, which keeps my cousin alive. It goes like this until both tribes agree on the payment, usually money." Hayder kept going, telling us of different scenarios and resolutions, with some real life examples: accidents hurting innocents and the like.

"You two, Jeff and Ray, are now in my tribe," Hayder said. "You are the same as my brothers."

"Great," I said. "I always wanted to be part of a tribe. And especially after what you just said about tribal justice. It makes even the Mafia seem overrated." We moved into the NGO Assistance Office to begin a day of work with our fellow tribesmen.

LATER THAT DAY, after the morning's paperwork got finished, Jeff met Maya upstairs in the Convention Center, over by the press center. She was in tears about the Willis fight. Jeff tried to comfort her by saying we really weren't mad at Willis, that we understood his position and had overreacted.

LATER ON THE AFTERNOON of the twenty-seventh Jeff and I met Dent poolside at the palace. He pulled up a chair next to ours and immediately lit a cigarette. He looked like he was about to cry. He was shocked that the Army was punishing him for trying to help innocent children affected by the war. All he wanted to do now, he told us again and again, was go home to his tribe's Indian reservation in Arkansas. Instead, he was probably going to lose rank, and might even face a dishonorable discharge—which meant that, beyond disgracing his tribe and upsetting his mother, he also wouldn't get his pension.

"Speaking of tribes," I said, "Jeff and I joined a Shia tribe from Sadr City this morning. Doesn't sound as appealing as the Arkansas reservation, though."

"Umm," Dent grunted and stared into the distance. Dent reminded us of a tragic Beetle Bailey. He was such a funny, nice guy, trying to help people, and now he was being crushed by the Army for doing work that exceeded the call of duty. We could tell the experience was snuffing the lightheartedness out of him.

We didn't feel like swimming, and we didn't feel like talking to Dent anymore. We weren't interested in seeing anyone or socializing with anyone.

THE FOLLOWING MORNING, Sunday, March 28, I was in the NGOAO using the computer when Lieutenant Colonel Weaver walked in and informed me that we couldn't use our computers anymore, that the office was going all-Iraqi. He had some lame excuse about how the office space and everything contained in it was now under a different acronym, and how, with a whole new Army Public Affairs command rotating in from the States, the structure of everything in Iraqi affairs was going to be redone.

"What? We haven't been told anything about this. It's bullshit!"

As he always did, Weaver slipped into his passive-aggressive tone as a way of fending me off. He was pretty good at it, having been a stress counselor before his deployment. "It's a done deal," he said, waving his hands. "Not my decision." Weaver was already backing away from my office. "No more computers," he said. "NGOAO is officially closed." With that, the NGO Assistance Office was no more.

So now the CPA was seeing a midcourse structural change due to military tours of duty? Wouldn't it have made more sense to change course based on Iraq's on-the-ground reality? Instead, the occupation was changed to fit a new troop rotation, wasting much of our work as well as some of the previous military administration's progress.

An hour later, I found Jeff sitting behind a computer in the Baghdad Central office. "Weaver kicked us out of the Convention Center," I said.

"What did he say?"

"That we weren't allowed to use the computers in the office anymore. That NGOAO is all moving under some new acronym. HAND is still our program no matter what that asshole says, and we still have all our other capacity building meetings. We just don't have desks. The Army's making some great moves this week, kicking us out and giving an Article 32 to Dent."

"That's nothing. The CPA shut down Moqtada Al Sadr's newspaper today."

Since nearly the beginning of the occupation, Sadr had been outspokenly and aggressively anti-American. He'd said over and over that the American assault and occupation of Iraq was about two things: an anti-Islamic crusade and the American thirst for oil. In recent months, almost in lockstep with the rise of insurgent violence across Iraq, Sadr had been making very public calls for jihad against Iraq's occupiers. He was on the news every night, his fist pumping, his body language aggressive, his speeches an angry flood of words whose underlying passion you didn't need to speak Arabic to comprehend. Lately, Sadr's paper, *Al Hawza,* was calling for an Iraqi arm of the fundamentalist Arab/anti-Israeli political party Hezbollah, much to the chagrin of Israel and all the pro-Israel hawks in Washington. Rumor had it the order to shut down Sadr's paper came from Washington by way of Tel Aviv. True or not, the Americans had set into motion a very high-stakes chess game with Sadr.

. . .

MARCH 29 WAS the day Hayder was to leave for Lebanon, so in the early afternoon, Jeff and I were at the Palestine Hotel, where the Beirut delegation was meeting before heading to the airport. Hayder was vibrating with nervous excitement. Everybody from Hayder's circle in Sadr City was along with him. Abed was carrying a soccer bag full of Hayder's clothes. Turtleneck, from my first Sadr City trip, was there, too.

We greeted everybody, then took Hayder aside for a minute.

"Don't forget, milk the room service at the Movenpick," I said. "Charge everything to USAID."

"And really, Hayder," Jeff said, "if you don't want to come back, you don't have to. Stay there, if you want."

As Iraq was imploding, Jeff and I had been talking about getting Hayder out of the country for good. We'd always told him he could live with us in New York if he ever got to the United States. Since we'd met him, Hayder had been telling us he wanted to see an action movie in a movie theater, "American style." We wanted him to know his options. Jeff kept saying, "Really, if you like Beirut, stay there."

He laughed us off. "Of course I must come back," he said. "This is the place of my family. This is my home."

Then the bus arrived, and all the NGO representatives slipped inside to board and leave for the airport. We said farewell and said we'd see him when he got back.

WILLIS'S ARTICLE appeared in the *Washington Times* that same day. When we got back to the Green Zone, we got the text of it via the

DoD's *Early Bird Wire,* courtesy of Lieutenant Colonel Weaver, of all people. Willis's article detailed the trip we took with him and Maya to Armless Sheikh's "Polio" Clinic, then touched on Dent's trouble without compromising too much:

> *The center was founded by Aziz Hashim Al Ndawy, a veteran of the Iran-Iraq War of the 1980s, who lost both arms but managed to hang onto his bullet-scarred legs.*
>
> *There are 1,500 children in the neighborhood, about 400 of whom are crippled from polio—a disease eradicated so long ago in the West that only senior citizens can remember its devastating impact on their parents' generation.*
>
> *"All these people need help, tools like wheelchairs. Wheelchairs are the most important," Mr. Al Ndawy said.*
>
> *Mr. Neumann and Mr. LeMoine returned to their home near the convention center at the end of a long day only to find that legal problems threaten to cut off the steady supply of used items from the United States.*
>
> *Appeals for goods had gone out under the name of Operation Starfish, a makeshift charity started by Air Force chaplain Fred Vicciellio and his aide, Technical Sgt. Van Dent, both of whom are due to return to the United States shortly.*
>
> *But it is against military regulations for active-duty soldiers to solicit charitable contributions. It is also questionable whether the military aircraft that*

deliver mail and packages to war zones can be used
for this type of operation.

 Army Lt. A. Heather Coyne, who is in charge of
the American-led coalition's resources center for Iraqi
charities, or nongovernmental organizations (NGOs),
says U.S. officials are just trying to make sure there is
no appearance of impropriety.

 "They're trying to dot the i's and cross the t's and
trying to make sure that there is a way of putting out
this information that isn't misusing government prop-
erty," Lt. Coyne said. "I'll still be here and we will make
sure that it gets to the right Iraqi NGOs."

"Could've been worse," Jeff said.

"Yeah, and the funny thing is, I still don't know whether Armless's clinic really has any cases of polio."

"After today, the way things are going, we may never find out. Guess it's time to e-mail Willis an apology."

THAT NIGHT, Jeff and I walked across the 14th of July Bridge. We were headed to the Hamra to bury the hatchet with Willis. He e-mailed us that NBC was throwing a big party there. We were about half-way across the bridge when, from the far side of the river, we heard three thud-ish pops. Three mortar shells soared over the Tigris, and then one, two, pause, three booms in the Green Zone. A flash illuminated the trees behind the palace. A fireball stung the sky to about twenty feet above the tree line.

"Wow, one actually hit something," Jeff said.

At the foot of the bridge, I took Jeff toward the outdoor diwan I'd found with Cole. Jeff was really into the place: With its bamboo walls and wicker benches, it looked totally Tiki Bar–ish, Jeff said. He was a devotee of Tiki Bar style, having honed his taste in Fiji. We got two pipes and two chai teas, and sat quietly under the evening sky.

"The war is seeping over the GZ's walls," Jeff said.

"What do you mean, seeping? It's seeped, man. Staying out at the NPR house, you've been missing most of the action. Every night the air-raid siren goes off."

"I know. So what's the dumbest possible thing we could be doing right now? Oh, yeah, walking at night through Baghdad." With that, we took our last pulls from the *sheesha* and headed off on foot for the Hamra, still about a mile away.

We paid and had made it to the next traffic circle, right where you turn to head to the Hamra, when we saw a huge crowd of chanting, picket-sign-toting young Iraqi males with trucks behind them. They were faced off with two Bradleys and troops from the 1st Armored Division. I stopped to buy a bottle of water from a street vendor so we had a reason to watch the action unfold. Jeff sat on the curb and watched the protesters. A scruffy young Iraqi from the crowd pointed at us, then drew his index finger across his neck, mock-slitting our throats. Jeff and the guy were locked in each other's gaze. I was watching and trying to chat up the vendor.

"We gotta get the fuck outta here," Jeff said, under his breath, his lips barely moving.

These were Moqtada Al Sadr's people, the Mahdi Militia, and they were out in force to protest the closing of Sadr's paper. Though there were only a few hundred of them, judging from the amount of U.S. armor present, things were serious. We kept on toward the Hamra in the opposite direction, not wanting to tempt the throat-cutter.

It was full night now. Baghdad was still dark and unelectrified. Jeff said he knew a shortcut down a back alley, where a trash fire burned six feet high and wild dogs hung in the shadows. The guards at the NPR house had demanded that Jeff and Maya be married if he was going to stay over, and with security deteriorating, that had been the last push for Maya to leave Adam and Jen's; she wanted a place with blast walls and full-time guards. She and Willis had just taken up a two-bedroom suite at the Hamra.

THE HAMRA'S RELAXED, carefree atmosphere was gone. Small huddles of reporters, photographers, translators, and aid workers crowded the pool patio and restaurant. Everyone seemed to be talking about the downward spiral of life in Baghdad. We'd even heard rumors that the NPR house was going to be disbanded over security concerns.

We sat poolside for a while, then we headed upstairs to the NBC bureau's rooftop suite. A buffet was spread, alcohol was flowing, the outdoor terrace was spacious and clean. Ah, network life in a war zone. NBC war correspondent Richard Engel's fist was in the refrigerator reaching for another cold one. We awkwardly stood around waiting for someone we knew to arrive.

Willis showed up, and we quickly made up. After a few minutes of I love you man's, the three of us settled into some beers before Willis called it a night and headed back down to his room. Slowly the suite began to fill as the Hamra regulars arrived. NBC's opulence made us palace squatters jealous.

A photographer we knew had recently bought a pound of hash

off a guy he met on the Internet. He asked if we wanted to partake of the sacred seed. A few friends joined us on a couch at the NBC suite. Through the haze of smoke, an older guy with a white beard approached. Under the circumstances, he looked rather wizardly, until he opened his mouth.

"You need to stop smoking that," he said.

"Why?"

"I'm a producer for NBC. We're a responsible network. You need to stop smoking that." Then he walked off. His overstuffed fanny pack had a walkie-talkie and a pack of cigarettes sticking out of it, emphasizing his tubby ass. He reminded us more of a KBR bus driver than a responsible pillar of American journalism.

"That guy looked like a fat Gandalf."

"Gandalf smokes weed, right?"

"Just in the movies, I guess. Let's get out of here."

THE MORE WE THOUGHT about it, the snarkier that interchange with the "responsible" news producer made us. NBC is a "responsible" network. Responsible to whom? To their viewers, or to their parent company, General Electric, the world's most profitable corporation?

We were actually glad to get booted from the "party" full of network stiffs, and we stumbled down to Willis's room. He let us crash for the night.

AT THE MOMENT, getting kicked out of a party for smoking hash was the least of our problems in Baghdad. The Army had taken away our

Convention Center offices and had closed one of our distribution programs in Operation Starfish. Insecurity had made the Rasheed Gate a daily lottery: You never knew when it was going to be open or shut. But what did we know? We were just two angry palace squatters who were about to be out of a job.

27

·

Wake Up

LATE AT NIGHT, on March 30, Jeff was in his hallway bunk outside Baghdad Central when Jensen and Kamal, from IRDC, began shaking him awake.

"Hey, man, wake up. You need to get up, this is really, really important," Jensen said.

"Huh? OK, Sarge, whatever you say."

"Look, there are some really bad guys following you and Ray around. We've had people tailing them for a while, and they've gotten into the Tuesday meetings."

"What? Who?"

Jensen and Kamal led Jeff to the long conference table set up in the middle of the Baghdad Central office, where they pulled out a chart of terrorist cells and their links to various attacks across Baghdad in the past few months. Kamal and the others from IRDC knew some of these people, and had pointed them out to military intelligence in our meetings.

"Was Red Eyes involved?" Jeff asked. "I know he's got some shady Baathist ties."

"No, man, they're bigger than that guy," Jensen said. "These guys are after you, they're the real deal. This is serious shit. Serious. They want to kill you guys."

"Why?"

"We're not sure. But, trust me, their intentions are to kill you guys." He said that whoever these guys were, they were the people responsible for the bomb scares and the "bomb catch." He said we needed to leave Iraq—immediately.

ON MARCH 31, we showed up at NGOAO to find that Lieutenant Colonel Weaver had even revoked our desks. They'd been given over to some Iraqis who, between instant messages and cigarette or tea breaks, were using our computers to translate the CPA website into Arabic. While that sounded like a good idea for the Iraqi Assistance Center, it was a very bad sign for us. Trying to regroup, we hit our smoke shop for an hour before deciding to return to the Convention Center, enlist any help we could find, and begin retaking HAND and the NGOAO.

As we walked back toward the GZ, we passed a small demonstration in front of the Rasheed Gate. It was some followers of Sadr, again protesting the closure of Sadr's *Al Hawza* newspaper two days earlier. Calling this a demonstration might be a stretch, since there were as many photographers and journalists as there were angry Shi'ites from Sadr City. But it turned out the big news from Iraq that day hadn't happened in Baghdad. As the day progressed, we began to hear bits about something bad going down in Fallujah.

Details started to trickle out of Fallujah that somehow Americans were involved, and had been killed. An hour after that, inside the CPA, the rumor was that there were four victims: American contractors from Blackwater USA, who'd been there providing security for a convoy delivering food and humanitarian aid to the city.

"Why the fuck would those Blackwater guys be guarding aid? They just drive around and shoot people."

"I don't know, sounds like convenient bullshit to me."

Then came the televised images: Two of the dead American contractors, stripped and charred in street fires, were now hanging from the bridge spanning the Euphrates. The official line from the CPA held that the heavily armed contractors were only providing security for a humanitarian mission. Word around the CPA and the military was that the mercenaries were looking for a fight.

THINGS WEREN'T HOLDING TOGETHER. We still had HAND, our aid program, but we had no desks to run it from. People were getting paranoid, us included, and rightfully so considering what we had just been informed of—our impending deaths.

And we weren't alone in feeling that Baghdad's Romantic Age was fading into memory. It was official: The NPR house was being disbanded for security reasons. Almost everyone was already living at either the Hamra, the Palestine, or the Sheraton, behind blast walls and armed guards. Maya was embedded with an Army unit up in Mosul around this time. Willis dressed up as an Iraqi woman, complete with an abaya, and snuck into Fallujah past the Marine security cordons.

Inside the GZ, the situation was the same as on the outside: bad getting worse. Leah Cato was now cut off from the DACs and NACs in Sadr City, and had little, if any, contact with her colleagues there. Cole was still able to work with his groups, but access was limited. Jensen was still jumping through hoops, but he was finding it harder and harder to deal with both the restrictions of the Army and the needs of the Iraqis. Heather was facing setback after setback, but somehow continued getting things done. Despite the stress of a possible Article 32 court-martial for the Starfish/*Stars and Stripes* debacle, and growing resentment from Civil Affairs brass, she remained resourceful and resilient.

Our trip to Egypt couldn't come soon enough.

THE NEXT MORNING, we reserved seats in an SUV convoy leaving Baghdad for Amman in a few days. That afternoon, we went to the Convention Center to tie up loose ends. Upon arrival, we saw a group of Hamra photographers smoking cigarettes outside. One asked, "You guys here for the protest, too?"

"What protest?"

"Crooked-tooth Sadr is supposedly having another one, after his failed attempt yesterday. Who knows? It's at 5:00 P.M. and they're coming by the busload."

"Yesterday, there were more reporters than protesters. We'll see."

FLOUTING WEAVER'S "ORDERS," we went to our office and commandeered our computers. Because of the scheduled Sadr demonstration, all the Iraqis had gone home and the Convention Center was empty.

A few hours later, Ski popped into our office. "Go outside."

"Why?"

"Just go outside and listen."

Ski, Jeff, and I walked out the front of the Convention Center to the roar of thousands. We couldn't see the protesters, but their chanting was deafening. We walked out the Rasheed Gate and soon were confronted by a sea of black-clad men waving red, green, and black flags, thousands strong. A bullhorn led the chanters.

Jeff and I waded into the crowd while Ski, in his uniform, stuck behind some Hesco Barriers. A Mahdi Militiaman patted us down. We walked about fifty feet before we were surrounded by a group of boys, mostly in black, some with green headbands. The boys started shoving Jeff and flashing knives. A sheikh hurried over and wrapped us in his robe, then scuttled us to safety. But the boys followed and began swinging at us, forcing us to flee toward the checkpoint.

Ski was taking photos of the whole scene. "You guys aren't dead yet. Good," he said. We watched the demonstration for a while longer. I climbed a pole to get a better view.

"Jesus, there must be ten thousand people here."

HOURS LATER, back at the palace, we could still hear the protesters. We were hanging out in the Baghdad Central office, talking about the convoy we had booked to Amman. We mentioned this to Andy Morrison.

"You guys are leaving *by convoy* to Amman?" he asked.

"Yeah, we're going in a couple of days. It's actually pretty cheap, too."

"Oh, no, no, guys," he said. "That's stupid. That's really, really stupid. Come on, I'll show you why." Morrison walked us over to a huge map on the wall, and with the precision of a seasoned strategist briefed with the latest intelligence he pointed at Highway 10. With the protesters' stadium-sounding roar in the background, Morrison spoke. "You'll have to drive right through Fallujah and the heart of Anbar province to get to Jordan. And to show you why that's not a good idea, all you need to do is look over at that TV screen."

We turned around and watched a CNN replay of the burned corpses hanging from the bridge in Fallujah.

It was approaching 8:00 P.M. and Sadr's protesters were still chanting nonstop. "I can't believe they're still out there," I said.

"If we don't watch it, they'll come right over these walls," Morrison said. "With Sadr and Shi'ites, we have to play our hand right. Otherwise it'll be choppers on the roof, á la Saigon."

Out of everyone we knew in Baghdad, we trusted Andy Morrison's judgment and local knowledge the most. Highway 10, our original route into Iraq, had now become, if not technically impassable, at the least a very poor travel option. Then Andy lectured us for a while on the complicated mix of tribes throughout Iraq and their complex sets of alliances and disagreements under different conditions as it all related to why a convoy of Westerners traveling through this region might be a really, really, truly bad thing. Then he made a quick phone call and within the hour had one thousand dollars in cash delivered to him by a colleague. He loaned us six hundred dollars (since one-way flights out of Baghdad cost $250 with the CPA discount), and he wouldn't let us refuse the loan.

The next morning, we went back over to the Convention Center, and at the Royal Jordanian Desk there secured open seats on the next flight out of Baghdad: Sunday, April 4. With six hundred dollars from Andy Morrison, we were leaving Iraq.

On one of our last nights before flying out, we had dinner with

Charlie at Fanar Chicken. He'd spent the last part of March away on embed trips around the country. When he was in town, we'd glimpse him in the Convention Center talking to military officers and sheikhs, running down facts for his stories. He was now working for Cox newspapers, and would soon make the leap to freelancing with *USA Today* and *Time*.

He was just back from Fallujah and we were eager to hear about it. The more Iraqis he interviewed, he told us, the more he grew convinced the CPA's disregard for everyday Iraqis, coupled with the institutionalized looting of their country by American interests, had destroyed any trust Iraqis had for their occupiers.

He'd been in Fallujah when the burned bodies of the Blackwater USA contractors had been strung from the Euphrates bridge. We asked him what he thought came next. He just shook his head, his mouth opening and closing silently several times before he could speak. "You guys," he finally said, "I think this whole thing is about to blow apart."

28

·

Black Sunday

AH, FREEDOM. On Sunday, April 4, we would finally get away from Baghdad for a few weeks' vacation with Rusty in Egypt. We were looking forward to something resembling normal life, with access to ATM machines and cash, a few good meals, the chance to meet some easygoing backpacker girls, and an opportunity to sleep through the night without the crash of incoming mortar rounds and the wail of the air-raid siren.

The morning of the fourth was chaotic. The Rasheed Gate was still surrounded by a few thousand Shi'ite protesters. We left most of our things in Andy Morrison's office bathroom, which he offered as a storage area until we returned. We left with only daypacks, sleeping bags, and one change of clothes. Because of all the chaos around the Rasheed Gate, we missed the BIAP shuttle that left from the Wolfpack Staging Area, so we hopped on the KBR shuttle to the Convention Center to catch a cab on the street. In the recent command change, the 82nd Airborne had left, and the Rasheed Gate was now being guarded by the 1st Armored Division, which had taken up positions behind the Hesco Barriers on the street to keep the protesters in check.

We walked past the soldiers and into the crowd, where we were instantly overtaken by a very uneasy feeling. Luckily, there was a taxi just past the razor wire, and we jumped in and headed off to BIAP. Later we would learn that by avoiding Highway 10, the road our bus had taken into Iraq three months earlier, we were now traveling on the Airport Road, the thoroughfare that had replaced Highway 10 with the dubious honor of Most Dangerous Road on Earth.

We got to BIAP just in time—or so we thought—for our 11:00 A.M. flight to Amman on Royal Jordanian. But when we got inside the terminal, we found out the flight wouldn't leave for another two hours. The airline did this to thwart attempts by insurgents at shooting down the plane, since knowing the exact departure time would have made their work much easier. The nearly abandoned terminal had an all-too-familiar dictator-chic vibe, seventies disco-infected monomaniacal totalitarian spaces in desert green, Saddam's favorite color.

Also waiting for the flight were a bunch of contractors, most of whom didn't seem at all bothered by the thought of departing Iraq by air. Just as we lay down on the gray padded benches in the waiting area, a set of explosions jarred us. Mortar shells rained closer and closer toward us along the tarmac, sending debris tumbling across the terminal's metal roof and making a clattering sound.

A couple of the contractors mumbled "controlled explosion" to each other, a term used liberally by the CPA and military to describe what was usually an attack. Despite the fact that we were in a glass-walled building, most people paid little attention to the blasts and went back to stretching out on the couches, which were actually pretty comfortable. After a few jumpy minutes, we were also able to relax and stretch out again, though Jeff and I listened closely for any new sounds from beyond the building.

Our plane's departure was announced, setting off what was more a sprint than an orderly embarkation. We were hustled aboard, and in minutes the jet was pushed back and was making its takeoff run down the tarmac. Just after leaving the ground, the plane went into a spiraling corkscrew until we reached safe altitude above ten thousand feet, the maximum height a surface-to-air missile can reach.

Then we peeled in a westward direction and headed for the safety of Jordan. Below us, two green lines—the Tigris and Euphrates rivers—cut through the pale, brownish-gray landscape of Anbar province. The place looked desolate. We couldn't know that down below, in just the brief time since we'd left the Green Zone, a two-front uprising had exploded. It had started in Fallujah, the cultural heart of Sunni Anbar, then had gone up with equal violence in the once peaceful Shi'ite slum of Sadr City. On the ground in Iraq on April 4—a day the 1st Armored Cavalry would come to call Black Sunday—all hell was breaking loose.

In Sadr City, a 1st Armored Cavalry patrol would be ambushed by heavily armed members of the Mahdi Militia. First Armored Cavalry soldiers described gunmen on rooftops laying down intense small-arms fire, accompanied by RPGs and rockets, assaults that effectively pinned the Americans down behind their vehicles and whatever cover they could find. By dawn the next day, eight U.S. soldiers were dead, and an estimated fifty more were wounded. One can only guess the number of Mahdi Militia casualties. Among the American dead was Army Specialist Casey Sheehan, a twenty-four-year-old from California whose mother would go on to become one of the Iraq War's—and President Bush's—most public critics.

For the rest of the spring and summer, the United States led an air campaign over Sadr City. It is impossible to bomb with precision a place as densely populated as Sadr City. Whenever I read about such airstrikes, all I could think about were the hundreds of children who swarmed every block of the Shia slum.

But if Sadr City was bad, Fallujah was worse: The 1st Marines had been ordered to pacify the city. Anywhere the Marines tried to enter the city, roads and alleyways blew up or erupted in fusillades of rocket and missile fire followed by machine-gun probes from somewhere inside. The city was an angry arsenal that had been gearing up for months in preparation for an American assault. The fighting wouldn't stop for three more weeks. It would prove to be the nastiest urban combat American troops have faced since the Marines at Hue City in 1968.

But we were now on our way to Amman, blissfully unaware of all that was happening on the ground below. As fate would have it, we'd left Iraq on the day the CPA's tenuous peace collapsed.

JEFF, RAY, AND HAYDER ON A HUMANITARIAN-AID RUN IN SADR CITY

(*Photo by Maya Alleruzzo*)

BOOK★FOUR

Space and Time

29

.

Road Beef

WHEN WE GOT OFF the plane, early in the afternoon on April 4, we headed by cab to central Amman and checked into the Cliff Hotel, the same run-down hole that Jeff and I had stayed at several times before. That night we slept on the roof of the hotel, where several foam mattresses were spread out under a bedouin-style tent. We'd been watching BBC World in the hotel's dingy lobby lounge, and had seen other news on the Internet, and couldn't believe how fast Fallujah and Sadr City had burst into flame. Much as we felt for the people there, our friends, it was something of a relief to be out of Baghdad now, sleeping under the stars in Amman. Neither of us got much sleep though. Then we both woke up at the crack of dawn to the scratchy, blaring calls to prayer from several nearby mosques.

Our first order of business in Amman was to get the hell out of Amman. We took a bus to Petra, the ancient city carved into rose-stone cliffs in south central Jordan. Petra is quite possibly the most overrated tourist attraction in the Middle East, but we wanted to see it. The bus ride to Petra took about five hours, then we walked through the site in thirty minutes and left. It held about as much exotic charm as Euro Disney. The next morning we got on another minibus, this time to the southern port city of Aqaba, where we planned to take a ferry down the Sinai Peninsula in Egypt to meet Rusty in Dahab. But while in Aqaba, we hit a little snag.

After checking into the eight-dollar-a-night Flower Hotel, where we'd stayed back in January on our way to Wadi Rum, we headed out on the street for some food. It was lunchtime. Across the road from the hotel we stopped at a bookshop that had a newspaper rack out front stuffed with all the major English-language papers. I took one off the rack and read the headlines. The angry shop owner came blowing outside through the store's open door.

"You picked up that newspaper, you will buy that newspaper!" the shopkeeper shouted.

"No, I won't. Is there a sign saying I have to pay? You can't put English-language newspapers out on the street and not expect people to look at them."

The shopkeeper kept pointing at the paper. "You will buy that newspaper!"

"No."

"You picked up that newspaper. You will buy it now!"

In an instant, push came to shove, and Jeff and I found ourselves tumbling into a street fight with the shopkeeper and his brother, who'd come streaking outside at the first shouted words. At the point we Americans usually expect the first punch to be thrown, the shop owner and his brother pulled off their plastic sandals and began hitting us with them: the ultimate Arab insult. These guys were smacking us on our shoulders and heads. We threw a few punches, which stopped them from bashing us with their sandals, then I dropped the newspaper and we ran off into an alleyway.

"Holy shit, what was that all about?"

"I got no idea, man. What the fuck?"

"That might have been the first fight either of us has ever won," Jeff said as we both laughed and ran away.

After getting a platter of late lunch—hummus, fuul, tahini, olives, dolmas, pita bread—on a pier and finishing the meal with a *sheesha* pipe, we drifted back to the hotel for a nap. Even with full stomachs, the Flower Hotel had not improved: The carpets were stained, and the whole place smelled like an old ashtray. We dozed on and off for the rest of the day, too tired to even get up and go out to dinner.

Late that night, around midnight, a knock came on our door. It was Aqaba's Finest. The local cops had chased us down—not such an accomplishment seeing as we were among the few Westerners in town, and probably the only two young Western guys traveling together. The cops were polite: Each had a mustache and a well-pressed uniform of navy blue trousers topped with a light blue shirt.

"Would you come with us, please?" they asked.

"Why?"

"We need to ask you some questions. Please come with us."

We were led out of the hotel and down into a police truck. We were being taken to the station for questioning.

THE POLICE STATION was a stone building arranged around a large, open courtyard. The station's interior was painted light blue, with whitewashed floors, and lit with humming fluorescent lights that threw everything into stark, shadowless relief. We were led to a back office, where our friends from the bookstore awaited us. One of them, Hassan al Rawadeen, had a big bandage all over his foot and a matching pair of black eyes. As was our common practice when dealing with the law, we stuck to the usual policy: Never Admit Anything. This approach was perhaps unwise under the circumstances, since we had cuts and scrapes on our knuckles and had obviously been in a fight. Suddenly, the whole thing seemed very serious. The police were talking about jail time. "You have committed assault, a very serious crime in our country," we were told. "Even if you deny this, there is evidence."

We had only one choice: It was time to pull the U.S. Embassy card.

"Look, we're employees of the U.S. government," I said, even though it was a stretch, pulling out our CPA badges. "There's obviously been an enormous misunderstanding." The cops examined our badges for a few seconds. "Just call the U.S. Embassy in Amman. Ask for Army Sergeant Jody Lautenschlager. She knows us. She's a liaison between our government and yours. She'll explain everything."

Since it was the middle of the night, Jody wasn't in the office, but we were able to get through to the head of security at the embassy, who said he'd alert Jody to our situation first thing in the morning. There was more waiting and unease. The shop owner and his brother sat there, talking to the cops in Arabic. Obviously they were angry that we were denying everything, and that we were now calling in the U.S. government to bail us out. They were also playing up their injuries. Hassan didn't need a bandage on his foot. Jeff snapped pictures of the man's bandaged foot and his face. He was lumped up, yes, but they'd started it. They'd hit us first.

After about ninety minutes, the night desk's captain, Captain Abdullah, who spoke pretty good English, walked over to us.

"You have a court date for tomorrow morning," he said. "The officers will come get you at your hotel at 7:00 A.M. You can go back to your hotel now. The officers will drive you." We were in major trouble, but thought we'd get out of it. The cops kept our passports.

THE NEXT MORNING, after being picked up and taken to Aqaba's courthouse and jail, then standing around in the hallway for about an hour, we were finally brought in to see the judge, without a lawyer. Thanks to Jody, the U.S. Embassy had sent some local Jordanian in to try to help us. His usual job in Aqaba, as we understood it, was travel agent.

The judge was sitting behind a plain wooden desk stacked with manila folders, and he looked pissed. He was a stocky, mustached guy in a gray suit. His eyes were hard. He motioned at us, and then at Hassan and his brother, who were standing behind us to the left. The room was empty except for the judge, his desk, and the framed portraits of King Hussein and King Abdullah II on the tan plaster walls. There seemed to be a shortage of air in the room. Our friend the Jordanian travel agent seemed afraid to speak; he literally was cowering.

The judge began to ask questions, which our travel agent friend translated.

"Did you hit these men?"

"No."

"You did not hit these men?"

"No."

"Look at these men." He motioned toward Hassan, just as the judge had done. "You did not hit these men?"

"No."

Again, it was obvious we'd been in a fight. Our knuckles were split and scabbed; where the skin on our fists wasn't open, there were abrasions, so we kept our hands in our pockets.

"You do not know who these men are?"

"No."

The judge's face flashed rage. "You are both sentenced to eleven years in prison!" Then he shooed us from his courtroom with a wave of his hand.

"That's it?" I said to Jeff. "That wasn't much of a trial. What the fuck?"

WE WERE LED AWAY. The police escorted us downstairs, into a concrete hallway in the basement. They began pushing us toward a pair of steel doors, which were already opened.

As we walked, our Jordanian travel agent friend was yelling at us, berating us. "You are so stupid!" he was shouting. "You are stupid men! Why do you lie? You are arrogant Americans."

The cops now pushed us through the doors into small concrete rooms that sat side by side in the dank basement. There were no lights in the cells or windows, only a small square hole in the steel doors. The time for changing our story was now.

"OK, OK," we said. "We'll admit it. Just get us out of here."

The doors stopped.

There was a long pause.

"All right, OK," our Jordanian travel pro said. "We can see if the judge will listen to you. But it may be too late. . . ."

The cops led us back upstairs and into the courtroom. The judge was still sitting there, and we could tell he was still pissed.

"You have changed your story?"

We nodded.

"Then you must come back tomorrow for resentencing. Your representative will drive you back to your hotel. Return tomorrow morning the same time as today."

AS OUR NEW FRIEND drove us back to our hotel, he was furious. "You Americans, so arrogant!" he was shouting. "I hate your country!" He was, obviously, the perfect candidate to be representing the United States in the Hashemite Kingdom of Jordan. As we drove, Jeff used the man's mobile phone to talk to Judy. She said she'd straighten it out, but we had to give her a little time. The man dropped us at the hotel and, without a good-bye, drove off. When was he coming back to get us? Was he coming back at all?

As we unwound from the legal flurry of the past twenty-four hours, we decided to head down to the only beach in Aqaba, about halfway to the ferry port used for ships heading to and from Egypt. The beach was disgusting: a minefield of cigarette butts and broken glass bottles.

We walked back to the road and hailed another taxi to take us back into town, where we'd planned to rendezvous with Rusty in a few hours. On the drive back, our cabby picked up a Jordanian on the side of the road. Apparently he would be traveling with us back into the city center. As we all got out at the downtown bus station—which happened to be right next to Aqaba's police station—the driver charged the local a fraction of what he was trying to charge us. Naturally, a heated argument ensued. Push soon came to shove, literally, and then we were in another street fight, this time with the taxi driver, directly in front of a mosque. A few punches were thrown before, in no time at all, Aqaba's Finest were on the scene and arresting Jeff.

"Hey, bail me out—fuck," Jeff shouted out the window of the police SUV as the cops drove him toward the station.

I walked the few blocks to the station. Because the cabby wasn't pressing charges, it was all handshakes and kisses between Jeff and his old captors, especially Captain Abdullah, the guy who'd booked us the night before. The cops couldn't believe we were there again. They laughed and told us to stay out of trouble.

We headed back to the hotel, where we saw Rusty walking up the sidewalk to the hotel's door, just as we were. We all embraced, excited to see one another after such a long time, and then headed to a pier to smoke narghile and drink cups of chai while catching up on the last few months.

Catching up wasn't easy. Jeff and I had just left a place that we were still trying to understand, as well as to take in all that happened during our last few weeks there. Our violent outbursts didn't help our cause; it just made us look crazy. Rusty didn't help us any. He just shook his head at our stupidity and changed the subject. If anything, his ambivalence made us feel more out of touch. Rusty was the first, but soon we'd see that most of our friends and family thought we were assholes for going to Iraq. And that the only thing we did there was drugs.

FORTUNATELY, Jody Lautenschlager and the U.S. Embassy weren't lost, or distracted. That afternoon, as we were lying around our room at the Flower Hotel, word came that down at the front desk a telephone call was waiting. It was Jody.

Jeff took the call.

"Have you guys ever seen the movie *Brokedown Palace*?" she

asked. "Claire Danes gets thrown into a Thai jail . . . for life. That's how I'm picturing you guys right now."

"Well, we're out of there. Thanks so much. Thank you. Thank you. Thank you."

"Well, it's not over yet. Baghdad Central and IAC got wind of what happened with you guys. Lieutenant Colonel Weaver knows about it. They all know about it."

"What does that mean?"

"I don't know yet. But we need to talk. I've gotten you guys a nice hotel room there, at the Alcazar. Go there. Relax. Eat, sleep, then get back up here to Amman so we can figure this out."

"But we have a court date tomorrow."

"Oh, don't worry about that. The diplomatic service ironed it out. All you have to do is go over to their store, apologize to them, and they've agreed to drop the charges. They were just angry. They know it was a misunderstanding. They just want you to admit you hit them. So do that. . . . Oh, and wait a minute. You guys were looking at eleven years in jail? Eleven years? I heard you made the judge angry, but how'd you piss a judge off that much? You guys are so lucky I'm here."

"Oh, we know, we know. Thanks so much. Thanks, Jody. Thanks. Really."

"Get up here tomorrow, OK?"

An hour later, Jeff, Rusty, and I were around the corner from the bookshop. We bought some cheap prayer beads at a shop nearby, then rounded the corner and entered the scene of the crime. We were greeted by hugs and kisses by the owner and his father, like beloved family members returning home from a long time away. We were given cups of chai. We kissed each other again, and said several times that we were sorry for our actions. We told them a little about Baghdad and what we'd been doing. They said they realized we were friends to the Arab people, and that night had been a mutual mistake. They said they wanted to take us on a special fishing trip, just for us, on their family boat. We respectfully declined.

NEXT MORNING, with Rusty in tow, we headed back up to Amman to straighten things out with the U.S. Army. We had a bad feeling about what was going to happen.

After we had settled into the Cliff Hotel, which was now starting to feel like home, Jody came over with another guy, Chris, from the U.S. Embassy, to take us out for drinks at an Irish bar in the basement of a Days Inn across town.

The night quickly turned sloppy. We had a lot of drinks—mostly Jameson on the rocks—and after going over our recent Jordanian experiences to Jody, we began catching her up on Baghdad and events at the IAC. We told her how Ibty had been doing, and what a passive-aggressive dick Lieutenant Colonel Weaver was. Somewhere along the line, Jody invited us to her wedding. At some point, I got too drunk and, needing a little air, went outside. Next thing I knew, I was being woken up on the lawn of the Egyptian Embassy by armed Jordanian soldiers. Brandishing their guns, they told me to get out. I went back to the Days Inn, but Jeff and Jody and Rusty were gone and the bar was closed, so I got a room there and called it a night.

ABOUT NOON THE NEXT DAY, I showed back up at the Cliff to find Jeff and Rusty. At the Days Inn bar, Jody told us she wanted to meet us the next afternoon at the Blue Fig, a coffee shop downtown, to address our run-in with the law with an Army JAG lawyer.

We found the coffee shop a few hours early and settled into an olive grove next to it to read the *Jordan Times* and wait. Soon enough, Jody was there with the lawyer in tow, and we all sat down for some grossly overpriced tea. The night before, Jody had been in jeans and a sweatshirt—it was the first time we'd ever seen her in anything other than a BDU—but now she was wearing a newly pressed suit (Army officers aren't allowed to be in uniform in Jordan), as was the female JAG colonel who accompanied her. The JAG colonel had a short Army-issue hairstyle. She was probably in her midforties, but had a weathered, lawyerly face. In the JAG lawyer's hand was a manila folder.

We were given a few seconds to explain our fight in Aqaba, but didn't have enough time to fully outline the context. Then the JAG lawyer began talking. At first, she commended us on our jobs, on what we had accomplished at NGOAO with little support and no real infrastructure to lean on. She was very nice about it. Then she shifted gears and began using words like "international incident" and "tarnished reputation" and "tainted."

"You understand," she said, "the Army is formally disassociating itself from you."

"This thing in Aqaba wasn't that big a deal. We made peace. We apologized. Before it was over, they offered to take us fishing."

"That's good, but I need you to understand, you don't work with the military any longer—under any circumstance. You are no longer associated with the military. Do you understand?"

"Were we ever associated with the Army?" I was confused. As far as I knew, Jeff and I were unattached volunteers.

"Not really." She opened her manila folder. "I have some forms for you to sign." She handed the opened folder to us. It contained two sets of stapled-together papers that were effectively our termination documents. Jody couldn't get a word in, nor did she have the authority to speak. We signed the paperwork without even reading it. The JAG stood up and Jody followed. Good-bye, Jody said, and they left.

We sat and tried finishing our lattes.

"When the Sinclair Group wanted some 'Good News from Iraq' the Army had no problem using us," Jeff said.

"Did Uncle Sam really just dump us? That was the weirdest thing. I never even knew we had any connection to the Army."

"Me neither. What the fuck was that?"

30

·

Tel Aviv Redux

THE NEXT MORNING, still stunned by our "formal disassociation," we shoved off for Tel Aviv from Amman, crossing over the Jordan River via the Allenby Bridge. We were scheduled to meet Inigo, due to return home in a few days. A lot had changed for us since New Year's Eve. Everywhere we looked, things seemed different.

We checked in once again at the Dizengoff Square Hotel, site of the crust punk death match back at the turn of the year. We dumped our bags, stole some towels from a laundry line, and headed for the beach, which we reached just before sundown. We waded into the surf. Without saying anything, each of us began to swim away from the shore, as another epic sunset began to dip below the Mediterranean horizon. As cheesy as it sounds, it felt great to be alive. The beach was empty, the Med was warm, and the air above our heads now felt cold. We swam out to where the water was deep, far over our heads, then stopped. Treading water, we turned back to look at the city.

Nothing else in the world seemed to matter. Though Army bureaucracy and our own stupidity mixed with stress and fatigue had torn our program, a successful network of Iraqi humanitarian-aid groups, from our control, all we wanted to do now was watch the lights of nighttime Tel Aviv switch on. We were utterly disillusioned with the U.S. government, the CPA, the U.S. Army, and the across-the-board failure of our nation's leadership to point out the stupidity of the Iraq War and the administration's handling of its aftermath. But, for a moment, we only wanted to watch it get dark.

Slowly day turned to night, and the lights of Tel Aviv came on. Car headlamps illuminated the city's beachside esplanade. We kept treading water, watching the smooth, glassy shapes of Tel Aviv's buildings begin to glow from inside, their reflections floating on the Med's smooth surface. It was the first moment of peace we'd felt since boarding the bus for Baghdad.

31

•

Watching
Ourselves

THE NEXT DAY, Inigo was back in town. We called him on his cell phone, and he suggested we meet him at an Internet café near our hotel in Dizengoff Square. He offered to put us up in his Bauhaus-style flat, conveniently situated on our favorite Tel Aviv location, Sheinken Street—or as we called it, Hot Chick Street. With Inigo's gracious help, we began to settle back into our old routine: staying out late, drinking and carousing with women in all the many Tel Aviv clubs where Inigo held sway.

Inigo was invited to a party at an embassy employee's luxury condo high up in the King David Towers, and we tagged along. An island in the kitchen served as the bar. We pounded several quick drinks. Jeff and Rusty walked out on a balcony to take in the night. A beer, then three, went over the railing and hurtled into the pool far below. Before long, Jeff and Rusty had sent an entire case of beer into the pool. Finally, someone saw Jeff and Rusty hurling beers over the railing and asked me what was going on. I said not to worry, they were just a little drunk, then I smothered the man with flattering questions about his post in the embassy. He let it pass.

THE NEXT AFTERNOON, Inigo finished editing his twenty-minute video segment "Good Morning Baghdad" for Britain's Channel 4. To celebrate, he organized a viewing at his apartment. He invited a bunch of State Department people from the party we'd crashed the night before, along with a scattering of UN and embassy representatives, a Norwegian diplomat, and the columnist Danny Rubenstein from *Haaretz*.

Everyone crowded around Inigo's television in his cramped apartment, and familiar scenes passed across the screen: Ski contemplating suicide with the loaded rifle in his hands; flattened buildings surrounded by sobbing, black-clad widows; the Clowns and their strange milieu; CPA officials dancing to "Tragedy" as chaos unfolded outside their door; and young Iraqi children peddling porno DVDs to soldiers inside the Green Zone. This was undoubtedly a new version of the Iraq War for most people, especially those outside Iraq who continued to buy the line out of Washington that everything was running smoothly. The people around us seemed genuinely shocked.

For Jeff and me, though, watching Inigo's film left a different set of impressions. We'd been living through Iraq's collapse under the CPA—at the center of everything good and bad there—and now, in just a few short days, we'd become locked out of that world with no way back inside.

Jeff, Rusty, and I walked out onto Inigo's rooftop terrace.

"God damn," Rusty said. "I had no clue what you guys were really doing over there. I figured you were just partying." Jeff and I didn't reply. We just turned and looked out over the hard glass-and-steel edges of Tel Aviv at night. We decided to take some time away from everything. Just a week or so to regroup, consider our options, and climb our way back into Iraq. Jeff was headed back to Amman to see Maya, on her way home from Mosul, and Rusty and I were off to Turkey.

32

•

B ECAUSE THE ARMY HAD crushed our hope of returning to Iraq in
any official U.S. capacity, we tried to engineer our return through
private channels. There was talk of us becoming NGO consultants
or contractors. We examined the prospect of going to work for the
IRDC, which operated beyond the grasp of the Army and the CPA.

Heather Coyne threw as many opportunities our way as she
could, but nothing seemed to stick. In e-mails from her, we could tell
she was dealing with the approach of organizational collapse as the
security situation deteriorated. The spring uprisings had shocked the
CPA to a standstill. Nation building and postwar reconstruction virtually ceased. The yardstick for CPA success had to be downsized and
redefined so many times and so quickly that there was no way to
judge any sort of CPA accomplishment.

Meanwhile, HAND was still up and running. Since the week before we'd left, Hayder had been running HAND, and he was now working daily with dozens of NGOs and making dozens of field distribution drops a week. Every week or so, we'd get e-mails from Jensen or Coyne with updates and reports singing Hayder's praises. Even if everything else in Iraq had ground to a halt under the violence, Hayder kept working. It was quite brave of him. The streets had become even more dangerous: Random violence was worse than ever, and a wave of kidnappings had begun across Iraq. To help protect him, Jensen had even gotten Hayder a gun permit and access to a weapon. Hayder refused to carry it.

JEFF AND I KEPT in good contact with our friends in Iraq. The constant refrain from people on the inside was how much Iraq had changed for the worse. The Green Zone was having trouble getting enough food inside, and some days the KBR buffets had to be rationed. Since mid-April, when the kidnapping wave began, even walking Baghdad's streets became a gamble.

Jo the Clown was kidnapped by guerrillas during the April fighting in Fallujah. Jo had been working there, honorably volunteering with a Red Crescent ambulance team, when she was taken. As she described the experience on her blog:

> *You look for ways out. You wonder whether they're going to kill you, make demands for your release, if they'll hurt you. You wait for the knives and the guns and the video camera. You tell yourself you're going to be OK. You think about your family, your mum finding out you're kidnapped. You decide you're going to be strong, because there's nothing else you can do.*

You fight the understanding that your life isn't fully in your hands any more; that you can't control what's happening. You turn to your best friend next to you and tell her you love her, with all your heart. . . .

Still my instinct tells me I'm going to be OK. Still my mind wanders to the question of whether they'll shoot us against a wall or just open fire in the room, whether they'll take us out one by one or we'll all be killed together, whether they'll save the bullets and cut our throats, how long it hurts for when you're shot, if it's instantly over or if there's some echo of the agony of the metal ripping through your flesh after your life is gone.

Fortunately, after twenty-four hours, Jo was released unharmed.

OTHER WESTERNERS weren't so lucky, especially those who weren't working under fire trying to save civilian lives. One was the Duke's best friend in Baghdad, Nick Berg. A nice Jewish kid from Philadelphia—everyone who knew him in Baghdad liked him—Berg was captured April 9 and beheaded, with the video available on the Internet.

As news of Berg's execution spread worldwide, our old friend Beth Payne from the U.S. Consulate came into the picture. Beth had told the Berg family that U.S. forces had detained Berg just before his kidnapping, which the Bergs then told the media. Beth Payne was removed from Baghdad. Controversy still surrounds Berg's death. Was Berg CIA? Or a member of Mossad, the Israeli intelligence and counterterror agency? According to the Duke, none of these rumors was true. Berg was a fellow businessman, interested in bringing wireless telephone service to the Iraqis. Of course, then again, who the hell was the Duke, anyway?

As the violence and kidnappings continued to escalate in Iraq during early April, phantoms of paranoia crept over everything that had happened and everyone who'd been present in Baghdad over the previous months. Everybody began seeing patterns that now left everyone and everything related to the CPA suspect. Naomi Klein jokingly asked Adam and Jen if Jeff and I were CIA.

Then, on the night of April 18, and thanks largely to satellite TV and the Internet, the Abu Ghraib scandal burst across global consciousness instantaneously. The images of Americans torturing Iraqis on Iraqi soil confirmed every accusation the insurgents and Iraq's anti-CPA leadership had been making since the war's beginnings.

Overnight, in Iraq and around the world, it was shown that the Americans were capable of any horror in their righteous "war on terror," those universally inalienable human rights they always claimed as their political bedrock only worth protecting when it was convenient. In Iraq after Abu Ghraib, if you were an Iraqi associated with the Americans, you were suspected of helping them in their nefarious, hypocritical, anti-Arab quest.

YET EVEN IN THIS environment, HAND kept thriving. Between the car bombs and the nightly mortar attacks, the program we'd created was among the few CPA civil society programs still succeeding in April and May 2004. In Sadr City and beyond, Hayder had become a figure of renown. Week after week, Hayder braved the violence of the Iraqi street, and the general distrust of any Iraqi who worked closely with the Americans, to bring aid to Iraq's poorest neighborhoods. And he was running HAND for free, all the while taking care of his brothers and sisters and finishing up his Ph.D.

On the morning of June 9, as he had most mornings since January, Hayder left his house for the Green Zone, climbing into his maroon mini-SUV. As he pulled out into Sadr City traffic, a car sped in from his flank and cut him off, forcing him to stop. Four men with machine guns stepped out. They opened fire. Hayder was assassinated in broad daylight, blocks from his Sadr City home. At least forty bullets pierced his body.

On June 12, I received this e-mail from Heather Coyne. It was sent to a dozen or so people, including Jeff:

> I AM GRIEVED TO REPORT THAT HAYDER MEHSSEN, LEADER OF THE VERY ACTIVE NGO "FRIENDS OF SADR CITY," WAS MURDERED THIS WEEK. WE DO NOT HAVE DETAILS YET, BUT HE WAS REPORTEDLY SHOT IN HIS CAR BY 4 ARMED MEN. I KNOW MANY OF YOU WERE GOOD FRIENDS OF HAYDER AND HAD WORKED CLOSELY WITH HIM. HAYDER TOOK THE LEAD OF THE HUMANITARIAN AID SECTOR AND HAD ORGANIZED SEVERAL OTHER NGOS TO PARTICIPATE IN THE HUMANITARIAN DISTRIBUTION TRAINING EXERCISE AND WAS MANAGING A NETWORK OF NGOS, CALLED THE HUMANITARIAN AID NETWORK FOR DISTRIBUTION (HAND). HE WAS EXTREMELY ACTIVE IN THE NGO COMMUNITY AND WE WILL MISS HIM DEARLY.

My first thought was how unfair it was that Hayder was dead. Of everyone Jeff and I had come to know in Iraq, he was the worst person to die because he was the best person we'd met there. My second thought, of course, was that Hayder's death was our fault. My third thought was to call Jeff. By then, both Jeff and I had returned to the United States. I was at my mom's house in New Hampshire. Jeff had gone home to Virginia, where he was living with his sister, brother-in-law, niece, and three nephews. On June 12, Jeff was on his way to Boston with some other friends of ours from New York. The Red Sox were playing the Dodgers for the first time ever at Fenway, and, of course, we had tickets.

I dialed his cell phone.

"Hey," Jeff said.

"Hayder got killed."

"What? How?"

"Assassinated. A carload of gunmen. They shot him in his car, in Sadr City. He was on his way to work."

Silence. Jeff was in a car with people who hadn't known Hayder.

"It's our fucking fault," I said.

"He is the wrong person to get killed," Jeff said.

THAT AFTERNOON, Jeff and I watched the Red Sox lose to the Dodgers with a half dozen of our friends. We stood in standing room in Section 7, by the right-field Pesky pole. It was our lucky section. It's where, in 1999, we'd all gathered when our vending work was through to watch the end of games. Nineteen ninety-nine had been a classic Fenway season. That was the year Fenway hosted the All-Star Game, and the first time the Red Sox ever played the Yankees in the ALCS. During the 2003 playoffs, people had been swinging from the concrete rafters above Section 7. On this day, Section 7 didn't feel very lucky. I didn't even want to be there. Neither did Jeff. It was the wrong place to contemplate Hayder's death.

Coming to terms with Hayder's execution was difficult. We had few people to talk about it with. Both of us were living with family, not peers. It took months before what had happened started to sink in and feel real. Baghdad became a traumatic place to think about. A combination of guilt and fear created in us a newfound sense of mortality. Even crossing the street I got chills if a big truck rumbled by. I feared the randomness of death. If I developed a cough it felt life-threatening. Jeff and I both felt lucky to be waking up every morning. Then, when I thought of Hayder, my sense of good fortune turned to guilt. The bullets that killed Hayder could easily have killed Jeff and me.

To this day, Jeff and I feel largely responsible for Hayder's death. The opportunity we gave Hayder put him on the death list. After all, giving Hayder the chance to help Sadr City with an endless supply of aid, on top of the chance to build a lasting program in the new Iraq, was too much for him to turn down. Even if he knew there was a possibility of his own assassination, as a person who lived for the betterment of his community, Hayder had to take over HAND. He was stuck. And we were the guys who'd stuck him there.

33

·

We'll Always
Have Baghdad

O N JUNE 28, 2004, a day before the Iraqi transitional government took nominal control of their country—having been the
Iraqi interim government before some official signatures during a
photo-op press conference—the head of the CPA, J. Paul "Jerry" Bremer III, skulked out of Baghdad on an unannounced 3:00 A.M. charter
flight.

In the wake of Abu Ghraib, Iraq was coming apart. The April wave
of kidnappings had become a groundswell that left no Westerners
there—especially Americans—secure. Iraqi suicide bombers were
blowing up innocent diners in restaurants and cafés daily, and any
time the Iraqis made a call for new army or police recruits, those recruiting centers would also be blown up during peak visitation
hours. Sectarian rage was shredding the country, and no one in Iraq
was immune to it. Even Bremer.

Claiming to have succeeded in setting Iraq on the path to stable self-governance, Bremer flew out of the country as an emperor without clothes. Only he and his boss, George W. Bush—who would soon award Bremer the Presidential Medal of Freedom for his sacrifices— couldn't recognize the bald disingenuousness of their claims of victory. The CPA, which had arrived a year earlier with grand plans for fixing a broken postdictatorship, ducked out of the country leaving a legacy of corrupt and hollow government ministries, Iraqi sectarian distrust and violence, institutionalized looting by shady foreign parties and corrupt Iraqi officials, and, in the end, brutal and systematized torture.

In the meantime, we were working to get our American-based lives back to normal. In April, while still at the Cliff Hotel in Amman, Jeff, Rusty, and I had read that Red Sox center fielder Johnny Damon had shown up shaggy and bearded at spring training and had taken to chasing teammates around the clubhouse, anointing them with "holy water." We instantly had a new T-shirt vision: red, with a saturated black schematic of Johnny's face on the front—à la the famous "Che" image—sandwiched between the phrases "The Passion of Johnny" and "W.W.J.D.D.," mocking the commercialization of religion. Around Fenway, the design was an immediate, runaway success, second in sales only to the old "Yankees Suck" classic.

Inigo had also hopped back into our lives. He'd come to the United States to make a film about Abu Ghraib. I met him in New York City's Union Square at an outdoor bar, where we were surrounded by young people. It was just like Tel Aviv, Inigo said.

The next morning, we traveled south by Sticky Van to interview General Janis Karpinski, who ran Abu Ghraib during the time of major abuses. She wanted the interview to be conducted at this New Jersey roadside motel. She clearly hated her superior, General Ricardo Sanchez, who ran the Iraq theater and who Karpinski said allowed the torture to happen, only to leave her holding the bag. General Karpinski then said the Abu Ghraib torture was ordered "from the top," and that when she'd told interrogators her troops weren't trained to be part of such practices, the interrogators showed her their orders, which had been signed by "SEC DEF," or, as we know him, Donald Rumsfeld. General Karpinski claimed ignorance of any torture committed by soldiers under her command.

Inigo and I got to Washington, D.C., that evening. We met up with Jeff and Rusty at ESPN Zone and watched the Sox play the Yankees. The Sox lost. During the game, Jeter dove into the stands after a foul ball and got his cheek badly cut. The next morning, we went with Inigo to West Virginia for his interview with Lynndie England's family and legal team. England grew up in Fort Ashby, West Virginia, in an old trailer with a pig farm as a front yard. The whole place smelled like pig shit. Lynndie's family seemed confused and angry with the Army and the U.S. government. They felt their daughter and sister was being made a scapegoat for illegal and immoral government torture policies. The stress was showing. Lynndie's sister's eyes were like black holes; she had a stare that seemed to take in light-years. Still, by the end of the day we were jet skiing on a local lake with Lynndie's lawyers. Then we went out to a barbecue with them. Inigo had never had a southern barbecue sandwich. "Better than falafel" was all he could muster.

Inigo's work done, we drove Sticky Van back to Washington, D.C., for a night of bars and clubs in Georgetown and Dupont Circle with Michael Cole. Cole had just returned from Iraq. With a look of shock on his face, Cole spoke to us of his ultimate nightmare: He'd frozen up at the shopping mall, in front of a Gap store, and he just couldn't go inside. Another time, Cole said, a balloon popping sent him running for cover. But he was still wearing the rebel shoes: Gucci loafers.

We chose to stay in D.C. for the Fourth of July, and witnessed a "Yankees Suck" T-shirt cross paths with a "Pro Life" shirt of identical design in front of the Lincoln Memorial. We thought that sucked.

After darkness fell, Inigo filmed the American Independence Day celebration in all its glory, with its bombs bursting in air above the National Mall as Black Hawk helicopters—probably manned by snipers—hovered in the sky farther above. It was an eerie sight. Even Washington, D.C., now felt under military occupation.

THINGS HAPPEN. Like the Red Sox beating the Yankees in the 2004 ALCS.

I went to ALCS Game 1, which the Red Sox lost. Then they lost the next two games, too. They lost Game 3, in fact, on Jeff's birthday. When it was down to a final, make-or-break Game 4, Johnny Damon kept insisting that they'd won four games in a row before, and that now they'd do it again.

Still, I couldn't take it and boycotted the Sox until Game 7, when—once again—with the ALCS series now tied 3–3, I decided I had to take the emotional risk and show up at Yankee Stadium, just as Jeff and I had for the same game a year before. This time, Johnny Damon hit a grand slam in the second inning, then topped it with a two-run homer in the fourth. The Sox won going away: 10–3. During the victory celebration, I ended up kissing a Boston cop named Tiger who had arrested me several times for selling T-shirts without a permit. It was that kind of night.

Then the Sox didn't slow down, and swept the St. Louis Cards in four games. Jeff and I were there. Sticky Van was there, too, having gotten us from the first two games in Boston to St. Louis' Busch Stadium in style. Rusty and Phil O'Connor were there, too. Two days later, we were part of the Red Sox victory parade through Boston, alongside 3.5 million other people. Sullys were drinking 40s with state troopers on the Mass. Ave. bridge. We heard an old man say it was the best celebration since V-E Day. "This is the end of *sports hyperbole*!" Jeff shouted at me through the crowd. It was the end of something, that's for sure.

34

•

"Frozen out of focus . . ."

T HEN MARLA WAS KILLED. She was driving across Baghdad on
the morning of April 16, 2005, on the Airport Road, when a suicide car bomber hit Marla and her Iraqi partner in CIVIC, Faiz.
The bomber was targeting a convoy of Western contractors, but
plowed onto the highway from an exit ramp and hit Marla and Faiz
instead.

She survived the initial blast, but burns covered 90 percent of
her body and she died en route to the Green Zone hospital. In Iraq
and around the world, the event generated massive media coverage.
Her funeral in Lakewood, California, was a standing-room-only affair.
Speakers from Sean Penn to Senator Barbara Boxer reminisced
about her. Jen and Adam went to the California funeral, too, as did
most of their former housemates. They said the service was incredibly powerful.

. . .

ABOUT TWO WEEKS AFTER Marla's death, a small memorial for her was planned in New York. Inigo was one of the organizers, and he came to New York a few days early, since the Tribeca Film Festival was also in full swing. I met him outside the loft building that was the festival's headquarters. Inigo had lost weight, but he was still the funny, smart, well-dressed Brit he'd always been. His film about the Green Zone had aired across Europe to great acclaim. Inigo said *Nightline* had shown interest, but backed out after viewing content that it deemed too anti-American.

Marla and Inigo had always been tight: two people who shared a volatile dual addiction to human rights and energetic nightlife. Marla's death had hit Inigo hard. We went to lunch in the West Village and tried catching up without being too macabre.

"I'm doing this film about Iraqi Jews who live in Israel but hate it," Inigo said. "They all want to go back to Baghdad. It's fucking hilarious."

It was just after 2:00 P.M. and Inigo said he was starving. I enjoyed watching him inhale his first meal of the day. As always while in New York, Inigo wasn't sleeping. He had the ability to run for days without food or rest. The last time he'd been in New York, Marla had thrown a party in the East Village. I'd skipped it because she and I had never made up after our blowup at the Hamra. At the time, Inigo had told me to forget about the past and come along, but stubbornness had gotten the best of me and I declined. Now my stubbornness had turned to regret.

We finished lunch and Inigo asked, "When does Jeff get here?"

"Tonight. We'll see you out at the memorial."

"Bring something to drink when you come, will you?" Inigo said. "I think red wine, maybe. Marla always liked red wine. She'd want it that way."

The memorial was held at a Williamsburg loft on a cool spring night. It was home to Marijana Wooten, a talented and attractive filmmaker in her thirties. Wooten looked like she could've been Marla's older sister, and she all but was: The two were very close. Her most recent film, titled *Bearing Witness,* had just premiered in Tribeca at the film festival. It chronicles the lives of five female correspondents in Iraq. Some of the women profiled were among the fifty or so people at the service. Marla's mother was there, too, wearing black like most everyone attending. She seemed a little wobbly, but when she spoke she seemed honest and tough. In fact, the room was filled with honest, tough women.

Several people showed films about Marla, including Inigo, who aired a touching ten-minute piece. Inigo's film closed with a scene from a Hamra party in winter 2004. It was filmed late, after a long night where Inigo had spent most of the evening DJ-ing South African ghetto tunes. The party ended with a perky-if-sloppy Marla harassing the great Iraqi pianist and fellow Hamra resident Samir Peter (himself the subject of a documentary, *The Liberace of Baghdad*) to play Don McLean's "American Pie" by singing the lyrics to him.

"Bye byyeeee Miss American Pie . . . do you know this song? C'mon." She sang it again. She wanted the party to end just like a high-school dance. Inigo's film ended with this scene. One of the song's lyrics sums up Marla's Hamra days: "And I knew if I had my chance, that I could make those people dance and, maybe, they'd be happy for a while. . . ."

A FEW WEEKS LATER, there was a large memorial scheduled for Marla in Washington, D.C., on May 14, 2005. It was to be held at the U.S. Capitol, and was to be hosted by Senator Patrick Leahy, the ranking Democrat from Vermont.

Jeff and I made the trip, arriving in Washington on Thursday the twelfth. We checked into the Churchill Hotel off Dupont Circle and caught happy hour. Maya met us for drinks, coming straight from work at the *Washington Times.* She wore gray slacks and a white blouse and looked very D.C. When happy hour expired, we walked to a nearby Salvadorian restaurant.

Jeff and Maya's romance cooled in the closing days of our time there; some things are better left in the place where they lived. I'd seen Maya a few times after Iraq. She and Jeff were able to forge a nice friendship, considering the potential trickiness inherent in such postromance relationships. Anyway, over heavy burritos and cold Mexican beers we compared thoughts on the chaos that had now fully engulfed Iraq.

"It's hard to have known so many people that are dead," Maya said.

She always grew close to the soldiers whom she was embedded with. Maya would feel the pain of war's death more than anyone we knew. Seemingly every month, another of Maya's soldier friends was killed. In mid-September 2004, Maya had gone to a service for a 1st Armored Cavalry soldier in Richmond, Virginia, Specialist Clarence Adams III, the war's thousandth U.S. casualty. Maya hand-delivered photos of Specialist Adams to his family. His mother cried as she looked at photos of her son playing with Iraqi children. Later, Jeff and I stayed at Maya's apartment while she was in Kansas revisiting another unit that had just returned home from Iraq.

"And now," she said, "Marla."

SATURDAY AFTERNOON, Marla's memorial was held at the Dirksen Senate Office Building on Capitol Hill, in a stately, neoclassical, high-ceilinged marble caucus room.

Upon arrival we found Charlie. He looked good, even under the circumstances. Charlie seemed much better than when we last saw him, during the fall in New York. At that point Charlie was just weeks from having been at the bloody battle of Najaf, and he'd been deeply shaken. We took seats toward the back, right as things got under way.

Senator Diane Feinstein spoke first. Then came Senator Leahy, who told a story of how he'd met and come to love Marla, and how, in her absence, he and his aide, Tim Rieser, had secured congressional passage of a Marla Ruzicka War Victim's Fund, to assist noncombatants injured in war. The fund's sum was $32 million. The room erupted into applause. Following Senator Leahy, officials from the Pentagon, Human Rights Watch, and the U.S. Air Force spoke. Then came Iraq's UN ambassador, the journalist Peter Bergen, and Bobby Mueller, founder and president of Vietnam Veterans of America.

Of all the speakers, the most impassioned was Shaun Waterman, a British UPI reporter. Waterman stood at the podium, nervously sweating and flustered. Jeff and I had never heard of him before. He spoke of America, and how as a Brit he never understood or liked the way Americans made their way in the world, and how that way outlined to him the American way of life. Then he spoke about Marla. Waterman said that watching and being around her during her several transformative years in Baghdad and Kabul made him realize what a great American looks like. He said Marla was the reason he now called himself an American. It moved many in the room to tears.

Afterward, a reception was held at a nice bar and grill in Adams Morgan. A few hundred people packed the room. It was as if the Hamra had been transported to Washington. Except, of course, that the most important Hamra person wasn't there.

The reception was a celebration of Marla's life. It's likely no other event could have so perfectly dragged the human panorama of the

American side of the Iraq War under one roof as could a party being held in memory of Marla. Army colonels mixed with peacenik activists. Senators talked with bootleg T-shirt peddlers (that would be us). Reporters slouched in low-slung couches, around tables littered with glasses and bottles. The party, Marla's final party, lasted well into the night.

Acknowledgments

WE ARE INDEBTED to the many people who helped make this book possible. First and foremost, we would like to thank Donovan Webster, who served as both a mentor and friend during the long and sometimes frustrating writing process. Without his guidance and talent, this book wouldn't have been possible. Also, thanks to his wife, Janet, for her patience and hospitality, and to their wonderful, brilliant children, Anna and James, for being so cool.

Second, we'd like to thank Jen Banbury and Adam Davidson. None of this would have been possible without your interest in our story. We'll owe you both forever.

This book is dedicated in loving memory of Hayder Mehssen, who was assassinated in Baghdad on June 9, 2004. Hayder and his NGO, Friends of Sadr City, were examples of courage and hope in a country at war.

ACKNOWLEDGMENTS

Within minutes of our arrival in Baghdad, Marla Ruzicka was there to point us in the right direction. She helped us understand what we'd gotten ourselves into, and showed us the best way to help: Do It Yourself. This book is also dedicated in her memory.

And to Charles Crain, without our shared adventures, and your friendship and knowledge, this book would have suffered greatly.

We owe Sergeant Shawn Jensen, Lieutenant A. Heather Coyne, and Sergeant Jody Lautenschlager—soldiers who define the word *hero*—for saving our lives, for springing us from jail, and for changing our lives by giving us the chance to work with Iraqis.

We extend our gratitude to Maya Alleruzzo and Willis Witter of the *Washington Times,* and to Phil O'Connor and J. B. Forbes of the *St. Louis Post-Dispatch.* Your articles helped people understand the growing humanitarian catastrophe in Sadr City and Iraq.

To write this book, Donald and Anne McCaig let us live among their dogs and sheep on their beautiful property in the mountains of Virginia. They offered great insight into the art of living and taught us so much.

The following people were integral to this book: Inigo Gilmore, Andy Morrison, Lieutenant Colonel Joe Rice, Jack Fairweather and Christina Asquith, Joe Cochrane, Sergeant Jay Bachar, Michael Cole, Andrew Robert Duke, Georges Maaloof, Jon Lee Anderson, Sewell Chan, Letta Taylor, Jens the Swede, Steph Sinclair, Mitch Prothero, Daniel Pepper, Mario Tama, Spencer Platt, Scott Nelson, Andy Cutraro, and Andrew Butters; all of Baghdad Central, the NGOAO, and the IAC; Abed and Friends of Sadr City, Adams, Samin and Rocket Man, Randy Jankowski; Chaplain Fred Vicciellio, Van Dent, and Operation Starfish; Luis, Jo, the Circus 2 Iraq, and all at Clowntown.

International Creative Management made this whole thing happen. Our literary agent, Kristine Dahl, listened to us with patience and understanding, offering invaluable guidance during the book's progress. In Los Angeles, Josie Freedman helped us weigh options and calmed our nerves. Jud Laghi and Michael McCarthy came through whenever we needed them. Also at ICM, we'd like to thank Montana Wojczuk, Liz Farrell, and Carrie Stein.

Several people in America took to our story, and we thank them for it: Jane Feltes, Ira Glass, and everyone at *This American Life*; Nancy Cotton, Mel Gibson, Christine Ryan, Peter Gould, and all at Icon Productions; Jeff Wachtel and USA Network.

At The Penguin Press, we send endless gratitude to our brilliant editor, Scott Moyers, who understood the book we wanted to write even more than we did. His great taste and keen insight were essential. Thanks to Ann Godoff for listening to our crazy story and giving us a shot. Janie Fleming held everything together.

Thanks to our friends in New York, Boston, Washington, D.C., Virginia, California, Beirut, and Chicago for entertaining us whenever we were in town doing "research." A special thanks to Jon "Jarbi" Bowne for being a class act. To everyone from the 38 GC, Cantina-17-a Raw Bar, original Yankees Suck-men, and old TYF/IME Crew: What were we thinking?

Ray wants MacKenzie Lewis, the most important person in his life, to know that this book couldn't have been written without her unconditional love. Also, he would like to thank his family for putting up with him, especially his grandmother, who deserves a big hug and kiss for keeping him focused.

Jeff would like to extend personal thanks to his sister, Marni, his brother-in-law, Baylor Rice, and their five amazing children, for letting him crash into their world and teaching him more about life than anyone ever has. Also, he thanks his dad, grandmother, the entire Neumann family, and Larry Redford. And Kristen Alff, for being the best friend he's ever known.

To the people of Iraq, we apologize for the reckless, unplanned, understaffed, corrupt, and wasteful way in which our country occupied and then failed at rebuilding your shattered nation. For every innocent mother or father, son or daughter, sister or brother, friend or family member who was killed, tortured, or injured by our country, we extend our deepest sympathy.

A NOTE ON SOURCES
Following the Iraq War and all its complexities is a full-time job. Without the following sources, this book wouldn't have been possible:

NEWSPAPERS: *The New York Times,* the *Washington Post,* the *Los Angeles Times, The Guardian, The Boston Globe, Haaretz,* the *Financial Times,* and *The Wall Street Journal.*

MAGAZINES: *The New Yorker, The Economist, The Atlantic, Harper's, The New Republic, The Nation, Foreign Affairs, Time,* and *Newsweek.*

If Iraq is indeed the most important story of our time, then the most important blog of our time is Juan Cole's Informed Comment (www.juancole.com). Essential and honest, Cole is *the* must-read of the Iraq War.